LETTERS FROM ATTICA

LETTERS FROM ATTICA

50TH ANNIVERSARY ANNOTATED EDITION

Sam Melville

Edited with a primer to the new edition by Joshua Melville

CHICAGO
REVIEW
PRESS

Copyright © 1972 by Joshua Melville
Annotations, new appendix, and primer to the new edition
copyright © 2022 by Joshua Melville
All rights reserved
Original edition published 1972 by William Morrow & Company Inc. Portions
of the book had appeared previously in *Ramparts* magazine.
This edition published by Chicago Review Press Incorporated
814 North Franklin Street
Chicago, Illinois 60610
ISBN 978-1-64160-695-0

Library of Congress Control Number: 2021948364

Cover design: Jonathan Hahn
Cover photo: Jayu/Creative Commons, via Wikimedia Commons, https://
commons.wikimedia.org/wiki/File:Attica,_New_York_(Correctional_Facility).jpg
Typesetting: Nord Compo

Printed in the United States of America
5 4 3 2 1

CONTENTS

ON HISTORICAL ACCURACY

A PRIMER TO THE NEW EDITION

by Joshua Melville

THE YEAR WAS 1973. I was eleven years old, looking at a picture of my father's face on the cover of this book, *Letters from Attica*. He was smiling at me, while I looked back in sorrow. Moments earlier, my mother had told me that he was killed in prison and why he was there. The first thing I thought of was the last time we spoke. He was teaching me how to build a fire as we camped alone on the Appalachian Trail. Looking sadly at the flames, he leaned closer like he had a secret and whispered that he would be going away for a while but that I should remember that no matter what happened—no matter what—he would always love me. After Mom told me of his horrible death, our covenant made in the woods would be tethered to the letters he had written from his cell, now published for the world.

When several activists and educators suggested a reprint of his letters to coincide with the fiftieth anniversary of the Attica uprising, I was very pleased not only to learn that the man who carried me on his shoulders had remained relevant for nearly half a century but also to take their suggestion and write a new foreword to true up the things I learned that are contrary to the commonly accepted narrative of his life, work, and capture.

Up until now, there were only two sources for facts. The first is this book's original editor, John Cohen, who contributed the 1972 introduction. He met my father around the events of the 1968 Columbia University takeover. Together, they formed a coalition to protest the university's gentrification into Harlem and Morningside Heights. The second was one of my father's lovers and a confessed coconspirator, Jane Alpert. Her "Profile of Sam Melville" for this book became a key source for journalists and historians. I, too, invested in Alpert's reconstruction, since the first thing I saw when I opened this book as a child was her dedication, "For Jocko Melville": my father's pet name for me, which only he used. Since the profile was dedicated to me, I thought I would be reading a tribute. But her critical words confused me.

Alpert's version of events centered around what she calls "the collective." Her facts here and in her 1981 memoir blame my father for their arrest, citing what she characterizes as his impulsive, narcissistic, and chauvinistic disregard of her instincts. She also wrote that he demonstrated little patience for planning, safety, or becoming literate about the history of revolution. Her evidence is that my father conspired with the now-infamous FBI informant George Demmerle by inviting him to place bombs in a Manhattan armory; the two were arrested in the process along with Alpert and others. Alpert paints Demmerle as a fool whom everyone in the collective suspected of being an undercover agent. She feigns pity for my poor father, so desperate for a new follower that he could not see what was obvious to all. However, she knowingly omits that Demmerle was involved with several others in the collective who were never arrested, and also that Demmerle was a career informant who had tricked even the most experienced movement organizers, notably Bobby Seale, the Black Panther Party, and the Young Patriots. Both Abbie Hoffman and Jerry Ruben each peppered their memoirs with details about how Demmerle infiltrated the Yippies and became Hoffman's "bodyguard" during the Chicago Seven riots at the 1968 Democratic National Convention.

Through my adolescence I wrestled with her claim that my father's gullibility led to everyone's arrest. It made no sense, given the thoughtful, intellectual, and cautious man I had known him to be during my childhood.

After a three-decade investigation—during which I acquired my father's DOJ files and court transcripts and tracked down and interviewed eleven collective members and dozens of other East Village and Chicago activists, girlfriends, and even FBI agents who worked his case—I learned that my father was not "disaffected and depressed," as Alpert (and Cohen) portray, but was in fact an inspiring and trusted organizer for several important factions that defined the radical underground. Nor did he scoff at the idea of understanding history, as you will see from his personal prison library in the appendix created for this edition. My facts painted a new truth: Sam Melville successfully planned and planted bombs with several collectives in several states, but of the dozens of people with whom my father conspired the only three people arrested were connected to Alpert. This was not a coincidence. All three, including my father, were Jane Alpert's simultaneous lovers.

Alpert had been under surveillance for months. Agents filed reports, noting how the four of them traded beds and volunteered for the underground newspaper *Rat Subterranean News.* But the thing that brought them to an arrest was Alpert's monthly column in *Rat.* There, she openly discussed their bombings and "predicted" the collective's next three targets. It was her writings that solidified the FBI's eleven-month case, not my father's one encounter with a random informant a day before the arrests. (The story of how I came to uncover these facts is the subject of my own memoir, *American Time Bomb* [2021].) Alpert knew that none of the readers of *Letters from Attica* in 1972 would have access to that data.

When she was asked to write her profile of Sam Melville, she delivered what you will read: a twenty-thousand-word profile (longer than my father's letters themselves). Rather than talk about his principled multistate campaigns against imperialism and the illegal war in Vietnam, she focused on my father's brief experimentation with LSD, her psychoanalysis of his mental state, and—of all the irrelevant yet telling insights into her motivations—his "infidelities." She wrote with a style that suggested her words were part of a consensus with others in the collective, others who were not indicted and so could not rebut her without admitting their participation in the bombings. Then she dedicated her revenge revisionism to me, personally: "For Jocko Melville." An eleven-year-old child.

There's no denying that I feel scarred by Jane Alpert, and after fifty years, it would bring me great personal closure if she would publicly come clean. But I have little hope. Through the decades Alpert (now in her seventies) has remained evasive about the inconsistencies between her 1972 account in this book and her 1981 account in her memoir. One possible explanation is that while her profile was crafted to push her narrative as the fulcrum of the collective, her memoir was crafted after she turned herself in and began assisting the FBI in the capture of others in the underground. In the late 1970s they were still hunting several cells virtually spawned by my father. Alpert's memoir was an answer to their problems: a tell-all book by a renowned feminist radical who, like Patty Hearst, had now grown strong through her penance and desired to return to mainstream life. This would strongly discourage others from following her path and bolster the establishment propaganda that politically motivated bombings must be the product of doped-out hippies, libidinous chauvinists, and those who are "mad."

As for my father's other historian, John Cohen's introduction to this book is less of a personal attack. But when it comes to the arrests, Cohen's distortions about them are aligned with Alpert's, to whom he was close during that time. Cohen excels as Sam's biographer once his narrative moves away from the secondhand information he had of the collective and toward his firsthand knowledge of Sam's prison life. There, Cohen's opinions and histories are also imperfect but understandably so, since what really happened at Attica is a labyrinth of ever-emerging facts, even to this day.

What you hold today is a *Letters from Attica* designed to offer modern readers a fuller perspective on a complex true believer, who some historians say defined the movement. This edition is annotated by the people who have researched and respected my father's life and often his choices more than any to date. The footnotes are coded as follows:

Cohen　　John Cohen's original footnotes from 1972.

DV　　David Viola, author of the PhD dissertation "Terrorism and the Response to Terrorism in New York City During the Long Sixties," for which the Melville Collective is a centerpiece. Viola brings refences to other radical movements of the time and insight into law enforcement's reaction.

JM　　My personal family knowledge, as well as conversations I had with collective members, FBI agents who worked the Mad Bomber case, and Attica inmate leaders.

JV　　'60s historian and professor Jeremy Varon, author of *Bringing the War Home* (Berkeley: University of California Press, 2004), puts the Melville Collective into a larger framework of New Left scholarship.

RK　　Ron Kuby, protégé to William Kunstler since 1982, adds legal expertise and insight into radical law of the period. He was also an attorney to members of the "Sam Melville / Jonathan Jackson Unit," known also as the "United Freedom Front."

SF　　Sharon Fischer, who has been a movement activist since 1968 and has worked extensively for the rights of prisoners, including the Attica Brothers. She has been researching Sam Melville for fifty years.

Also important to note is the fantastic but invisible work of Jeffery Berryhill, who was the transcriber of the original letters. Without his attention to detail this reprint would have taken years rather than months to collate.

As to the letters themselves, when editing them in 1971, John Cohen made some mysterious redactions. I presume that they were referencing people or clandestine events that today would be benign to talk about openly. There is, for instance, much back-and-forth between Cohen and my father about specific dictionaries that are now out of print. Dictionaries were common tools for ciphering. For the sake of posterity, I have reinserted the redacted portions and marked them with gray shading. Cohen also changed several names to protect against possible legal entanglements. For historical purposes, those who are now deceased have been restored to their original names.

I began this forward with the influence my father had on me, but I'd like to conclude with the influence he had on someone else. My father would have hated the bougie idea of a fan or follower, but if there were fan clubs for revolutionaries then Sharon Fischer would be the president of his. She worked tirelessly on this project to provide some of the best contextualizing footnotes. She writes:

> *What comes of rereading these letters almost fifty years after they were written? That they are the thoughts of a remarkable man who took the worst of circumstances and made the best of them. His great heart and fighting spirit come through on every page.*
>
> *Throughout Sam's incarceration he felt depression and despair, yes, but he took joy where he could find it (books, music, letters from his son) and he never lost his sense of humor. He took responsibility for his actions and wanted others to learn from his mistakes. His political insights remained sharp and focused; his observations about people were perceptive.*
>
> *Despite the constant degradation of life at Attica, Sam's letters prove he was always thinking about the problems of others with caring and concern. He was a good man.*
>
> *For me, the enduring legacy of Sam Melville's letters and his life is that he is still teaching us to not bow down, to never give up, and above all "for Christ's sake do something."*

The last words my father wrote were an errand to the movement. They were written on the second day of the uprising and snuck out (most probably) by Clarence Jones, publisher of the *Amsterdam News*, who was an observer in D Yard. They were omitted from the first edition. These words best capture my father's spirit and the legacy of Attica and seem the logical place to end this preamble to a tribute of that for which he lived and died:

> *Power People!*
> *We are strong, we are together, we are growing. We love you all, we need your continuing love & support. Brother Huey is on*

his way and Counselor Kunstler, too. YAWF is storming the walls.
What shall we do? Cha Cha Cha.
   Ho Ho Ho Chi Minh.
   Please inform our next of kin.*

* SF: Prisoners Solidarity Committee, "Letters from Imprisoned Brothers," *Attica Since the Massacre*, September 30, 1971, 4–5, via the Freedom Archives, https://freedomarchives.org /Documents/Finder/DOC510_scans/Prisons_Attica/510.AReportFromInsideAttica.pdf."
"YAWF" is Youth Against War & Fascism, the youth group of the Workers World Party.

FOREWORD

by William Kunstler

IN A WAY, IT IS STRANGE THAT I have been asked to write a foreword to Sam Melville's *Letters from Attica*. Most of my knowledge about him is secondhand. We had never exchanged a word until early in the morning of September 10, 1971.*

But in another way, it probably is appropriate. Sam and I first laid eyes on each other in the D Block yard of what is euphemistically referred to as the Attica Correctional Facility during the inmate rebellion at that maximum security institution. Under those circumstances what otherwise would have amounted to nothing more than a fleeting acquaintance suddenly sprang forth as a significant relationship which more than made up in dramatic intensity what it lacked in longevity.

Sam was virtually the first inmate I met formally at Attica. At dawn on Saturday, September 10, after a nightlong session of listening to and cataloguing prisoner demands, my fellow negotiators and I were waiting to be escorted from D yard when Sam walked over to me. "I'm Sam Melville," he said in a quiet, subdued voice, "and I'd like to

---

* SF: In his autobiography Kunstler says he went into D Yard "shortly before midnight"; other sources say 11:30 PM or 2:00 AM. In any event, it was night. William M. Kunstler, *My Life as a Radical Lawyer* (Secaucus, NJ: Birch Lane Press, 1994), 217.

say hello to you. We have many mutual friends."* We had time just
to shake hands and exchange a few words before the committee was
asked to follow its guides back through the no-man's-land of yards
and catwalks that separated the portion held by the rebels from the
rest of the prison.

Strangely enough, Sam was one of the last inmates to whom I spoke.
On my final visit to the yard the following Sunday evening, as we were
about to leave, I asked someone where he was. I was taken to him. He was
in a line of men who, with arms linked, stood between the main body of
prisoners and the immediate area of the negotiating table. I embraced him
and said that I hoped we would meet again someday. Without breaking
ranks, he looked at me and said, "I hope so. But whatever happens, tell
everyone that people here are as together as I once hoped they could be
on the outside."

In a way, it was inevitable that Sam would become deeply involved
in the rebellion. He was a political person, dedicated to social change.
When he arrived at Attica he joined Fred LeShure's sociology class,
and there he ran into Herbert X. Blyden, one of the three blacks in
the fifteen-man class. Sam had known Blyden at the Tombs, and
Blyden showed him a manifesto of demands prepared by a number
of black and white inmates who called themselves the Attica Liberation Faction.

Although Sam initially expressed some doubts about the manifesto,
which was modeled after one created a year earlier by Martin Sousa, a
Chicano inmate at Folsom Prison in Comstock, California,† he eventually supported it wholeheartedly. Within a short time he had been
made a vice-president of the Liberation Faction as well as chief of the A
Block Workers' Coalition. After George Jackson's death at San Quentin

---

* DV: Incidentally, Kunstler was also associated with some that Sam categorically did
not consider friends: Kunstler had previously defended FBI informant George Demmerle, alongside Abbie Hoffman, in a case related to Demmerle's faux radical leftist
activities while spying on members of the radical left community. Neither Kunstler
nor anyone outside the FBI was aware at the time of that case that Demmerle was an
informant.

† JM: Folsom Prison is actually located within the city of Folsom, California. It's unknown
what Kunstler is referring to when he references "Comstock, California," which is not a
recognized locale in the state.

in August, he helped to organize the Attica "spiritual sit-in," which consisted of a silent fast in A and B messes and the wearing of black armbands.*†‡

When the inmates seized control of D Block on September 9, 1971, Sam was part of the first leadership group. It was Sam who first suggested that Herb Blyden become a member of their negotiating committee. As Blyden recalls it, shortly after the take-over he heard Sam's voice over the loudspeaker saying, "Will Herb Blyden come to the bullhorn?" When he did, he was asked to be one of the two representatives from B Block on the committee. "Our lives are at stake," Sam had told him, "and it is vital that we get the blocks together." Blyden, who first demurred, finally agreed and later, by unanimous vote of the full committee, was elected its chairman.§

---

* JV: George Jackson (1941–1971) was an African American author and revolutionary most famous for his bestselling book *Soledad Brother* (Chicago: Lawrence Hill Books, 1994; orig. publ. 1970), written from prison. Jackson commanded a following on the left beyond the prison walls. In 1970 his brother Jonathan Jackson was killed after an armed attempt to free radical prisoners from a courthouse in California. Prisoners' anger at George Jackson's killing a year later during an apparent prison escape helped precipitate the uprising in Attica prison in New York State.

† SF: The fast with inmates wearing black armbands was held on August 27 to honor George Jackson, killed one week earlier by a San Quentin prison guard. To the Brothers of Attica, it was a memorial; to prison authorities, it was a nightmare, because it showed the unprecedented unity of every faction and every block of the prison. Sergeant Jack English, stationed in the mess hall that evening, described it as "the weirdest thing. . . . They just walked through the line and went to their seats and they sat down. They looked straight ahead, and nobody made a sound. You could have heard your wristwatch ticking. A thing like that took a lot of planning and organization. We had no idea they were that organized." Sam may have helped organize this key event but sadly was not able to participate as he was then undergoing a ten-day stint in keeplock. Derrick Morrison, *The Attica Rebellion* (New York: Pathfinder Press, 1972), 3.

‡ "Keeplock," referred to in Sharon Fischer's note above, was a disciplinary measure by which a prisoner was "locked in his cell all day and deprived of privileges," as John Cohen explains in his introduction.

§ SF: Blyden "demurred" initially because he already faced a seventy-eight-count indictment for his role in the 1970 Tombs rebellion, but at the urging of Sam and others he relented; Tom Wicker, *A Time to Die* (New York: Quadrangle, 1975), 50–56. Roger Champen later described to Wicker how the leadership worked: "Before we made a decision . . . I would talk to Herb [Blyden] and Herb would talk to me and we would talk to Sam and would talk to Richie . . . then . . . I would raise it to the general population." Roger Champen, manuscript from taped interview, 39–40, in Wicker, 330.

When the shooting started on Bloody Monday, Sam seems to have been one of the first victims.* In fact, the prison authorities, despite statements that they would not release the names of slain inmates until next of kin had been notified, lost no time in proclaiming that "Mad Bomber Melville" had been shot down while rushing toward an oil drum with four homemade Molotov cocktails. But many of his fellow inmates have since told interviewers that just before the attack Sam was seen wandering in the vicinity of the bend in the defense trench paralleling the catwalks that divided D from A and B yards, and that he had had nothing whatsoever in his hands.

I have my own suspicions that Sam was gunned down because he was an apostate—a white man who had managed to leap racial barriers. Herb Blyden reflected this when he told me he had insisted that Sam sign a condolence letter sent by the Attica inmates to George Jackson's mother after her son's death. "Without Sam's signature," Blyden said, "the letter to Mrs. Jackson just wouldn't have meant as much."

Although Sam's letters are hardly enough to memorialize his life, in many ways they go to the heart of the Attica story. But it would be purposeless to interpret these letters; I am sure that Sam never anticipated that anyone but their addressees would see them, but they speak quite eloquently for themselves. Whether he is writing about politics, pollution, vegetarianism, penal conditions, or standing up to his guards, he is outspoken, articulate and, above all, singularly honest with both himself and his correspondents. It is utterly impossible to read these letters without coming to the conclusion that they were composed by a caring and sensitive and deeply moral person.

Since his death many people have told me that Sam was a revolutionary. To me, this means that he favored the radical alteration or destruction of social institutions which had proved themselves incapable of responding

---

* SF: In 1972 this may have been a reasonable assumption by Kunstler. Today we believe that Sam was one of the last. Regardless of when or where Sam died, there is no doubt that his was the first death announced to the world, less than one hour after it supposedly happened, while other Brothers' families had to wait days to learn if their loved ones were alive or dead. On Wednesday, September 15 (two days after the assault), a first partial inmate casualty list was released. The first name on it was Samuel Joseph Melville. "First List of Prisoner Dead Made," *Buffalo Courier Express*, September 15, 1971.

to the needs of those they professed to serve. How cruel and exasperating it must be for such a man to find himself in a prison, where even relatively minor change is hardly possible.

But men like Sam are not deterred by the seeming hopelessness of their situations. Like Herman Melville, whose last name he adopted as his own, he saw man's role as perpetually seeking to overcome evil. Prison did not destroy Sam's basic optimism. In one letter written from the bleakness of Attica to a discouraged friend, he said, "I offer my love, and ask that you consider anew the prospects of winning."

Sam may have gone down lashed to the whale, but tomorrow Ishmael returns to the sea.*

---

* RC: One of William Kunstler's favorite images, in his writing and his speeches, was that of Ishmael returning to the sea. Melville, of course, left Ishmael's future undecided. For Kunstler, whose long life taught him that the struggle against evil is perennial, it was unthinkable that Ishmael would do anything other than return.

PROFILE
OF SAM MELVILLE

by Jane Alpert

For Jocko Melville

I FELL IN LOVE WITH SAM MELVILLE on a crisp September morning in 1968, at a sit-in in front of the St. Marks Arms on West 112th Street in New York City. The sit-in, called to stop the evictions of the building's aging tenants, was the last significant action of the Community Action Committee, a group of perhaps two dozen Columbia students, Upper West Side white radicals, and working-class tenants who were trying to get the community together in the apathetic aftermath of the Columbia strike. CAC had been together since May; I was a latecomer and had gone to my first meeting only a week before the St. Marks Arms action. I liked the people in the group more than any I'd met since college and I quickly became caught up in the sense of urgency they felt about their relevance to each other as a community.

I don't remember Sam from that first CAC meeting a week before the sit-in, although he told me later he had stared at me intently throughout it. I'm sure he didn't say anything to me or anyone else. In all the meetings Sam and I went to together in the following year I rarely heard him

contribute to the discussions except for occasional angry outbursts that
talk was bullshit, and why didn't we *do* something. The morning of the
sit-in he was much more noticeable. My attention was drawn to him as
soon as I saw him striding exuberantly up the street, looking strong and
alive in anticipation of the approaching conflict with the marshals. I had
already been watching him for some minutes when he seated himself on
my stoop and asked if he could look at my *Times*. We talked for perhaps
fifteen minutes, and in those fifteen minutes I forgot almost everything
else that was happening. I thought—I still think—that he was the most
dynamic human being I'd ever met.

We started talking about communes, and he launched into an enthusiastic description of a piece of land upstate he was thinking of buying with
some insurance money he was about to receive. After we'd talked for less
than five minutes he invited me to visit or live at the commune, which
wasn't even yet a reality. He seemed so little like a man who wasted his
time on idle fantasies that I did not doubt he would bring the commune
into being; nor did his invitation seem forward. Sam was simply—in his
good moods—an incredibly warm and open human being who could
initiate intimate discussions with strangers out of simple affection and
friendliness.

Sam told me he'd been working at *The National Guardian*[*][†] since
April as a deliveryman and handyman, earning, like the rest of the staff,
fifty dollars a week. It was his first involvement with an organization
which at least made a pretense of collective dedication to a revolutionary
movement, and Sam had put his whole being into it. I bought a copy of
the paper from him and then gave him a check for a subscription, more
as a ruse so that he'd have my name and address than from any serious
interest in the paper.

Sam was a powerfully built man, over six feet tall, broad-chested and
broad-shouldered, muscular rather than heavy. What impressed me most

---

* Cohen: *The National Guardian* is a weekly radical newspaper.
† JV: The *Guardian* was a New York City–based radical weekly newspaper. With roots in
the Progressive Party of the 1940s, it provided news stories and editorials from a broadly
socialist perspective. Sharing little in the anarchic spirit of underground newspapers like
Rat Subterranean News, it favored mass movement building and disdained the radicalism
of groups like Weather.

about him was that he was a self-avowed revolutionary, a man in apparently active struggle against the power structure. I had never met anyone like him before. He always stood tall and straight, and his face emanated a proud vitality. The bones were clean and prominent; he had a strong chin line and a straight jutting nose. His face, when I met him, looked younger than his years despite a receding hairline and a bald spot he'd had since he was twenty. His mouth was wide and thin-lipped, sensitive and mobile. But most amazing were his eyes. Even behind the steel-rimmed glasses he usually wore, it was obvious that they were two different colors: the right clear blue, the left a sort of hazel going to green. His left eye was totally sightless and therefore expressionless. It contrasted oddly, sometimes frighteningly, with what went on in the rest of his face, and one was never quite able to pinpoint the strangeness of his aspect.

In Sam's good moods his presence was charismatic. He was one of those people who could hold a crowd of friends enthralled not so much by what he said as by the dynamic shading of his voice and his great vitality. With people who appealed to him he was irresistibly gregarious. He loved good meals, good times, good dope, and lots of company. One felt he was incapable of any manner but that simple, warm earthiness. A close friend used to call this Sam's "farmer image";* his honest heartiness reminded her of the classic pictures of Western farm folk.

I thought about Sam every day after the sit-in and longed to see him again, but I had little hope. At work I told a friend I'd spent the morning talking with the most attractive man I'd ever met. I thought of calling him, but there was no listing for him with the telephone company. I was quite startled when he called me up one evening a week later and said he wanted to drop by my place.

He appeared at the door five minutes after he called, just giving me time to wash my face and change out of my jeans. When I opened the door I saw he hadn't changed his clothes since I'd last seen him. A faded blue workshirt, multi-pocketed overalls, and six-inch boots were virtually his uniform. He seemed out of place and a shade uncomfortable in my apartment which, though hardly luxurious, still featured more furnishings,

---

* SF: At Attica, Sam applied for and was given a "garden plot," sadly revoked when he was charged with insubordination.

knickknacks, and carpeting than suited Sam's monkish preferences. Our conversation that evening was a lot more strained than before. He drew out my opinions on the university system, on government, on Marxism, and proceeded to attack all my rather nebulous ideas with what then seemed to be a terrifyingly logical consistency. I smile now, remembering how he intimidated me. As the ideas of the New Left became familiar to me it also became clear that Sam was no great thinker, something he would have been the first to tell you. It was the power of his ideas, not his logic, that was compelling. When I mentioned to him later how he had awed me verbally that night, he couldn't even remember the substance of his arguments, only his tension over whether I wanted to sleep with him as much as he did with me.

Sam told me that he was thirty-two, almost thirty-three, that he'd been married until four or five years before, that he had a six-year-old son whom he hadn't seen in many months because he couldn't work out an arrangement with his wife. He told me he'd worked as a civil engineer for nearly eight years, starting out as a draftsman by pretending to have an engineering degree;* then, as he gained experience, changing jobs and gradually increasing his salary to twelve thousand dollars or more a year;† finally sickening of his whole way of life and deserting his marriage, his job, and the assortment of responsibilities he'd accumulated and becoming, as he put it, a bum. He told me how much he envied the kids at Columbia who realized that middle-class life was a pile of shit before they got sucked into it, as he had been, and that he identified more with eighteen- and nineteen-year-olds than he did with friends he'd known since his early twenties.

I was keenly aware of the differences in our lives. I was twenty-one when I met Sam, a year out of college, working at a publishing job people

---

* JM: In fact, my parents separated twice, once in '65 and again in '66, and ultimately my mother asked my father to leave in part because of his infidelities but mostly because they had grown apart ideologically. When my father met Alpert he was still married to my mother, and they would not officially divorce until after his arrest in 1969; my mother never refused him a parental visit. According to her, he would disappoint me by not showing up. He did, in fact, have an engineering degree from the Brooklyn Polytechnic Institute, a night school.

† JM: Adjusted for inflation, $12,000 in 1976 is approximately $55,000 to $60,000 today.

ten years older might have envied but which I was coming to despise. I
was a part-time student at Columbia during the strike, but I'd taken no
role in it. Seeing the frustration of professors and graduate students who
were miserable with their lives but afraid of change had had a strong
effect on me and made me aware of my own alienation, but I had not yet
found the courage to break with my upbringing. Sam talked as if it were
easy, and I was deeply impressed with the courage that he must have had
to abandon, overnight, the accoutrements of middle-class security. Sam's
way of confronting people with their most personal fears usually made
them either his enemies or his devoted admirers. I thought as we talked
that he must despise me for my cowardice and I was taken aback when,
during a short pause in our rather heated conversation, he asked me if I
would go to bed with him.

It was sex that broke down the barriers between us in the first weeks
we spent together. Sam always preferred naked confrontations—of any
kind—to ideological debate, and I loved making love with him. He always
insisted that I enjoy it as much as he did, a trait most men profess but
few act upon. One of his more amazing characteristics was his complete
frankness about his sexual fantasies. They were classical male supremacist
fantasies—he liked to imagine himself a sultan and me his odalisque—but
his freedom about his fantasies initially gave both of us great pleasure.
Nevertheless it was impossible that his inmost attitudes toward women
as sexual objects and the natural slaves of men confine themselves exclusively to the bedroom. Over the next year I often thought, and said as
much to Sam, that his sexual power trip was the central paradox of his
alienation and that the liberation he sought would evade him as long as
he was unable to deal with it. These arguments filled him with despair.
He said he could never change his fantasies; perhaps it would be different
if he were younger, but at thirty-three it was just too late for him. Still,
his own awareness of his sexist psychology and his willingness to bring
it out in the open—I do not say this to excuse it—set him far apart from
men who are unable even to admit that in their secret lives they are rap-
ing every woman who passes them.*

---

* SF: Alpert makes quite a point of informing us about Sam's sexism during the thirteen
months they knew each other. Every male in the universe was a "male chauvinist pig" back

I saw Sam again the next night, and the next, and after that until I gave him a key to my apartment and he moved in. He charged with me an exciting new vitality in those first weeks. Compared to Sam's tremendous energy, I saw white America, even relatively young white America, sunk in an abyss of boredom and apathy and I wondered what it was that sucked the life-force out of us before we even emerged from adolescence. When I picture Sam before me now I often see him as he looked one night that week. I was expecting him to come at about midnight, and on impulse I decided to wait for him outside. I was wearing a sweater, but, seated on the pedestal of a statue by Riverside Park, I soon began shivering; I was thinking about going back inside when Sam came swinging jauntily down the street, his shirt half unbuttoned, a big cigar stuck in his teeth, squinting a little in the dark to see who it was sitting out there in the middle of the night. When he figured it out, he swung himself lightly up on the pedestal, pulled me close to him, and immediately started talking about a Godard movie he'd just seen, as if fully prepared to spend the night sitting half-naked in the October chill. He said he wasn't cold.

But then, Sam almost never admitted he was cold. He did not own a coat, out of choice rather than poverty. He had two sweaters, one of which he gave me, one of which he wore only when the temperature dropped below twenty degrees. People continually asked him, running into him in his shirtsleeves during a snowstorm, if he wasn't cold. The first couple of times they'd ask, he'd say no. Only when he was irritated by the recurrent questions would he tell the truth: "Sure I'm cold. I get cold just like everyone else, but I *like* being cold." It was important to him to challenge his body to see how much it could take. Going coatless all winter was just one aspect of this. He liked strenuous wilderness hikes and swimming naked in icy water. For several months he used to go to a gym in the middle of his workdays at the *Guardian* and work out with

---

then. Most are today. But Sam's letters revealed his growing awareness of that and his struggle to change. He even ordered feminist literature. It was not easy for a male inmate to support the women's movement in the macho environment of a maximum security prison almost fifty years ago. As a feminist, I would never defend or excuse sexism in anyone, male or female, but I think it's fair to say that had he lived Sam Melville would have continued to grow and fight sexism—in society, and other people, and in himself.

weights for two hours. After a month of that he told me he could press as much as some men who'd been at the gym for years. He was reputed to be one of the best frisbee players in Manhattan; but his favorite sport was basketball. Every couple of weeks he'd go to a neighborhood park and play a rough game with black kids half his age and twice his speed. I think he was a little hurt once when one of them told him he was "pretty good for an old man."

When Sam moved into my apartment he brought everything he owned: a few pairs of jeans and shirts, two pipes, a dictionary, *Moby Dick*—and a fine Martin acoustic guitar, which went with him everywhere.* Sam was a trained musician and a very good one. He'd studied for several years to be an operatic tenor, had taught voice, played tuba and French horn, and been a professional choir singer for a number of years. He was an excellent amateur folk guitarist and his voice was heartbreakingly sweet, yet powerful enough to fill a large room. In rare moods, he would sing Schubert lieder or old ballads in his exquisite tenor. Much more often he sang baritone and played folk songs by Dylan, McCartney, Muddy Waters, and Jack Elliot. His favorite musicians were the old Delta blues singers; his knowledge of and taste for classical music seemed to embarrass him a little, except when he was with a few old friends who'd once been in a choral group together.†

He told me once that in his days of dreaming about grand opera he'd been to every concert Fischer-Dieskau had given in New York. Sam's enthusiasm for anything was completely captivating, and when Fischer-Dieskau came to Carnegie Hall in January I decided to surprise him by buying tickets. I hoped very much that he'd be pleased, and was gratified when his eyes lit up and he rewarded me with a delighted hug. But when I called him from work the day of the concert and asked him if he wanted

---

* JM: Alpert's use of the term "moved in" is somewhat subjective. He owned little more than could be contained in a small backpack, and two other women he was involved with at the time whom I interviewed claimed they gave him keys to their apartment. He would alternate between Alpert and theirs. All three women were aware of each other.

† JM: My father took voice and conducting courses at City College. The only instrument he played with proficiency was guitar. He never sang professionally, although it was his dream to be an orchestral conductor. His knowledge of classical music was extensive. According to my mother, he criticized pop music as decadent and only embraced artists like Bob Dylan and Delta blues singers after he became radicalized.

to meet me at Carnegie Hall, he said, "Babe, I hope you don't mind too much. I really don't want to go." We gave the tickets away. Sam wasn't sorry to have missed the concert. He said he didn't like Carnegie Hall anymore, the minks and jeweled cuff links and idiotic talk bothered him, and anyway he didn't think it was healthy to immerse oneself in the art of another era.

He was the same way about poetry. He knew dozens of poems by heart, mostly Gerard Manley Hopkins and Hart Crane and Walt Whitman, but it was only in occasional romantic moments that I ever heard them. He was contemptuous of my enormous book collection, although I occasionally found him sneaking looks at volumes of poetry and ancient philosophy. He claimed that in holding on to so many books I never read I was clutching at material possessions. I finally had no choice but to agree, and he persuaded me to sell the collection to a secondhand bookstore. Sam then packed and delivered every last one, even the poetry and foreign language dictionaries that had fascinated him. The argument had become so heated that he must have thought it would seem a surrender to hold on to a few. Sam never surrendered.

In certain moods, Sam enjoyed talking about his childhood. I think this happened especially with women who were attracted to him, because he'd discovered that they were pushovers for his stories. He was a good storyteller, as much because of the dramatic timbre of his voice as anything else, and over the years he'd romanticized his early autobiography to the point where he himself was unsure of how much was true. With some corrections which I later learned from Sam's stepmother, whom I met a few times after our arrest, this is the story:

Sam was born October 14, 1935, in the Bronx. His mother and father separated when he was still very young. His mother then moved back to her hometown, North Tonawanda, between Buffalo and Niagara Falls, New York, with the children. Sam told me that his mother was a prostitute and gave me the impression that she'd never married his father, and that she had had no idea as to the paternity of his two half-sisters, one a year or two older than he, the other five or six years younger. This seems to have been one of Sam's romantic exaggerations; but he did not use the word prostitute deprecatingly. He commonly used the word "slut" as an approbation, meaning by it a woman who was honest and direct about her sexuality—not understanding that his altered intention did not alter the insult. He nearly always spoke of his mother with great affection, even when describing the extremes of her behavior. Her frequent moving around, her dependence on having a new paramour every six months, her neglect of her children weren't things that Sam resented. He was glad to have learned independence early in his life and thought his upbringing had been preferable to that of the Jewish middle-class sheltered homes in which most of his adult friends were raised. Yet his mother's neglect, if it did not do him emotional damage, at least cost him half his vision. When he was four or five he got a cinder in his left eye while his mother was either away from home or not in the mood to listen to his complaints, and by the time he got medical attention the cinder had penetrated so deeply that the eye never recovered any sight.

Sam always led me to believe that Melville was his mother's name, which he'd used naturally while he was growing up because she used it. It was only in court, when the prosecutor tried to imply to the Jewish judge that Sam had rejected his father's name out of anti-Semitism, that I learned that Sam had legally changed his name from Grossman to Melville sometime shortly before he married.* While anti-Semitism certainly had nothing to do with it, it is quite possible that Sam took the name Melville not from his mother but in a spirit of rejecting both his parents, and that his only connection to the name was his admiration for the great writer. He'd read *Moby Dick* four or five times and could recite whole chapters by heart and was also familiar with the lesser works. It was like him to identify with Herman Melville's romantic hero, who devoted his life to the pursuit of his superhuman enemy, and to desire the relationship so strongly that he could pretend a possible blood tie by saying that his mother had been a Melville. The day the issue of his

---

* JM: My father actually changed his name from Grossman three years *after* he married my mother, when I was almost two. My mother suggested the name "Melville," because *Moby Dick* was his favorite book. The catalyst for his name change was resentment for his father Bill Grossman, who Sam felt was a sellout for quitting the Communist Labor Party and becoming a capitalist by buying a restaurant. They spoke rarely after this falling out. Bill Grossman died before my father met Alpert.

name came up in court, I asked him, surprised, why he didn't tell his lawyer that Melville had been the name he was brought up with. He only smiled.

Whatever ambivalence Sam may have felt toward his mother, his feeling about most of her boyfriends was uncomplicated contempt. This contempt was not simply part of the myth. It came out only once, when he was reliving his adolescence aloud at the height of an acid trip and dredged out of his subconscious the immediate cause of his leaving home. His mother was living with a man named Tag, whom Sam once described as even more lazy and abusive than his predecessors. His mother was working at some drudgelike job at the time, and Tag would lie around in bed all day, drinking liquor, yelling at Sam and his sisters, not even getting up until Sam's mother came home from work. Sam was about fifteen at the time, growing stronger and angrier, and he'd had enough. He told me he'd attacked the man, beaten him up, and thrown him out of the house. Then, afraid of his mother's wrath, he packed a few clothes and left home himself. He quit school and got a room in the Buffalo YMCA and a job setting up pins at a bowling alley.

Sam's second favorite story from those years was about walking home from the bowling alley when he got off work at two or three a.m. The buses had stopped running at that hour, and he loved to describe, in his inimitably expressive voice, the stillness of the empty roads at night, the snow piled on the ground and flying around him, the trees whistling at him, as he sang and whispered and recited poetry and shouted at the stars the length of the seven miles. But his favorite story from that period was about his first meeting his father. Sam's father had recently married his second wife, and together they went to North Tonawanda to see his two children. Sam's older sister had by this time run away from home and married, but his father and his stepmother had better luck with Sam. Sam vividly described seeing his father for the first time in his memory; he was coming out of some building in Buffalo; his father was standing at the bottom of the stairs leading up to the building. Sam said that, after dreaming of his father his whole life, he knew him at once and just stood and stared at him for some time before finally yielding and racing down the stairs.

Sam's father and his wife spent several days with Sam. They convinced him to finish high school, offering what financial support they could provide. They promised that once he finished school he could come to New York City and live with them and that they would give him the singing lessons he longed for. Sam said that by this time he'd outgrown the adolescent homeliness which, among his other problems, had made him miserable in school, and he leaped at the chance to return. He did his last two years at a high school in Buffalo, continuing to work after school. He joined the glee club and the school orchestra, made friends his own age for the first time, and started dating. His grades were erratic; he said he was fairly good at English and math, but terrible at languages. But he had lots of charm and was allowed to graduate despite the lack of a few required courses because of the efforts of a few teachers whose hearts had gone out to his proud self-sufficiency. He graduated at nineteen and went to live with his father, stepmother, and three half-brothers in the Bronx. Within a few years he lost touch with his mother and sisters and never saw them again.*

New York City opened up a new world to Sam. To fit his changed life he stopped using his childhood nickname, Buddy, and may have adopted the surname Grossman for the first time. Sam's father had joined the Communist Party in the thirties or forties.† He was friends, Sam said, with many prominent left-wing intellectuals in the city, and worked for

---

* JM/SF: Bill Grossman left Sam's biological mother with three children and remained disconnected from her from the time my father was five until their reacquaintance described above when he was sixteen. Regarding the "first meeting" Alpert describes, his stepmother could not have been present for it, since she did not meet Sam's father until two years after this incident. My father quit school and was hired as an apprentice at a small Tonawanda company, Beacon Devices, where he lived on the premises. Beacon was an army contractor that made windproof lighters and fire extinguishers. This is likely where he gained his knowledge of keeping water and fire under pressure—knowledge he put to use in D Yard constructing his famous "rocket launcher." He had only two half-brothers through Bill's second marriage. He never lived with them but saw the older one on occasions when he would accompany Bill to CLP meetings.

† JV: From its founding in 1919 through the 1950s, the Communist Party USA was a major force on the American left. It helped shape the labor movement and vigorously supported the freedom struggles of Black people in the South. The McCarthyite Red Scare of the 1950s badly hurt the party's membership and reputation. In the early 1960s, the New Leftists largely broke with established communist parties, questioning their perceived dogmatism and their focus on the working class as the key agent of social change.

many years with the Communists organizing taxi drivers' unions in New York. Once when Sam and I were driving up Lenox Avenue, he told me how his father used to take him to Harlem to teach him how the white ruling class forced the poor to live. Sam said the message never quite got across to him because he could only envy the kids playing ball, chasing each other, fighting, and having fun in the streets. He said it seemed a much more joyful life to him than that which went on in more antiseptic neighborhoods.

Sam held a succession of odd jobs in those first years in New York, interrupted or combined with one or two short spells in college. His chief interests were music and socialism, both of which he approached in his characteristic romantic style. He eventually became disillusioned with the latter; or rather, he became disillusioned with his father, who was his main tie to socialism in his early years. He said that his father at the end could not stand up to the pressure of McCarthyism, left the party and abandoned his ideals, and moved with his wife and Sam's half-brothers to a home in a white middle-class neighborhood on Long Island. Sam said they parted bitterly, and that he had not seen his father for some years when he died of cancer in February 1968, just eight months before I met Sam. At the funeral he quarreled for the last time with his stepmother, whom he did not see again until she came to visit him in jail. His father, though he died nearly penniless, bequeathed his eyes to his oldest son.

Sam's father had at least some lasting influence on him. While Sam despised the cowardice of the Communist Party, its political analysis of imperialism and the inevitability of socialist revolution was the first and last political doctrine he ever learned. He did not progress through the usual stages of liberal reformism when he joined the movement. In the late sixties he merely began to put into practice what he had held to be true for a decade.

Sam told me that he married when he was twenty-two or thereabouts (he tended to be vague about dates). His wife had just graduated from college with a degree in education, and according to Sam she pressured him to get into some respectable line of work. I can't quite imagine anyone ever successfully pressuring Sam to do anything he didn't want to do, but he describes his wife (whom I never met) as having had great power over him in the first years they were together, partly because of her strong will, partly through deviousness, and partly because he was totally enamored of her. Her chief determination seems to have been to make a materially comfortable life for herself and I expect that Sam, disappointed over his father's sellout, was glad to try the new role of good-Jewish-husband-provider for a while.*

He got a job as a draftsman in a civil engineering firm, and although he had no formal education in engineering he was probably good at his work. He had a natural mechanical bent which corresponded to the very physical way he related to everything—though I think he fell a little short of being the "electrical genius" members of the New York City bomb squad were later to call him. He worked at a succession of engineering jobs for the next eight years or so. He never stayed at one job for more than two years.

He didn't mind his work but he hated the companies he worked for. One incident perhaps foretold the nature of his future political involvement. He was ordered by one firm to begin work on a building project which turned out to be the construction of new offices for Chase Manhattan in the Union of South Africa. When he found out what the project was, he became so infuriated he could barely control himself from striking the boss who had given him the directive, and immediately turned on his heel and walked off the job. He was so disgusted with his employer's utter casualness about profiting from apartheid that he could not have returned to the firm in any capacity. It was a moral rather than a political reaction, as so many of Sam's responses were. Sam never related to the

---

* JM: Alpert's recollection jibes with my mother's here, though my mother would not call herself "devious" but rather "practical." Sam criticized my mother for wanting a large apartment but easily afforded himself luxuries when it came to his interests in music, such as recording equipment and an expensive stereo. She told me that shortly before I was born my father said to her, "I'd rather have my son think of me as a successful engineer than a starving musician." I have no doubt that she encouraged this change of heart. He quit his musical ambitions and went to night school to earn a degree in plumbing engineering. I interpret this as my father's attempt to form some semblance of a "normal" life after his turbulent adolescence. The responsibilities of being a family provider proved too confining for him and could not compete with the freedom and allure of the counterculture growing around the Upper West Side by 1966 and what he saw as his calling to be a meaningful part of social reform.

complex theories about racism that intrigued the New Left, but he did relate closely to the styles, attitudes, and the strengths of black people, and he responded to white supremacy, overt or veiled, as though it were simply incomprehensible and not to be borne.

His marriage was falling apart by the time Ruth became pregnant with their son, Jocko, and they separated during her pregnancy, then came back together for another year after Jocko was born. Their ideas of the ways they wanted to live were increasingly in conflict, and trying to raise a child together only made this more emphatic. Middle-class comforts now bored and disgusted Sam, and he and Ruth fought angrily over everything: life styles, sex, child-rearing, and her accusations that he was a communist. They separated for the last time when Jocko was less than a year old.

Sam saw his wife and son regularly for the first few years after the separation, but their conflicts grew so bitter that he had stopped seeing even Jocko by the spring of 1968. He had a picture of his son taken when he was six years old which he treasured and kept in his guitar case. He didn't like to talk about him. Once he told me he had called his wife's house after he'd seen his son for what turned out to be the last time. Jocko had answered the phone, to Sam's pleasure. He greeted him, "Hi, Jocko, this is Daddy," and the boy responded with silence, then hesitantly volunteered that his mother wasn't home. Sam told him he didn't want to talk to his mother, he wanted to talk to him, and repeated, "This is Daddy." Jocko then said, "No, my daddy's gone away and he's not coming back." Sam said the conversation broke his heart and he hung up without another word, and never tried to call again. When he renewed contact with Ruth after he was in jail, in order to get a formal divorce from her, she refused to allow him to see the boy. She never told Jocko that his father was in jail.*

I take Sam's very negative descriptions of his wife with a grain of salt. I'm sure his love for Jocko was genuine, but his relationship with women was always sexist and he must have been even worse in the years of his marriage than he was when I knew him. Whatever Ruth's faults,

---

* JM: My mother never insisted that he could not see me. Rather, she insisted that he write to me from prison. His letters can be found herein. He would not have done so without her permission.

her resentment of Sam had at least some valid grounds. I expect that after Jocko was born Sam delivered his notions on how the child ought to be raised but never offered real assistance. When Sam and I talked of having a child together he was always excited about the idea, yet there was something casual in his attitude which frightened me. He made it clear that he was not about to take on the burdensome aspects of raising any child he conceived and that, if we separated, the child would become my sole responsibility. While I've sometimes regretted not having become pregnant before he went to jail, I don't doubt that it was a sensible decision. And while I'm not sure I could like Ruth if I met her, I don't hold her accountable for what Sam suffered in the years of his marriage.

After Sam left Ruth and before he started working at the *Guardian* he lived on short-term jobs or unemployment checks. His last straight job was a one-semester spell teaching plumbing design at a trade school.* It was one of the few things in his recent employment history that his lawyer was able to use to argue that he was a sufficiently respectable citizen to deserve release on bail. Sam himself liked to sum up the experience, "The only thing you have to teach a plumber is payday comes on Friday and shit don't go uphill." While he had this job, in the winter and spring of 1968, he started to take an active interest in the radical activities around Columbia University. He went to Peace and Freedom party† rallies, joined CAC,‡ and was arrested for the first time in the occupation of an apartment building from which Columbia was evicting the tenants.

---

* JM: After leaving his engineering job at Syska & Hennessy, Sam's only other job before he worked for the *Guardian* was teaching air-conditioning installation at the Voorhees Technical Institute. I researched what I could of the available unemployment archives for confirmation of Alpert's facts. I found nothing. According to my mother's divorce papers, unemployment benefits were not listed as one of my father's assets.

† JV: Formed in the mid-1960s, the Peace and Freedom Party (PFP) was a radical political party that ran candidates in local and national elections, though perhaps more as an act of protest than a bid for electoral power. In 1968 Black Panther leader Eldridge Cleaver ran for president as the PFP candidate, with Yippie leader Jerry Rubin nominated as his running mate.

‡ JM: It would probably be more accurate to say that Sam cofounded the CAC with John Cohen. Their only significant action was the demonstration Alpert describes. The CAC broke up shortly after. While this incident is what started both Sam's and John Cohen's FBI files, this was not my father's first arrest. He was arrested for refusing to proceed to a bomb shelter in 1959 during a Cold War air-raid drill.

One friend told me that when Sam had arrived at the building with the other demonstrators, he promptly went to sleep in a vacant upstairs apartment. When someone awakened him to tell him the police were on the way, he said, "Okay, let me know when they're here"—and went back to sleep. The police came, ordered the building cleared, and then arrested everyone, including Sam, who had awakened by this time. I saw him in a newsreel film of the event, wearing his best guerrilla expression, stern, proud, eyes straight ahead as he marched into the paddy wagon with the rest. (Others who were at that scene said it wasn't true that Sam had been asleep. In any case it's a nice image of the complete nonchalance he liked to project in tense situations.)

Sam was at this time living with a woman who was herself a radical activist, teaching an untraditional psychology course at City College (she called it "Revolution 101") and housing the Columbia Strike Committee in her large Upper West Side apartment. Sam told me the romantic aspects of his relationship with Diane had ended after a few weeks but that he had continued living with her as a "friend," and that he liked and trusted her. Diane's version, which I didn't learn for some time, was a little different. Diane fought fierce internal battles over her feeling of having been rejected by Sam, but to the extent she hadn't won them she felt possessive about Sam. For months after they'd stopped sleeping together, they'd continued to relate to the world as a couple, and that they no longer had sex hadn't changed the relationship much in Diane's mind. Yet the relationship that was so real for her simply did not exist for Sam, and I never had any idea when it had ended in his own mind. Perhaps it went on until the day I met him. Not that Sam lied to me; as far as his own feelings were concerned, he couldn't distinguish truth from fantasy. He had wiped out of his mind the period before he'd ceased to love Diane and came close to forgetting that he'd ever loved her at all.

For all Sam's intensity, there was something strangely mercurial about him, an unsettling sense that he was out of touch with some deep part of himself. It was typical of him to take people to his heart for a short time, practically worship them, then just as suddenly lose interest and act almost as if he didn't know them. In different ways he did this with men, with women, and with ideas. The warmth and tenderness of his love when he felt close to a person was equaled by the immense hostility of which he was capable. There were several periods in our life when Sam would, for no apparent reason, or simply because he felt slighted in some trivial way, announce to me that he wanted to "break up." These announcements always came out of the blue, were always serious and icy, were sometimes accompanied by a rage which Sam himself did not understand. I sometimes tried to rationalize him out of those moods, but our discussions invariably ended with me in tears or near them and Sam more disconsolate than before. He would emerge from those moods as suddenly as he went into them. Somehow our relationship survived them all, but not without scars.

Sam and I moved to the Lower East Side in November. Sam, inspired by Diane's ideas in particular, had for months been wrapped up with experimenting in communal living. When he gave up the idea of buying land with his insurance money, his plan was to get a large apartment in New York with room for six or seven people. Somewhat to my surprise, since I had now learned how short-lived his dreams were, he actually found a place for it, on a mad, stoned bicycle trip he and Diane took downtown one rainy day. Diane and Sam were very excited about it, although Sam told me when he got back from paying for the place (seventy dollars a month for rent, plus a staggering eight hundred dollars in "key money") that he'd been so stoned he couldn't remember what it looked like, except that the kitchen had a *stage* which would be great to fuck on and that it had four fireplaces. It also had no heat. It turned out to be, on a more sober viewing, a six-and-a-half-room apartment composed of two smallish parallel railroad flats with the wall broken down between the two kitchens. It was in a decaying tenement which stunk of cat semen on one of the city's most notorious streets, 11th between B and C. The two or three other people who'd expressed interest in the commune backed out when they saw it, and my first sight of it did not exactly inspire me. But by this time I'd quit graduate school and CAC was fading into oblivion so I no longer had anything holding me to the Upper West Side; and I was afraid I'd see little of Sam if I stayed uptown while he moved to 11th Street.

As an experiment in communal living, 11th Street was an abysmal failure. Within two weeks Sam and Diane were no longer on speaking terms, and when a new boyfriend of Diane's moved in we more or less partitioned the apartment into two separate dwellings and lived as two separate couples from then until Sam and I moved out in the spring. Sam had been attracted to the idea of a commune for the same confused reasons that he sought extra-monogamous relationships. He had had a history of moving restlessly from one woman to the next ever since his marriage broke up, and he tended to interpret his inability to be satisfied with one woman for more than a few months as some innate resistance to the system at large. He used to say that his marriage had convinced him that monogamy was simply one of the oppressive structures of capitalism. It was a system which isolated people from each other and then co-opted any struggle against that isolation by suggesting that its solution was to attach oneself to a partner as lonely and insecure as oneself, and shut out the rest of the world as a couple. The ideal he pictured was a society in which people shared their possessions and each other, free of jealousy, possessiveness, and insecurity. It was an exciting vision, but Sam was no more capable of carrying it out than any other normally repressed, and oppressive, male. Whether he was living with more than one woman, as on 11th Street, or merely having affairs with several while living with one, he wound up hurting either the "other" women (because he cared for them too little) or the "one," in this case me (because he cared for the "other" at the expense of our relationship).*

Despite the failure of the commune, living on the Lower East Side was a whole new experience for me and to a lesser extent—he had lived there before—for Sam. Some of our old friends from Morningside Heights moved down around the same time we did and we made new friends among the dope dealers, politicos, street theater freaks, and the rest of the pleasant, easygoing community that existed around us. Sam and I always seemed to have more money than anyone else (we had our salaries plus Sam's four thousand dollars in insurance money) so we kept the refrigerator full of food, the canisters full of grass, and the doors open. The house was full of people almost all the time, and we grew comfortable with the

---

* JM: I have interviewed several of the women with whom my father was involved at this time. Only the one Alpert calls "Diane" claimed that he "broke her heart." Others told me the general feeling among their group was that monogamy was akin to "state control."

life we'd made together in our slum. Sometimes we got up at dawn and rode bicycles down to the Williamsburg Bridge to watch the sun come up over the East River; at night we'd walk through the giant new housing developments along the river and listen to the buildings sigh as they swayed with the wind and the strange electrical hum of the city at night. We'd sit on a bench and smoke a joint or two, then stop at a candy store on Avenue B where the guy who worked the night shift packed two huge scoops in a fifteen-cent ice cream cone. Or we'd lean out our window and watch the circus of East 11th Street, the Puerto Rican kids burning cars. They always picked the biggest and newest ones, and Sam would cheer them on even as he shook his head at the utter futility of their anger at those cars. I made plans to quit my publishing job before the spring was over, and we talked of going to Mexico with the money we were saving. For a while we were pretty serious about that fantasy. I saved at least fifty dollars a week toward the trip, and we got books and studied Spanish together. (Sam used to get frustrated with that because I was much faster at picking up the language than he, even though neither of us learned an appreciable amount.)

Sam's brief involvement with the overground movement was gradually coming to an end. He had initially been drawn to the Left because the radical analysis of capitalist society helped him make sense of his own frustration and hostility. But most of the movement offered Sam no outlet for his energy. He was constitutionally unable to get involved in long-range organizing projects, partly because he had no patience for the endless discussions that such projects entail. Movement gossip bored him; talk that was not supported by action aroused his anger. By January 1969 he had become completely disillusioned with the *Guardian*, which had ossified years before he joined it. Without talking much about it, his initial enthusiasm evaporated and when he walked off the staff he gave no more notice than he had when he'd quit his succession of straight jobs.* His interest in demonstrations was confined to whatever opportunity they seemed to offer for militant action. The more he informed himself

---

* JM: Others who claimed to be part of the collective quit their jobs on the same week as Sam—including one who also worked at the *Guardian*. It was a coordinated effort to "drop out." Alpert, however, maintained her job at Cambridge University Press.

about the war, about foreign policy, and about the economic structure, the more he felt it was all doomed and that the only right action was whatever would push its physical destruction a little closer. He began to fantasize about sabotage.

This was not a sudden development in Sam, although it seemed to occur over a short period of time. He was by nature an intensely passionate man. His hostility to stupid and vicious forms of authority had long predated his political activism. The analysis of the New Left had given him a framework which justified his commitment to violent change, but the Left itself could not move fast enough for him. He once told me the story of the first mass action in which he'd participated, the defense of the Columbia campus against the second police invasion. Sam claimed that as the police charged the barricades, the people trying to defend their territory scattered in confusion, and he could not persuade them to fight back. Sam says that, left alone, he started dragging huge garbage cans up on a roof to hurl down on the heads of the invaders. It wasn't a particularly sensible move, isolated as he was and surrounded by club-waving cops, but Sam says he kept expecting people to help when they saw what he was doing. No one did. He was almost immediately grabbed by campus security guards who shoved him into a building, clubbed him a bit, and tied him to a chair, where he remained until a doctor gained admission to the building and demanded that he be released for medical treatment.* Sam couldn't understand what kept the others from being more militant in a situation where they had no choices but to be passively arrested or to fight back. It was something that baffled and depressed him at every demonstration he went to. Impatient with organizing, contemptuous of such sterile radical organs as the *Guardian*, and frustrated with people's helplessness at mass action, he inevitably began to think in terms of underground action.

---

* JM: This supposed incident during the Columbia takeover, in which my father threw trash cans from the roof, has become Sam Melville folklore. However, he could not have thrown garbage cans off the roof of any of the student-occupied buildings, because those roofs are steeply pitched and students had no access. But, like most legends, there is some truth. In this case, it is the conflation of the Columbia takeover with an incident in which he was tied up and beaten by cops the next week at the CAC occupation. This arrest is the same incident about which Jane claims earlier in this profile that Sam might have been "asleep."

During the winter of 1968–69 Sam discovered acid, and it instantly became his current enthusiasm. He would buy fifty hits at a time and drop nearly every day. He claimed he couldn't trust anyone he couldn't trip with. He announced that his goal was to become so comfortable on acid that he could carry on his normal activities as effectively stoned as straight.*

He liked to drop a few hits and then do some pushups and walk around the neighborhood, stopping in to buy things, to chat with people in storefronts, dropping in on friends. His acid phase lasted well into the spring, but the turning point came in March, when he experienced his first death trip.

In the last few years I've seen many bad drug trips but never anything that matched Sam's. The first death trip happened after he'd been into acid for some three months. He was at the apartment of a dealer from whom he was purchasing one hundred purple domes. He called me at work and told me to meet him at the apartment with the money. When I got there Sam was alone with the dealer; they'd both dropped some thirty minutes before. Sam was strangely quiet when I walked in and the look on his face disturbed me. The other man was looking at him closely and assuring him that it was really fine acid. I asked Sam how he felt; he shook his head slowly and muttered, "Heavy stuff, heavy stuff." We sat and smoked for another half hour and Sam grew increasingly tense. Suddenly he gripped my wrist as if he were drowning and asked me to take him home. I'd never before—and I never again—heard Sam utter an undisguised plea for help, and it was the only time in my life I saw him look frightened. I had to help Sam across the street and into a cab. By the time we got home he was practically catatonic. All he would say—in a barely audible voice that didn't even sound like his

---

* JM: According to my interviews, the group's experimentation with acid lasted less than three months, from December 1968 to February 1969. During this period many friends (more than eight that I met), some of whom eventually formed into the collective, were using the Eleventh Street apartment as a crash pad. The fifty hits were shared by all. According to her 1981 memoir, Alpert was out of the country during most of these dates. Also, thinking that a person was trustworthy if he or she was willing to drop acid was commonplace in the counterculture. Abbie Hoffman wrote about this belief contributing to his downfall, as he trusted several dopers who turned out to be cops.

own—was that death was the worst thing ever, that none of us realized how bad it was. He lay in bed and stayed there for the rest of the afternoon and a good part of the evening. Once in a while he'd grip my arm and ask me not to leave the room; the few times I did go out he seemed not to notice. The news that Sam was freaking out on acid was so astounding that within a few hours nearly everyone we knew had gathered in the living room and discussing in hushed voices what had gone wrong. Everyone has had bad trips from time to time—but not Sam???! Finally Sam emerged from the bedroom. He was a little more coherent but still couldn't describe what was happening to him. He kept insisting that the jar we'd bought was death and that we had to destroy it.

Of course there was nothing at all wrong with the acid. We managed to salvage a few tabs that Sam didn't flush down the toilet, and everyone else who took it had a good time on it. People kept trying to get Sam to describe what had gone on in his head that day. The most he offered as an explanation was that it seemed to him that the world had died, that his friends were as corpses, and he was helpless to bring us back to life. He dropped acid perhaps six more times in the months that followed. One or two times it was all right, but not like the good times he'd had with it at first. Once or twice more he repeated the death trip, although never as severely as that first time. He wouldn't touch that batch of acid again and most of the rest of us thought he shouldn't take any at all; but Sam refused to give it up until he felt he'd conquered whatever it was that was making him have bad trips. He never did conquer it and when he finally abandoned the drug, he did it with a vengeance. He said that it destroyed people; or he would say that acidheads were escapists, that no one could do acid—even occasionally—and contribute anything serious. He was not a moderate man, and it seemed he had to look on acid either as a panacea or as a potion of the Devil. By June his attitude toward the drug had become so hostile that I used to leave the house for the day when I wanted to trip and not tell Sam I'd done acid until I was coming down, or not tell him at all.

It was around the time that the good trips were coming to an end that I went to England for a month on a business trip for the publishing house I worked for. For the first two weeks, Sam wrote me every couple of days. You couldn't really call them letters. They were aerogrammes which he marked off in squares and called "The Adventures of Jane Daring." The drawings didn't have much on R. Crumb,* but one of them learned something from the other. Jane Daring was the leader of a guerrilla band which was planning a complicated raid on a building remarkably like the Pentagon. The main object was to get to certain controls in the basement of the building. The Band fought its way through fantastic obstacles, submachine guns, poison cesspools, torture chambers, and Jane was, at the end, the sole survivor. Repeatedly raped and put through all sorts of sexually sadistic exercises by the Pentagon guards, she nevertheless managed to kill or get past them all and arrived successfully at the automatic controls in the basement. The last two frames of the series, which was continued over six or seven aerogrammes, show Jane lighting a fuse to a bomb in the control room, then running to safety as the building explodes and contentedly embracing the ground as she exclaims, "That sound always makes me come."

I knew those aerogrammes were meant jokingly, but I didn't think they were funny even when I went along with Sam's laughter. I had my own violence fantasies but they did not include having my lover raped and tortured. Sam at times would sense clearly that the way out of the alienation that was at the root of his hostility was through the humanism of the Left and not the fascism, sexual and classist, of the Right. At other times his anger would overcome political boundaries and he would see it as all the same whether he dreamed of shooting police, bombing buildings, or playing René in *The Story of O*.† He would vacillate between sexual fascism and vague dreams of striking out at the power structure. For a time he went about chalking "George Metesky was here" on buildings, unable to relate to any hero but the man who ended up in prison for the criminally insane after his conviction for bombing dozens of Con

---

* JV: Robert "R." Crumb (1943–) was a leading cartoonist in the "underground comix" movement of the 1960s. Often drug-inspired, his work featured sardonic and sometimes crude takes on American life.
† JV: Written by Anne Desclos and published in France in 1954, *Story of O* was a highly risqué erotic novel that depicted sexual submission and sadomasochism.

Edison installations—reportedly because of a "personal grudge" against the company.*

It was a set of coincidences that finally helped Sam untie the knots of this dilemma. Before I returned from England two French Canadian fugitives, Jean and Jacques, arrived in New York. They had been working for the last year with a third man and were responsible for the political bombings that had shaken Montreal for the past year. As their group always signed themselves "Front de la Liberation de Quebec" (FLQ)† it had been assumed for months that they were a giant organization. In fact, Jean and Jacques said, FLQ‡ was just a term that became popular when Pierre Vallieres and others started using it in the early sixties; it was used by many different revolutionaries in Quebec, most of them

---

* SF: Another person obsessed with George Metesky (the original "Mad Bomber") was Abbie Hoffman, who also scrawled Metesky's name all over New York City and sometimes even used it as an alias. Free [Abbie Hoffman], *Revolution for the Hell of It* (New York: Dial Press, 1968), 205, 210, 217–227, back cover.

Hoffman never forgot Sam Melville, and after Sam's death Abbie seemed almost haunted by it. Hoffman's own brother confirmed this, writing that Abbie "felt sure that in prison he would be assassinated and had repeatedly stated that if he ended up in Attica he'd be killed just like Sam Melville." Jack Hoffman and Daniel Simon, *Run Run Run* (New York: Tarcher/Putnam, 1994), 278.

While underground in 1974, Hoffman tried to sublet an apartment from Jack Siemiatychi, who later recalled, "He wouldn't give out details of where he'd been, but he made a reference to Sam Melville, who had been killed at Attica, and said, 'If they catch me, I'll end up like Sam.'" By December 1979 Hoffman was thinking of turning himself in and held a "war council" of six friends, including Chicago Eight codefendant Dave Dellinger and movement lawyer Michael Kennedy. Hoffman "repeatedly stated that if he ended up in Attica he'd be killed just like Sam Melville." Marty Jezer, *Abbie Hoffman American Rebel* (New Brunswick, NJ: Rutgers University Press, 1991), 262–263.

† DV: Representing an interesting and unexplored international aspect of the spate of bombings in NYC during the 1960s, the FLQ had their fingers in an earlier headline-grabbing plot as well. In 1965 FLQ member Michelle Duclos drove from Montreal with a case of dynamite in furtherance of a plot to bomb the Statue of Liberty and other national monuments in an attempt to bring attention to the ongoing violence facing civil rights activists in the American South. As the result of a police infiltrator, Duclos was arrested with the plotters before they could put the plan into action.

‡ JV: The Front de Libération du Québec was an armed left-wing group in Canada seeking national sovereignty for Quebec. It engaged in bombings, kidnappings, and occasional assassinations. The group was embraced by American militants supporting national liberation movements worldwide. After killing a government official in 1970, the group went into decline, suffering severe government repression and the loss of public support.

doing different things and unknown to each other. Jean's and Jacques' cell had never been infiltrated—they never tried to expand beyond their original number—and they were beginning to get that dangerous feeling of immunity when a member of the group was picked up by the police. Apparently he'd been turned in by a storekeeper who lived downstairs from the Montreal apartment the group had used as a drop for explosives. The storekeeper had finally grown suspicious of the young men who periodically came to the apartment empty-handed and emerged shortly afterward with briefcases, and had done his patriotic duty and alerted the Mounties. Jean's and Jacques' partner was immediately arrested but Jean and Jacques managed to escape to New York, where they telephoned the one name they had, a well-known black radical. This contact seemed to want nothing to do with them. They had been forced to spend the little money they'd brought with them on hotel accommodations while their contact tried to dump them on one friend after another. Meanwhile their arrested comrade pleaded guilty to all the bombings and claimed to have had no accomplices, a ruse to take the heat off the others which got him a life sentence. After a chain of leads that had led them nowhere, had not even got them money or food to keep them alive, someone had given them Sam's name and number. For the next two months, at which point they got safely out of the country, Sam devoted his whole existence to caring for their needs.*†

It was impossible not to like Jean and Jacques. They were unfailingly gentle and thoughtful; Jean's explications of Quebecois Marxism-Maoism

---

* JM: Sam was living with Jane and another woman ("Diane") in a large apartment on Eleventh Street. But both the lease and phone were listed only in Alpert's name, which is significant because Alpert was the first person of interest in the FBI's investigation of the Federal Building bombing on September 19, 1969. I was told by confessed collective members that the two FLQ fugitives had the contact information for another member of the fledgling collective. She, along with her lover (also a soon-to-be collective member), allegedly housed and cared for the two men in a Harlem apartment and then yet another soon-to-be collective member's apartment on Sixth Street for several months. It was not until Jane went on a writing assignment in London that Sam gave the fugitives asylum in the Eleventh Street apartment he and Jane shared. Most of my father's friends who helped care for the two bombers (about seven) told me that this was a bonding moment for the collective.

† DV: Few accomplished works exploring the FLQ have been published in English; one of those few is Louis Fournier's *F.L.Q.: The Anatomy of an Underground Movement* (Toronto: NC Press, 1984).

were strong and persuasive, yet sensitive, and he was never either dogmatic in his words or belligerent in his style. They were in an unbelievably difficult position in New York. They had imagined, when they fled, if not a warm welcome from an organized underground at least some quick assistance in securing funds and getting to a safe country. Instead they got cold shoulders. In order to avoid detection, they had never related closely to most of the other revolutionaries in Quebec and had never met the man who gave them the name of their New York contact. When that contact proved useless, they had nowhere else to turn. Neither of them had ever traveled outside Quebec before. Jean alone spoke some English and that was halting. They had no money, no clothes, and were afraid—justifiably so—to so much as go to the foreign newsstand at Times Square to buy the Montreal newspapers, as it seemed two French-accented men buying the Montreal papers every day in the midst of an international search for two men of their description would arouse suspicion.

Sam alone, of those of us who met Jean and Jacques, felt total responsibility for their welfare from beginning to end. The rest of us were intrigued and sympathetic, and ready to help in any way that seemed reasonable, but we tended to feel their fate was in their own hands, that we had done what we could, and other possibilities having been exhausted they should probably think about staying in the United States indefinitely, eventually getting their own place(s) to stay and perhaps looking for work. Jean's response to this was that they'd rather be in jail. What Sam saw as the low level of concern on the part of everyone else repelled him. At times he was ready to sacrifice his life to aid Jean and Jacques. The others of us, who were not quite at that point, received his scorn for our cowardice and lack of comradely attitudes. Sam finally got them safely away through a scheme he worked out alone and forced to completion almost by sheer will.* (It wasn't quite all will, but the details of that story will have to wait.) He never saw them again, but he talked of them often and I believe that they had a greater influence on him than anyone else in those last months of his freedom.

---

* JM: After cooperating with the FBI, Alpert recalled differently in her 1981 memoir. There she returns from England to find the two FLQ guests and many of their friends in the apartment. Only then does she participate in the plan to get them out of the country.

Sam was exuberant throughout Jean's and Jacques' stay in New York and for a few days after they left he was still riding high on the success of their departure and the thoughts they had left with him. He was now determined to imitate their exploits. He thought it would be easy to steal explosives from an unguarded construction site and gather a small group which would begin hitting selected targets in and around the city. He still wasn't completely clear about the kind of attack that would have the most political impact. We would have long arguments about such absurdities as whether WBAI,* the closest thing to a radical radio station in New York, was or was not "the enemy." But Jean's and Jacques' beautiful sanity had convinced Sam that his innate militance was moving in the right direction, and for the first time in months he felt a sense of purpose.

He was soon disappointed. First, he discovered that dynamite would not be easy to get. It isn't left unguarded at construction sites in New York as it is, or was, in Quebec. Second, Sam found it much easier to find movement people who would talk about what a great idea it was to blow up Chase Manhattan or a draft board than to find people who wanted seriously to do it. He felt the absence of the two courageous Quebecois as a great loss, and the quick disillusionments that followed plunged him into a state of mind so desperate and vindictive that he became nearly impossible to live with. His frustration became worse whenever he took acid, which he still did from time to time. On one occasion he came close to striking me as the nearest available object for his blind rage. I had just decided to leave the house as soon as I could find a place of my own when Sam suggested that we take a vacation from the city and try to work things out. He found a place in the country a few hours from New York, and there we spent the only week we ever had together totally free of other people and distractions.†

---

* JV: WBAI was a New York City–based commercial-free radio station that served as a major media institution of the political left. Its pioneering programming ranged from news about local and national protests to performances by countercultural artists to free-form discussions among activists and intellectuals.

† JM: The fight she is referring to is elaborated on in her 1981 memoir. I investigated this incident by talking to other collective members. Several were not happy with Jane by this point in 1969 because, against my father's objections, she had decided to write an article for the underground newspaper *Rat Subterranean News* detailing how the group had helped the FLQ fugitives hijack a plane. It would turn out that this article would tip

We had a beautiful time. As the quiet woods and fields, the deer, the sunsets, and rain dripping in a well brought Sam out of his depression, I fell in love all over again with his great gift for making the most of small pleasures, and with his innate strength. He gained a new calm that week, in which he decided to stop his battle with acid and felt that his determination to "begin guerrilla warfare" was right and the obstacles could not be unconquerable. It was a turning point in our relationship to each other as well. When we came back to the city we moved into our own apartment on East 4th Street. It was a spacious sunny place in which we became closer to each other than we had been for months and began to feel, for the first time, a sense of semipermanence about each other. Sam seemed to have unusual patience—for him—and he began to look more earnestly for people who might be persuaded to join his cell.*

Sam realized at this point that the only way he could get dynamite was to rob an explosives warehouse at gunpoint. He did some exploring and chose a place which he discovered to have only a single old man guarding the stock at night, and at last found two similarly minded men to help him. The robbery went more smoothly than he could have hoped. The guard offered no resistance, which greatly relieved Sam, as he was certain he could not have used his gun on the old man. The only disquieting note in Sam's eyes was the last-minute reluctance of his two comrades. He told me that for no apparent reason they each, at different stages, became totally paranoid and wanted to turn around and return home empty-handed. He found this especially disturbing

---

the FBI and mark Alpert as a person of interest. Also worth noting is that both my mother and every woman I interviewed who was involved with my father were consistent in that he was never physical or violent with them. Alpert's profile is the only source for the allegation that my father was ever physically abusive to women, a reputation that has clung to his character.

* JM: Alpert dissolved the lease on Eleventh Street in April, after she and my father had a fight over her "hijacking article" in *Rat*. Jane moved to Fourth Street, in a unit two floors below another member of the still-nascent collective, the same week. Sam took his own apartment on Second Street, which he used for storing munitions. My father and Alpert never "lived together" after that, although Sam slept at her Fourth Street apartment many nights. Other nights, he would rotate among other alleged collective members and two lovers who remained uninvolved in the collective's plans.

because their enthusiasm for the plot had suggested the opposite of faintheartedness. This was a theme that recurred many times in the next months.

The group that Sam gathered together to use the stolen dynamite was nothing if not eclectic. Few of them had actually met all of the others before the first meeting. That first encounter was nervous and tentative. Excited by the success of the robbery, by far the boldest action any member of the group had had anything to do with, each man tried to outdo the other in bravado. There was some desultory talk about the kinds of targets that ought to be selected, a general agreement that it was important to include corporate centers (to make it clear that the enemy was not just the military machine) and a not very successful attempt to see how much political ideology was common to the group. During one slight impasse one of the women offered, "Well, it certainly would be a waste not to *use* the stuff." She had brought out in the open what was in the back of more minds than hers. Everyone laughed nervously, except Sam whose face slightly darkened.

Things went on in this vein for a month. I became convinced that few members of the group were serious and said as much to Sam. But he was deep into revolutionary patience that month. He was delighted to have found a group of people who were willing to risk even a meeting about sabotage and thought it impossible that nothing would come of that achievement. On the other hand, he had no intention of tying himself down to anyone else's growth schedule. By the end of July, Sam had decided to celebrate July 26th with the Cubans by bombing the United Fruit Company.*† He was sure everyone would approve of this action whether or not they were informed in advance. He was very cheerful about the idea and it didn't for a minute occur to him that he was insulting

---

* JV: On July 26, 1953, Fidel Castro led an attack on a military barracks in Santiago, Cuba. The July 26 Movement became a name for the revolutionary insurgency Castro later commanded. The revolution triumphed in 1959, overthrowing the US-backed government of Fulgencio Batista. July 26 became a holiday in Cuba, heralded by leftists worldwide.

† JV: The United Fruit Company was a US-based corporation that traded in tropical fruits from Central and South America, where it wielded enormous power. In 1954 it played a notorious role in encouraging a CIA-backed coup that deposed Guatemala's democratically elected president Jacobo Árbenz. The company was a favored target of anti-imperialist activists in the 1960s.

his collective or violating their notions of discipline by neglecting to tell them what he was doing with their dynamite.*

Approval was granted fairly readily after the fact, partly because the United Fruit bombing did hardly any damage and only made page 126 of the Sunday *Times*.† The collective did say that they hoped in the future Sam would consult them before he acted, but on the whole they seemed relieved to be let off the hook. Sam didn't quite see how ominous their attitude was. He had thought his action would goad on everyone else and that once they saw how easily it was accomplished they would move more quickly. Instead it seemed to make the others less serious. Everyone was busy with other things, the Woodstock Festival was coming up, and it was all so much easier not to deal with it.

Sam and I hated Woodstock. He went to it almost against his will and only because all our friends were going, most of them to work on the movement booths that were to be set up in "Movement City" near the Hog Farm free kitchen. Within hours after we arrived Sam began to feel oppressed by the utter mindlessness around him. He felt mistrust directed at him because he looked older than most of the people around, while he regarded the crowd as robots manipulated by clever capitalists. The whole scene was a concentration camp to Sam. He couldn't wait to leave and when I found a friend driving back to the city Saturday night he leaped at the chance to go home.

Woodstock will forever stay with me as the place where Sam first talked with George Demmerle, the undercover agent who two months later named Sam, Dave Hughey, Pat Swinton, and me as a bombing conspiracy. George, dressed in his shining purple Prince Crazy cape and feathered helmet, was hard at work manning the Crazies booth. He stayed at the booth long after the other Crazies had drifted away to dig the music

---

* JM: My father, along with two others in the still-forming collective, stole the dynamite and kept it in his Second Street apartment, since the rest of the still-forming collective at this time weren't ready to commit to using the explosives or being an active part of a group. Contrary to Jane's opinion that this was perceived as an impetuous act, others who were close to the situation saw it as evidence of my father's leadership initiative.

† JM: It is worth noting that even though Alpert is a fugitive at the time of this writing, she can retain and deploy details of what page of the *New York Times* her bombing appeared on. It would be her fascination with publicity that ultimately led the FBI to her and to my father.

or take a nap or search out some dope. I wandered back to Movement City after one of my own sojourns to the main part of the festival and found Sam full of admiration for George's dedication. "That George," he said to me, "he really is crazy. He's been at this fucking booth all day, he won't even sit down. I offered to take his place but George said he couldn't let me do that because I wasn't a Crazy and the Crazies booth had to be manned by bona fide members."

A week after we returned from Woodstock, Sam bombed the Marine Midland Bank building in lower Manhattan.* Unlike the United Fruit bombing, which was undisciplined but still carried out rationally, the Marine Midland bombing was an act of unmitigated anger. Since Woodstock no one in the collective had even attempted to call a meeting, nor had there been a meeting the week before Woodstock in the midst of preparations for the festival. Sam was tired of prodding everyone on and incensed that anyone who considered himself/herself a serious revolutionary could spend more energy on a Movement City than on destroying the enemy. He began to see the whole collective as a collection of phonies and cowards and deliberately set out to shock them. He put almost no care into the Marine Midland bombing. To judge from what he told me later, he merely assembled a bomb, timed it to go off at 1 A.M., stuck it in a briefcase and wandered down to the financial district to find a good target.† It never occurred to him that people might be working in the building when the bomb went off and, as it happened, a night shift of mostly female typists and clerks was working on two floors

---

* JM: Woodstock ended on August 18. The Marine Midland bomb was planted on August 20, not "a week after." The week before Woodstock, Jane, playing publicist, had convinced the collective that they should wait until after the music festival to perform their next attack so that the country was not distracted. But the day after Woodstock no other members seemed to be interested in following up. My father decided to turn Marine Midland into a group gut check.

† JM: I have no doubt that my father gave Alpert the impression that he bombed the bank with "almost no care." But this may have been because he chose to withhold details as to why he chose Marine Midland as a target. I have come to learn that others close to the situation thought of Alpert as someone not to be trusted with details. Despite Jane's theory, my father was not someone who did things at random. He had worked on the plans for the Marine Midland building when he was a plumbing designer at Syska & Hennessy and had harbored residual hatred for them since he was a teenager, seeing how they bulldozed parks to replace them with a corporate headquarters in Buffalo and branches in the Tonawandas. Also, his bomb was set for and went off at 11:00 PM, not 1:00 AM.

of the building during the explosion.* A warning call was placed around midnight, but the watchman who answered the call ignored its message. It was mostly luck that the worst that happened was slight injuries to ten or twelve people. Sam had earlier rationalized the possibility of injuring people, in a theoretical discussion, by comparing his activities to those of the NLF and the Algerians, who carried out revolutionary terrorism in which not only the powerful but also the "innocent bystanders" were injured or killed. But the effect of the actual injuries on him was profound.

He was so badly shaken with the unintentional results of the Marine Midland bombing that his disgust with the collective turned into a desperation that it survive. He seemed to realize for the first time that a collective was not just a practical aid but a very real political need. As long as he acted in isolation he was in danger of losing his political vision to that side of himself he later described from a jail cell as "just one more nut who freaked out, O.D.'d, or climbed up a tower and gunned down people." Had there been no Jean and Jacques, no Third World guerrilla movements, no people in America sympathetic to revolution, Sam would have been compelled to express his moral rage in the wildest acts of destruction physically possible. On the other hand he had a vision that his anger could be much more than that, and that with the help of other people he could turn it in a direction that would move others to action and hence become a part of social revolution. But only with the help of other people.†

---

* JM: Actually, at 11:00 PM in 1969 it would most probably be male brokers doing transactions in Tokyo, where it was lunchtime. The Marine Midland action may have been dangerous, but that doesn't mean that it was *intentionally* careless toward women specifically just because typists were largely female at that time. This is how Alpert tends to focus on the elements that make her points and obscures the steps that get us there. It also doesn't take into account how much was known or unknown then in regard to executing these kinds of actions. This was, after all, the first skyscraper bombing of its kind in US history. Obviously, after it went off, this detail about late-night workers became painfully clear to my father, and adjustments were made. But by applying that learned experience retroactively, Alpert is misleading readers and laying the groundwork for her characterization of my father as a misogynist, which she will expand upon in her 1981 memoir.

† JM: According to others close to the situation whom I interviewed, after the Marine Midland attack my father immediately began planning more attacks with people outside the collective, mostly in Milwaukee and Wisconsin.

None of this was as clear in Sam's mind as I have perhaps implied. He always had great difficulty expressing his inmost feelings, especially when they revealed self-doubt. He often spoke of the "demons of guilt and shame" as the inner enemy he wanted to defeat. When I pressed him about what he meant he would sometimes talk about Ivan Karamazov by way of oblique explanation. Dostoevski was one of Sam's favorite writers, but that summer I do not think he could have borne to reread him and confront those astounding insights into the destructive aspects of anger. For a time after the Marine Midland bombing Sam was unusually subdued. He renewed friendships with certain philosophically minded people who had bored him in the past two or three months and he went to some lengths to hold the collective together, although he had little hope that he could still prod them to action.

Surprisingly, only one person dropped out of the group after this flagrant example of Sam's unconcern for collective discipline. I personally pleaded with some of the collective to stay with the group if only to restrain Sam's impetuousness, as I was sure if he went on as he had been he would wind up insane or quickly captured or both. Those who stayed may have been persuaded of the truth of this or, impressed by Sam's willingness to admit his error, may have been convinced that he would act less irresponsibly in the future. Moreover they were really ashamed at this point of how far they had pushed their procrastination and seemed more serious about carrying out the actions that had been under discussion for nearly three months. And so, paradoxically, Sam's perverted way of pressuring the collective actually worked. Had he never struck out as individually as he did, none of the group's accomplishments could have happened.[*]

Our first brush with the FBI occurred within weeks after the Marine Midland bombing. Liberation News Service and the radical papers in the city had been sent copies of a communique regarding the bombing. *Rat*,[†]

---

[*] JM: At this time my father was involved with several groups that had no connection to the collective. It seems reasonable that he had realized that the friends Alpert was trying to recruit would never commit and he began focusing on more serious militants, some of whom were allegedly connected to offshoots of the Young Lords, SNCC, and the group that would in subsequent years become known as MIRA.

[†] JV: Formed in 1968, *Rat Subterranean News* was a New York City newspaper of the underground press. Blending radical politics and culture, the highly experimental paper

the paper at which I'd been working since quitting my publishing job in April, was the first to print the letter, and when it appeared on the stands the FBI raided the *Rat* office for the original document. I was on my way to the office the day of the raid and found police cars downstairs and the doors barricaded. I later found that a staff member gave my name to the pigs in response to their question about who usually opened the mail in the morning. I had not opened the mail the morning the communique arrived and in any case it wasn't logical that opening *Rat's* mail could be grounds for a criminal accusation. But the government had so few hints that any name that came to them was sure to be fully investigated. For the first time we began to feel watched.*

In September the collective at last pulled itself together and carried out the bombing of the Army Headquarters in the Federal Building. It was an action of which everyone felt proud. It is a little odd that when we were arrested Sam, in order to convince the FBI that no one had assisted him in the eight bombings, drew a diagram showing where the Federal Building bomb had been placed. For once Sam was not the person who planted the dynamite. For the first time the collective effected a fairly equal division of responsibilities and made careful work of casing the building, observing its activities at night, and planning the location of the explosives. The collective wanted to avoid any further special attention to the radical press, and had also been disappointed by the slight attention paid to the Marine Midland letter—which had explained that the injuries were unintentional and a warning phone call had in fact been made—due to its narrow circulation. A communique was sent in advance

---

was known for its wild covers and provocative content. It openly espoused violent revolution in the United States and printed the communiqués of the Melville collective and similar "urban guerrilla" groups.

* JM: *Rat* was not just the "first paper" to publish Jane's communique; it may have been the *only* paper to publish it at the time. When researching my father, I checked issues of the *East Village Other*, the *Militant*, and *Rolling Stone*. None of the other papers to which she sent her press releases published them in the days following the attacks. According to agents I interviewed, it was because of *Rat's* isolated interest in the bombings that the FBI was able to connect the bombers to the paper. During the NYPD's raid of *Rat*, Alpert's name was given to NYPD detective Pete Perrota by a *Rat* volunteer. This confirmed the FBI's developing theory that Alpert was the common link to other New York bombings that summer.

of the Federal Building bombing, this time to all the major news media. Because this bombing damaged only property and because the communique was printed in all the New York papers and read over radio and TV stations, the action was nearly universally accepted as coming out of a revolutionary contingent.*

The morning after that bombing, Sam and I received a phone call from the people who had moved into our apartment on 11th Street. They told us that the FBI had just been by, two gray men who asked for us both by name, said they wanted to ask us a few questions, and left their business cards. Sam took the phone call while I was out walking the dogs and told me about it when I came home. He was alarmed and tense. He wanted to call the FBI office immediately and ask what they were up to. I managed to convince him that he had nothing to gain by talking to them and that they would inevitably get more information from him than the reverse.† I was sure that the worst the agents knew was that we had some contact with Jean and Jacques in the spring, since if they were working on any more recent information they would have come to our 4th Street address rather than a house we had left four months previously. Sam agreed to wait until we could consult a lawyer but he was on the whole less rational. He had never had any experience with government harassment before, and he didn't know what to think. For all his boldness he had a tendency to imagine his enemies omnipotent. He never thought of what it would be like to be caught, to face a trial, and least of all to serve time in prison. Because the possibility was so unreal to him any hint of

---

* JM: Alpert asserts the opposite in her 1981 memoir, written after she began cooperating with the FBI. There she will take full credit for the multiple press releases to "message" each bombing and express frustration that only an underground paper would take her communiques seriously. Her use of the term "revolutionary contingent" appears to be code she is sending to readers in the 1972 underground. It references the radical group of the same name, which had some cross-pollination to the collective.

† JM: In her memoir written years later, Alpert would claim it was *she* who wanted to hire a lawyer to confront the FBI and that my father wanted to leave the city immediately. I tend to believe the version in her memoir over this one, because my father did leave New York the next day and Alpert, against his suggestion, engaged an attorney named Henry De Salvo who spoke with the FBI and who later represented her at trial. It was through this conversation, according to FBI records I read, that agents learned Alpert's current address on Fourth Street and began a stakeout on her block the next day.

its existence elicited an irrational reaction, often out of proportion to the real nature of the threat.*

Sam was just beginning around this time to get involved with a group of people who were trying to form a national guerrilla organization, Black-led but including a few whites. During September and October he met several times with this group. The very first meeting was scheduled for a few days after the FBI visit, and by the time we were able to get an appointment with a lawyer Sam had left for the meeting. I talked to the lawyer myself, and he subsequently telephoned the FBI and left word that he was acting as attorney for the two of us and that the FBI should direct any questions they had for us to him. The lawyer assured me that it was very unlikely the FBI would return to bother us because of the legal nature of an attorney-client relationship.†

A few days after Sam returned the agents were back, this time in front of our own door. I was out when the agents arrived. Sam came up the stairs to find them ringing our doorbell. They presented him with their identification and asked if he knew whether Sam Melville lived in the apartment. Instead of admitting that he was the man they were looking for and insisting that they call the lawyer instead of bothering him, Sam tried to put them on another trail. He told them that Sam Melville was no longer living in that apartment, that he had moved out some weeks before and had left no forwarding address. The agents then asked whom they were addressing, and Sam answered, "David McCurdy." When I learned what Sam told them, I wished he had stayed around long enough to talk to the lawyer with me.

---

* JM: Alpert is knowingly spreading a falsehood with her assertion that Sam "never had any experience with government harassment before." My father already had an arrest record, having been jailed at least twice during protests and deported from Canada after striking a Royal Canadian Mountie at the border crossing. Alpert was aware of these incidents at the time of this writing.

† JM: In her memoir, Alpert claims the "black-led militants" were led by H. Rap Brown. My father connected with Brown in December of '68, almost a year before Jane's time stamp above of September–October 1969. After my father and Alpert split up (May '69), my father began collecting and storing munitions in his new apartment on Second Street, which he code-named the "McCurdy place," using the name on his fake passport to obtain the lease. (The FBI found these munitions after his arrest and alleged they were connected to Brown.) All this was months before Jane claims above.

It was a very foolish thing to do. The agents later claimed that they had received the lawyer's message but only the part of it that pertained to me. They pretended not to know that the lawyer was prepared to speak for Sam, and hence they justified their continuing to look for Sam. If Sam had simply admitted his identity and referred them to the lawyer he would have had some legal protection to suppress the confession he made upon his arrest, on the grounds that it had been extracted from him in the absence of his attorney of record.* Even worse, "David McCurdy," the first name that popped into Sam's head, just happened to be the name in which he'd rented the East 2nd Street apartment that he used as a storage place for the dynamite, blasting caps, explosives literature, and guns. It was the biggest lead he could have given the FBI.†

Sam vacillated constantly between great confidence and a hopeless fear that the Man was closing in on him. His inability to distinguish what was important in both moods made him sometimes courageous and sometimes incredibly reckless. He never confronted his fear rationally even when it threatened to overwhelm him, most particularly immediately after such encounters as the one on the stairs. When he did defeat his fear, he would swing into exactly the opposite mood and scorn any talk of possible detection. While Sam was an extreme example of this vacillation, to some degree it haunts anyone who works outside the law. One never knows how much credit to give one's enemies. If one assumes the most conservative position, that they will eventually discover any aberration, hopelessness inhibits all action. On the other hand, following Che's

---

* JM: This exposes Alpert's understanding, or lack thereof, about what is required of an underground radical. The purpose of having an alias was for situations such as FBI confrontations. Also, the attorney Alpert is referring to was Henry De Salvo—*her* attorney, not my father's. According to FBI files, the agents were staking out her block to surveil known associates of Alpert's. Had my father identified himself, he probably would have been taken in immediately.

† JM: The FBI never found the McCurdy apartment via their investigation. They believed that the man they were talking to was named McCurdy (they even made note of it in their report) and never followed up. The McCurdy apartment (bomb lair) was never connected to my father by law enforcement during the investigation. It was not until after my father's arrest that the investigators made this connection, and only because their informant George Demmerle (who lived around the corner) met my father there to assemble the bombs intended for the bombing of the Sixty-Ninth Regiment Armory.

dictum, "Audacity, audacity, and more audacity," has its own pitfalls. Ultimately only hindsight determines which is right.*

A month after the Federal Building bombing the group fell apart. While Sam was out of town the group had agreed to allow a man who was not a formal part of the collective to use dynamite in the bombing of the Whitehall Induction Center. That bombing took place in early October, a day or so before Sam came back from out of town. It was the boldest and most ingenious of the bombings to which Sam confessed, carried out under the watchful eye of armed guards who stood twenty-four-hour watch at the Induction Center. It completely destroyed the building and prevented the induction of hundreds of young men into the war.[†‡]

All this was entirely incidental to the progress of the group, no member of which was ever inside the Whitehall Induction Center while it was

---

* JV: A doctor from Argentina, Ernesto "Che" Guevara (1928–1967) became a major figure in the Cuban Revolution. In 1956 he joined the guerrilla forces led by Fidel Castro that toppled the Cuban government in 1959. Guevara served in the new Cuban state and became a leading critic of US imperialism. In 1967 he was killed, with assistance from the CIA, while trying to foment revolution in Uruguay. His image proliferated worldwide, and he enjoyed widespread adoration among leftist radicals worldwide.

† JM: The person Alpert describes here as "someone outside the group" who performed the Whitehall bombings was arrested with Alpert in her apartment as part of the "Melville Collective," as that term was defined by the FBI. According to FBI records and interviews I conducted with two of the FBI agents on the case, this man had been a primary person of interest in several of the bombings for about a month by this time (not someone outside the collective). He was with the Revolutionary Contingent, a radical group that had been infiltrated a year earlier by Demmerle. Demmerle's FBI file contains reports in which he claimed that this same man spoke of blowing up Whitehall at RC meetings. FBI, Demmerle file, section 2, sub. A, "Blowing up Whitehall Induction Center," December 12, 1967, 103–104. Jane's description of him being "not a formal part of the collective" was likely intended to insulate him from more charges.

‡ SF: The right-wing book *Communism and the New Left* includes a photo of the Whitehall damage. Its caption reads, "An example of a bomb which blasted the fourth and fifth floors of the Army induction center at 39 Whitehall Street, New York City, knocking out two walls and shattering more than 40 windows." Since the ruling class cares mainly about its property, there was no word about destruction of the draft records, which was the reason for the mission. We will never know how many generations of Americans and Vietnamese are alive today because the Whitehall draft records—which would have sent young American men to Vietnam—were destroyed. These thousands of lives were saved through the courageous actions of Sam Melville and his collaborators. US News and World Report, *Communism and the New Left* (New York: Collier Book, 1969).

still standing.* The success of the Federal Building bombing, instead of encouraging everyone to further action, had perversely seemed to satisfy them that they had accomplished what they set out do and could now take a rest. The group did not actually divide over the question of whether more bombings were necessary; theoretically everyone agreed that they were. There was also agreement that it was time to shift from antimilitary bombings to anticorporate bombings: it seemed important to dramatize that responsibility for the war lay not only with the army and with the formal structure of government but with the monopoly capitalists. The United Fruit bombing, because it was so little publicized, and the Marine Midland bombing, because it had been so shocking, had failed to make this connection. At least verbally, the collective expressed the feeling that it should be made soon.†

Nevertheless no one was very anxious to make the first move. Ostensibly what divided the collective was the question of timing. A mass antiwar action was being called by the National Mobilization Committee for November 15 and was to be preceded by a week of local antiwar actions. Some members of the collective argued vehemently that to do anything in the weeks immediately preceding the Mobe‡ action would keep people away from the march. Others held to the opposite point of view, that a week set aside for protest was the best time to "increase the level of struggle." Sam simply thought Mobe irrelevant. He was not always consistent in this view, and it was easy to get him to agree that people are radicalized slowly and by different processes. But he'd been to enough demonstrations to convince himself that ghetto riots had a more profound effect on the government

---

* JV: The Whitehall Induction Center was a military processing facility that operated in Lower Manhattan for eighty-six years. More than four million inductees were processed until the facility moved in 1972. The center processed draftees in the Vietnam War and was a frequent target of protests, including a bombing by members of what the FBI called the "Melville Collective."

† JM: In her 1981 memoir, Alpert scolds my father for bombing Marine Midland because it "has nothing to do with the war."

‡ JV: The National Mobilization Committee to End the War in Vietnam ("Mobe") held major antiwar mobilizations, including the tumultuous March on the Pentagon in 1967 and protests at the Democratic National Convention in 1968. It organized in November 1969 in Washington, DC, the largest protest of the era, attended by more than half a million people. By that point many antiwar militants believed that large, peaceful demonstrations were an ineffective means of protest and favored instead direct action.

than mass marches, and he felt little kinship with people who were content to wave the V-sign while chanting, "All we are saying/Is give peace a chance." The last demonstration Sam ever attended was a peace rally in support of Fort Dix* G.I.'s in September 1969. He took a hand grenade.[†‡]

Sam himself didn't expect to be in Washington on November 15. He had another meeting coming up with his other group, which was now taking up more and more of his time, and on November 13 he expected to be out of the city. He was even considering not returning to New York for some months after that meeting. He was anxious only to carry out the corporate bombings the collective had talked about for so long, and to clear out the "David McCurdy" apartment before he left. His mind could not have been further from an antiwar march, nor from the possibility that jail would interrupt his travel plans.

While the group was in the midst of furious argument over the correct reaction to November 15, Sam got in touch with George Demmerle. I believe he'd only seen George once since Woodstock but he must have continued to be impressed with his seriousness and militance. No one else thought very highly of George, though very few actually suspected him of being an agent.[§] He was most typically described as "unstable." The

---

* JV: In June 1969 more than a hundred US servicemen engaged in protests against deplorable conditions in the stockade at the US military base in Fort Dix, New Jersey. The protestors included anti–Vietnam War military resisters and conscientious objectors. The rebellion was suppressed by military police and dozens of the protestors, dubbed the "Fort Dix 38," were put on trial. A major episode in military resistance to the Vietnam War, their protest was widely supported by the civilian antiwar movement.

† JM: I can find no corroboration for my father attending this rally, which if Alpert's recollections are correct would have taken place shortly before he met her. Since carrying a hand grenade into a military facility is unlikely, my guess is that he told her this story as way to impress a new lover, and Alpert's choice to include it here is another example of her positioning my father as unstable. Sharon Fischer's footnote directly below offers some reconciliation for this event.

‡ SF: Alpert has some dates wrong, and I believe that the rally may be one of them. There were many peace rallies at Fort Dix then, including a small one in September 1969 at the court-martial of Allen Myers for distributing antiwar leaflets. But I believe what Sam and Alpert probably attended was the huge march on October 12, 1969, in support of the Fort Dix 38. "Tear Gas Used to Drive Off War Protesters at Ft. Dix," *Buffalo Courier-Express*, October 13, 1969.

§ JM: In her memoir, Alpert will claim that most people in "the group" thought Demmerle was a fed. However, at least three others who were allegedly in the collective and close to Demmerle had performed several subversive acts with him and shared ties with story George told about himself had much in common with Sam's own background: George claimed to have working-class origins, to have had at one time a wife and family and a respectable job, and to have thrown it all over to join the movement. He was a few years older than Sam but of the same generation. He smoked grass but would not take acid. George was so militant he made people nervous. When our lawyers were preparing our case they were besieged by sympathetic movement people offering stories of how George had approached them with the wildest proposals, including plots to get dynamite and guns and to blow up the Brooklyn Bridge. George once told me over a casual cup of coffee after a Crazies meeting that he was trying to get hold of a powerful chemical to drop into telephone manholes in the financial district and shut off telephone service there indefinitely. No one, not even Sam, who made people nervous himself, talked up violence as much as George.*

After Demmerle was exposed as an agent, movement people who knew him and those who had only heard of him were convinced that his insincerity had been crystal clear all along. Some said this was obvious because he talked so much about violence. Others pointed to his consistent refusal to expose himself on acid. (More interesting was the information that the Young Patriots had purged him when he refused to take the required injection of sodium pentothal, a "truth drug.") Even the nagging doubts about the difference between his age and most of his

---

at least two other radical groups: the Crazies and the Revolutionary Contingent. Two confessed collective members introduced my father to Demmerle at Woodstock. Finally, Demmerle's career as an informant is far more successful than Alpert paints it to be: Demmerle, according to his FBI file, was installed a "Defense Captain" in the Young Patriots, by Black Panther Party chairman Bobby Seale. Seale recruited Demmerle after the informant hosted a fundraiser for Huey Newton's legal defense fund in 1968. News of Demmerle's appointment reached Yippie leader Abbie Hoffman, who made Demmerle his personal "bodyguard," at the Chicago DNC rally that resulted in the arrest of the Chicago Seven. Demmerle was scheduled to be a witness against Hoffman at the Chicago conspiracy trial until my father contacted him on November 8 to bomb the Sixty-Ninth Regiment Armory.

* JM: Interestingly enough, it was this very conversation between Demmerle and Alpert (which took place at the Panther conference in Oakland, California, in July 1969) that Demmerle used to surmise that Alpert was linked to my father. He would recapitulate all this at their pretrial hearing, where he claimed that Alpert referred to herself as *Rat*'s "star reporter." Supreme Court of the State of New York, CR 1741–1770, part 30, April–June 1970.

"friends" came to the surface. The radicals who found it so easy to see through George after the fact had never met anyone like Sam and had no understanding of the range of human responses to oppression. The difference between people like Sam and people like George lay deep in their personalities, in some inner place almost unrelated to the roles of daily life. The games they played were similar, but for George it was all games. It was easy for him to disguise his real motivations because they were so shallow. Sam's whole drive was a cry against the objectification of human beings, of the alienation of people from each other and them-selves. It was profoundly impossible that he could have construed the American government, the institutionalization of racism, or the system of competition as anything but his enemies. George was an oddly passionless human being. After he surfaced he told a right-wing gathering that he had become an undercover agent in order to protect society from the violence of the radical Left. He said, "Most of these people think they mean well but they're pursuing a course that will lead them to murder." All ethics of revolutionary warfare aside, it might be pointed out that Sam Melville never killed anyone, intentionally or otherwise, while George bears some ultimate responsibility for Sam's death. (Confronted with this fact at a press conference, George said, "What are you talking about? I didn't even know Sam was at Attica.")

Sam fell completely for the trap George had been laying for three years. He had little faith left in the judgments of the people who advised against bringing George into anything heavy. He respected these opin-ions only to the extent of keeping from George the names of any of the other people in the collective. (It was just guesswork that led George to name Dave Hughey, Pat Swinton, and me as members of the conspiracy. He knew only that we were involved in the movement and that we were Sam's close friends. No evidence of a conspiracy was ever brought up in court and the lawyers seemed to feel that any of the three of us could be easily acquitted if we asked for separate trials.) Sam showed George his trust by telling him literally everything that he had done for the last six months and asking George if he'd like to participate in a test, after which he might be invited to join the collective. Exactly what collective Sam expected George to join is a mystery. Our group was breaking up and Sam himself was going to be leaving the city, perhaps permanently. Sam seems to have been playing his own game with George, implying that he held some important position in a national organization, telling George that his group included fifteen or twenty people in different parts of the country, going into all the dramatic details of the bombings already carried out.*

The collective meanwhile managed to agree—at a meeting which took place in the absence of the person who was most vociferously opposed to any bombings before the Washington march—that it would carry out three simultaneous corporate bombings on November 10. The unity was illusory. The pro-Mobe faction announced that they would have no more to do with the group if others went ahead with these plans. It is slightly comforting to know that such absurdities have plagued the development of revolutionary groups much more ambitious and successful than this one. Of course the whole argument about whether bombings would interfere with the Mobe action was completely specious. If it were true that people would stay away from demonstrations because of radical violence, then the real decision to be made would be whether the violence or the mass demonstrations were more effective. Presumably anyone who'd been a member of a guerrilla organization for five months would have already come to a decision about that. Nevertheless, in the paranoia that always grew more intense as the date of an action grew closer, arguments that were unimpressive a week ago were seized on as an excuse to back down. The collective split in half over the issue.

Those who remained committed to the action carried out, on the scheduled date, the bombings of Chase Manhattan, Standard Oil, and

---

* JM: It is important to keep in mind that all of Alpert's "facts" are secondhand, based on what she claims my father told her had transpired. It's hard to trust that these accounts are accurate even if Alpert is correctly recapitulating what my father told her, since Sam apparently peppered his accounts to her with misinformation. If my father was trying to recruit Demmerle into anything, it would have been the militant group in the Midwest allegedly connected to Rap Brown. The collective, as Alpert correctly states, had dissolved by this point. According to Demmerle's FBI file, at least two of the people who were close to these events had carried out several noted "guerrilla theater" actions with Demmerle. My father would have likely relied on their endorsement when he first met the informant at Woodstock. Demmerle did indeed "guess" about who my father's accomplices were, but Alpert is omitting the key part of her contribution to Demmerle's sleuthing: her articles in *Rat*.

General Motors. The success of these actions brought one of the dropouts back into activity in the last two days before the arrest. This person was going to demonstrate change of heart by sabotaging the Criminal Courts Building at 100 Centre Street.* Sam was, of course, pleased and agreed to help.†

As the group was now dissolved into so many isolated individuals, Sam felt that much freer to continue his contact with George. A week before the bust he went back to George's apartment and, after unscrewing the telephone receiver to make sure their conversation could not be tapped, made a specific proposal to him: that they place bombs in army trucks parked by the National Armory on Lexington Avenue and 26th Street. George readily agreed and they set November 12, the last night before Sam was to leave town, as the date.

On November 10 we first noticed a white, late-model sedan parked outside our building. It was occupied by two obvious agent-types who remained in the car all evening, sometimes changing places or leaving the car for a short walk. Sam was positive they were watching us. If it had occurred to him that George was an agent, he might have realized that the two men intended simply to keep a close watch on Sam until the night of his action with George. Instead it seemed a mysterious demonstration of the omnipresence of the police in our lives. Surely if the government knew that Sam was responsible for the bombings they would not waste time watching but would make an immediate arrest. If they didn't know, it was hard to think of what they expected to learn by watching our apartment. Unable to figure out what they were after, we simply did what we could to avoid them. We took to keeping the shades drawn and most of the lights out, even when we were alone in the apartment. We would take roundabout routes through deserted streets whenever we went out and watch to see if anyone followed us. We never saw tails, which only

---

* JV: The Criminal Courts Building is a massive structure in Lower Manhattan that houses various courts and law enforcement offices. The trial of the Panther 21 was conducted there, making it a target of supporters of the Black Panther Party.

† JM: There are too many tangled facts in this and the three paragraphs before to unpack into a footnote. For those interested in the details of the final days and hours of the collective, I would refer readers to my memoir, *American Time Bomb* (Chicago Review Press, 2021).

heightened our confusion. An eerie sense of impending doom haunted Sam's last days as a free man.*

Sam and his friend placed the bomb in the Criminal Courts Building the morning of November 12, timed it to detonate at 8 P.M., and returned safely. When Sam came home the white sedan was gone. This cheered him a little. He spent the rest of the day at the David McCurdy place, fiddling with new timing devices and rearranging his things. By the time I came home in the evening it was dark and I didn't think to look for the white car, assuming it had just been some temporary lookout, probably having nothing to do with us. I was surprised to find the lights out when I opened the door to the house. Sam was peering out the window from under the half-drawn shade. "Hush," he said. "They're back." I felt a powerful tremor of fear, and it suddenly struck me as ridiculous that Sam was going to go out that night to bomb three army trucks with a man he barely knew and whom no one liked. The newspapers were still full of the successful bombings of two days ago. The bomb he'd planted in the morning in the courthouse had yet to go off and was sure to outweigh the propaganda impact of destroying three miserable jeeps. Sam was supposed to be leaving New York in the morning anyway and whether he made a recruit of George or not seemed irrelevant if he wouldn't even be around to follow up the "test." But it was useless to talk to Sam when he'd made up his mind about something and I couldn't see taking out my tension in another fruitless argument. All I could muster up was, "Are you sure you want to go?" Sam's answer was simple. "I've got to. I promised George I'd be there." He hugged me briefly and left. The next time I saw him he was under armed guard.

The pigs reported the arrest to the media as if it were the result of months of masterful sleuthing. In fact Sam couldn't have made it simpler for them. They had some dozen different agents assigned to watch his route to the Armory, enough so that they could switch off every block or so and convince Sam that he wasn't being tailed. At the Armory itself

---

* JM: Even though Alpert claims to be concerned about being watched by the "white sedan," according to her 1981 memoir, she offered in a phone conversation to wire my father $100 knowing that he was on a bombing tour with another radical group. A wire would reveal my father's location as well as the others'.

they had arranged for the army trucks to be parked on the opposite side of the street, next to a row of private houses. Perhaps this was so they could claim the intended bombings were aimed at innocent people; perhaps it was a tactically superior place for them to effect the dragnet. They assigned twenty or more armed agents for the actual arrest. Sam said that because the trucks had been switched to the other side of the street, he'd decided not to place the bombs after all and was walking away when the agents suddenly appeared from all corners, guns drawn, and surrounded them. He said he saw their hands shaking as they held the guns even as they pushed him against the wall, face forward, and began to search his body. At about 10 P.M. twenty to thirty agents and police broke down the door to our apartment and arrested me and David, who had dropped over about an hour earlier. Pat, who lived on the second floor of our building, had not been home all day. Apparently she was alerted by the radio or by a friend and managed to get away.*†

Once under arrest Sam seemed to break down completely. The tension of the last days had been monumental and when it climaxed in his dramatic arrest he thought there was no hope left. To complete the nightmare the agents told him, in their friendly manner, that a man had lost his arm in the explosion in the Criminal Courts Building. Later they changed the story and said it was a little girl and that she had nearly died. (Neither story, of course, was true.) They made sure that they paraded Sam in front of me at the FBI office and while I was not surprised to see him there—one of the agents had muttered before, "We already got your friend"—the sight of me in handcuffs broke down any last resolve Sam may have had to keep his silence with the Man. Perhaps hoping that he could remove the onus from his friends by repeating the tactic of Jean's and Jacques' comrade, he at once confessed to all eight bombings and claimed that he acted alone.

---

* Cohen: A few months later Jonathan Grell, a nineteen-year-old member of the *Rat* staff and the Motherfucker family, was picked up in New Mexico and charged with being part of the conspiracy. He was jailed in lieu of $100,000 bail and had been in prison over a year awaiting trial when all charges were suddenly dropped. Rumor had it that his parents turned him in. Sam did not even know who he was.

† JM: The "Motherfucker family" in Cohen's note above refers to the East Village activist group the Up Against the Wall Motherfuckers.

The confession sealed Sam's legal fate, although it took six more painful months to work itself out. George's testimony alone might have been discredited in court. He would have been a poor witness and we had many offers of testimony as to the instability of his character. Our lawyers tried to suppress Sam's confession, but as there was no physical brutality involved and as Sam had been advised of his rights there were no sound legal grounds on which this could be done, and the judge ruled against us. For six months the judge ruled against us. When we raised $50,000 bail for Sam (Dave and I were released after a week or two in jail on less than half that amount) the judge doubled it to $100,000. When we raised $100,000, he insisted that we produce a wealthy responsible person who would agree to take Sam into custody while the trial was pending. When we produced such a person, the State of New York brought down its own charges and ruled that Sam should not be granted bail at all.

Hanging over all our legal decisions was the fact that Sam faced more than three hundred years in total time. The combination of his confession and George's potential testimony made an overwhelming case for the government. Even if David and I had claimed responsibility for some of the acts in Sam's confession we could not have reduced his sentence to less than life.*† The more political we made the trial, the worse the consequences would have been for Sam. We might have defended the bombings as the right to revolution, attempted to introduce evidence about the connection between Chase Manhattan and the Whitehall Induction

---

* JM: The DA, John Doyle, offered eighteen years concurrent time to each, but only if all three—my father, Hughey, and Alpert—agreed to plead guilty to conspiracy. According to their lawyers, with good behavior they could be out in five years. Hughey and my father wanted to take the deal, but Alpert refused and jumped bail, killing the negotiation and thus resulting in longer sentences for both her lovers. Omitted by Alpert was that my father's confession was to eight bombings, even the ones that Alpert and others allegedly executed.

† SF: Most people do not realize the power and scope of federal conspiracy laws and why the government loves to use them in political cases. From the early Alien and Sedition Acts in the 1920s to the COINTELPRO prosecutions of Black militants and antiwar activists of the 1960s and '70s, conspiracy laws have been a tool used by the government to crush dissent. Even today, it is hard to believe that Julius and Ethel Rosenberg were convicted only on conspiracy to commit espionage and yet were executed. Craig R. Whitney, "Suspects in Bombing Conspiracy Foiled in an Attempt to Escape," *New York Times*, March 12, 1970.

Center and the courtroom in which we sat, challenged the government for prosecuting us for mere property damage while they slaughtered people in Asia. It would have made a splash in the papers perhaps; but Sam did not want to spend his life in prison for the sake of verbal histrionics. He hated the courtroom. When he was not completely ignoring the proceedings he sat with his fists clenched and his mouth tightened in barely suppressed fury. He vented his anger at the judge only two or three times in the course of the hearings. It simply wasn't his style of protest.

Much harder on Sam than the courtroom battles was the experience of jail. In his most despairing moments he would write that he didn't think he could bear it much longer. He had never in his life submitted to any authority except that of his conscience and I could not imagine how he would respond to the swift unthinking brutality of prison law enforcement, or what would happen to his enormous energy in the confinement of an eight-by-five barred cell.

Faced with the growing likelihood of life imprisonment, Sam twice attempted to escape from the Federal House of Detention. This only landed him in the Tombs, surely one of the worst prisons in the country. He wrote me that his worst fear was that somewhere in the Tombs or some place like that he would meet an absolutely ignominious end, killed in a petty quarrel with another inmate or a guard. It was a common enough happening in American prisons and Sam was a likely target for it. All hope of bail ruled out, Sam began to be receptive to the possibility of pleading guilty in exchange for some sentence less than life. This was just what the government had hoped for. While we felt ourselves that a political defense was nearly out of the question, the judge was terrified of possible violence in his courtroom. If more than six sympathetic spectators appeared at a hearing, the judge would summon all the extra armed marshals he could muster to keep "order." He was delighted at the prospect of dealing us out and avoiding the spectacle of a trial and put constant pressure on the prosecutor to make us an offer we would accept.

Until the Friday before the Monday that the trial was to start, the prosecutor* held out for a minimum of thirty years for Sam. For rea-

---

* Cohen: The prosecutor, John Doyle, has an interesting history of his own. He joined the Justice Department when it was prosecuting segregationists in the South. Ours was his first

sons we never determined he made an about-face at the last possible moment and offered a deal of fifteen years for Sam and five each for Dave and me, on the condition that all three of us would plead guilty.*† I never got to see Sam between the time his lawyer, Bill Crain, told me of the offer and the morning we went to court, but Crain told me that the offer had immediately lifted Sam's spirits, that he was very pleased at the prospect of possibly emerging from prison before he was an old man. He sent a message to me asking me to stay around long enough to enter a plea with him and David and so not jeopardize the offer. I saw Sam alive for the last time on May 8, 1970, when we appeared in court together to plead guilty to conspiracy. The judge solemnly asked the three of us, one by one, to affirm that we were pleading guilty solely because we had really committed the acts of which we were accused and that we had not been offered reduced sentences in exchange for the plea. The farce completed, I embraced Sam once more and tried not to watch

---

case against political radicals. For all his apparent machinelike efficiency we seem to have freaked him out. A year later he lost the prosecution of David Poindexter for aiding and abetting Angela Davis's flight from jurisdiction, and shortly after quit the Justice Department. He is now reported to be working for a liberal law firm.

* Cohen: After his failure to have Sam's confession suppressed—which Sam made impossible by reiterating it, point by point, when he was examined on the witness stand by the assistant US attorney—Sam's lawyer gave up hope for acquittal, saying publicly, in court, that Sam was "doomed." Sam figured that he faced 370 years on federal charges alone, and even more than that on state charges. But because the government's case against Jane and Dave seemed quite flimsy, the government was willing to arrange a deal. All three defendants would plead guilty, saving the government the expense of a long and difficult trial, avoiding publicity the government didn't want, and securing convictions on conspiracy against Jane and Dave, where the prosecution was weak. In return Sam would be given fifteen years on both state and federal charges and would be able to serve state and federal sentences concurrently. After Jane split, Dave was sentenced to from four to six years in a federal penitentiary. Sam got from thirteen to eighteen years, to be served in a New York State jail.

† JM: It is important to note that this statement in Cohen's footnote above, "After his failure to have Sam's confession suppressed—which Sam made impossible by reiterating it, point by point, when he was examined on the witness stand," is a secondhand anecdote. According to what Cohen told me in 1989, he was not a witness to Sam's testimony and instead relied on Alpert's recapitulation as fact. My reading of my father's trial transcripts, acquired via FOIA, found no such confession on the stand. It's unlikely that the authorities would have offered to reduce my father's sentence from 350 years to 14 if they'd already secured an admissible confession. For more details on this, see my memoir *American Time Bomb* (Chicago Review Press, 2021).

as four guards led him out of the courtroom and back to his cell. A few days later I jumped bail.

I knew that as deep as Sam's moods of despair might be he had far too much inner strength to be broken by prison. Even in his worst moments in the Tombs there had been moments of sunlight: the company of other political prisoners, a sign of growing awareness among the inmates, indications that alone as he was he was not totally helpless when he had other human beings around him. The reports of his death are as confusing as everything else that happened at Attica and I cannot pretend to know what happened or even guess at Sam's state of mind during those last days. One thing is clear: that he died for things in which his belief had never altered, an end to racism and liberation from senseless authoritarianism. I find some solace in knowing that he did not meet the ignominious end that he said he feared above all else. It is weeks since a bullet took his life and the lines of an Edna St. Vincent Millay sonnet keep recurring to me.

> Say what you will, kings in a tumbrel rarely
> went to their deaths more proud than this one went.

If I could come out of hiding to write Sam's epitaph, I would engrave those lines on his stone.

INTRODUCTION

by John Cohen

SAM AND I BECAME FRIENDS during the Columbia Strike, in the spring and summer of 1968, when we worked together in the community around the campus with a committee which tried to build resistance against Columbia and support for the student strike.

One nucleus in the committee consisted of people from the 1950's, who had matured after McCarthy and before Kennedy, around thirty, embittered by their experiences in the forms of middle-class life, intellectuals who had to a great degree given up on the value of thought, some of us on the fringes of the beat movement, keeping ourselves alive with part-time jobs, most of us suffering great difficulty or total failure in our few attempts at human relationships. We were cynical and depressive and infected with a deep and destructive fatalism. We were fearful of our inner feelings, seldom dealing with them ourselves or communicating them to others. It had taken the brutality of Viet Nam to break through our cynicism, and the warmth and idealism of the anti-war movement to bring us to hope for social change.

We came together to organize politically, but another important goal was personal change. We were struggling to break through our bitter, fatalistic cynicism, to open ourselves to each other, and to accept hope as a strong guide. We were trying to regenerate our self-respect and breathe life and power back into our souls.

Sam related ambivalently to this group. He was drawn to us because he was very much like us—depressive, alienated, aware that the forms of life we had fled were impossible but that the aimless hopelessness we had come to was equally impossible. On a personal level he was friendly and warm, and he made several strong friendships. But at meetings he was restless, silent, and sometimes morose. He hated our endless discussions of what we should do, and he absolutely abhorred attempts to use the committee as part of a struggle for personal change.

For us the summer of 1968 was a constant high of naive optimism. Until then, from peace marches to the Pentagon to Columbia to Chicago, the Movement had grown quickly and hopefully. Everything, especially the Columbia Strike, bolstered our enthusiasm. But the next fall and winter the strike turned into a mockery of itself, Progressive Labor warped SDS toward self-destruction, the counter-inauguration degenerated into childishness, and the Movement began to falter.

Our committee was a microcosm of the Movement. Throughout the summer we threw ourselves into action—rallies, marches, building seizures, picket lines. At first we grew in strength and energy; but as we did, Progressive Labor infiltrated, and began to push its ideological line onto us. Meetings twisted from close, friendly gatherings directed toward hope and trust into strident ideological battles. To deal with PL's destructive intrusion,* we were forced to use just the kind of political manipulations we despised. By packing meetings and limiting voting rights we threw PL out; but we left ourselves disenchanted, sour and dispirited. At the same time our actions were becoming increasingly repetitive, and their effectiveness was diminishing. Especially as we watched the student strike fail, we became weary, depressed, and confused. We talked of communalizing, but we were totally unready for that. At the end of the fall we disbanded.

---

* JV: The Progressive Labor Party was a radical, mostly student organization that espoused Marxist-Leninist and Maoist doctrine. Formed in 1962, it spread throughout American campuses and sought, as a faction within Students for a Democratic Society, to take over the organization. It was disdained by many in the New Left, including the group in SDS forming Weatherman, for its dogmatism, sectarian zeal, and dismissal of cultural rebellion.

Sam moved downtown, and during that winter I saw him infrequently. When I did he was depressed and restless. But in March he told me he had come to a decision. He said he couldn't bear inactivity anymore; he wanted to *do* something, to know indisputably that he had helped in a real way: he was going to set himself up as a station on the underground railway. I took Sam's words at face value, thinking he meant to help soldiers fleeing the army and kids fleeing the draft. He did help a couple of men who claimed they were AWOL, but Sam really was talking about two FLQ revolutionaries who were fleeing Quebec. They were already in his apartment as we were talking.

During that conversation, for the first time in months, Sam seemed cheerful, hopeful and determined, and during the following spring and summer his mood continued to grow brighter and heartier. I remember this clearly, because I was growing only more depressed. In July I walked into his apartment and found him busy over a set of drawings. He was very cheerful. When I asked what was up, he said, "I'm working with some really good people on a great project." He didn't elucidate any further; I didn't ask any more questions. Two weeks later the United Fruit pier blew up. Through the rest of the summer Sam was in and out of town on unexplained errands. Once he told me not to call him Sam anymore: his name was David (for two days. Then he phoned and said, "Hey, John, this is Sam"). He shaved his beard and cut his hair; a hippie appearance, he said, wasn't possible anymore. He gave up drugs (several times); drugs were not compatible with serious revolutionary work. Once or twice he spoke of having to disappear, but except for a few short absences he never did. Once I stopped by his apartment and found him wearing a suit jacket—very unusual for him. When he flopped down on a sofa the jacket fell open. He was wearing a shoulder holster with a pistol in it.*

As the summer progressed and Sam became more and more involved with his guerrilla activities, we saw each other less frequently, though we used to have breakfast together. On those mornings, when he pounded

---

* JM: The group would bring the FLQ fugitives food while they holed up in the large Eleventh Street apartment that was leased under Jane's name while she was in England. According to Jane's memoir, John Cohen was peripheral in helping to arrange for their escape via hijacking of a commercial jet to Cuba.

on my door at 7:30, I would still be sleeping, but he would already have done his exercises and walked his two young dogs. Almost everywhere he went he wore ankle weights to strengthen his legs. He would drag me out of bed, and we would walk to his favorite neighborhood store to buy fresh Polish rye, butter, milk, cream cheese. The morning newspaper. Then back up to his fifth-floor apartment, two or three steps at a time. With ankle weights. Sam would cut thick slices of the rye bread, spread butter and cream cheese thickly, and whip up a health drink. We ate in the sun by the window.

The FBI's surveillance of Sam started at the end of March, 1969*—just about the time he told me he was setting up on the underground railway. As part of his effort to help the Canadians, Sam traveled several times to Canada to contact the FLQ. The Royal Mounted Police noticed, and at the end of March when Sam tried to take a train to Montreal he was stopped at the border. When he tried at another crossing, by bus, he was turned back again. A week later he met his FLQ contact in upstate New York. This time he was watched by the FBI.[†]

The Mounties thought Sam was involved in political bombings in Canada, and did not suspect that he was helping FLQ fugitives. They had contacted the FBI, who began to watch Sam, although not with much zeal or thoroughness. It took them six months simply to find that Sam had moved from one apartment to another. During that time he hid the FLQ fugitives, got them papers and money, helped them escape, stole dynamite from a Bronx warehouse, and attacked the United Fruit Company and the Marine Midland Bank. He also dropped hints to many people that he

---

[*] JM: Sam's FBI file was collated for this investigation in March 1968. It has several summaries dealing with prior arrests, but the use of Cohen's word "surveillance" is inaccurate. The FBI never knew where Sam was until two days before his arrest (as Cohen himself will attest to in the next two paragraphs by corroborating that they never observed Sam doing a number of arrestable activities). Rather, other collective members had monthly reports in their files. Two had been upgraded the year before to "Key Activists" and were under almost daily surveillance. How Cohen knew enough about Sam's FBI file to opine on when his FBI surveillance began is a question of mine that he has never been willing to answer. His footnote below is not sufficient explanation, as Sam's lawyer would not have turned Sam's FBI files over to Cohen due to attorney-client privilege, and Cohen would not have had public access to them until years later when they were declassified.

[†] Cohen: Much of the information in this section comes from FBI files turned over to Sam's lawyer during his trial.

was into something heavy—as far as security was concerned, Sam was a
lousy guerrilla*—but the FBI remained totally uninformed.

In September FBI agents questioned the superintendent at Jane
Alpert's 4th Street apartment building. He told them, yes, there was a man
living with Jane, but he didn't know who he was.† Agents tried to question Jane. She refused to answer and called her lawyer. When the lawyer
asked the FBI what they wanted with his client, he was told that it was a
matter of "national security." But apparently they still had not connected
Sam with bombings in New York City. In the middle of September the
New York FBI office set up a twenty-man unit to investigate these bombings, but the unit was totally separate from their investigation of Sam. On
September 19 the Federal Building was bombed, destroying several offices
of the U. S. Army, and on October 7 Whitehall Street Induction Center
was bombed and put entirely out of business.

Twice during October agents tried to find Sam at the 4th Street apartment. Once they actually spoke with him, but he identified himself as
David McCurdy and said that Melville had moved out. On October 27
agents contacted Sam's wife, from whom he had been separated for several
years. She didn't know where Sam was; she was looking for him too. On
November 5 Jane's lawyer called the FBI. He said that he was Sam's lawyer also, and that neither of his clients wished to speak with FBI agents.

On November 8, going against the unanimous decision of his group,
Sam contacted George Demmerle.‡ He told Demmerle that there would

---

* JM: Several other militant groups who embraced Sam and his legacy would strongly disagree. Not only was my father impervious to observation for all the things Cohen mentions
above, he was also conducting bombings in Milwaukee, Wisconsin, and Chicago, and yet
none of the other bombers connected to him were arrested.

† JM: This is confirmed by FBI files, but what Cohen is conflating is that the FBI questioned
Alpert's landlord (and the provost of Columbia University) as part of its investigation of
her, not my father. At the time, the FBI had not connected my father to Alpert or the
bombings.

‡ JM: This is inconsistent with other testimony and facts. Cohen has maintained publicly
since 1971 that he was never part of the collective. So what is his source for this disparaging
claim? The source is most probably Jane Alpert, to whom Cohen was closest. But Alpert
herself disagrees with Cohen; in her 1981 memoir, written after she cooperated with the
FBI, she claims that my father had disconnected from "the group" by November 9, 1969,
which was the day he tried to recruit Demmerle. The reality seems to be that by this point
my father was trying to recruit Demmerle into a different group, most likely one that was

be a bombing in two days, that he had 150 sticks of stolen dynamite, that he had bombed United Fruit, the Federal Building, Whitehall Street Induction Center and a National Guard Office in Milwaukee, and that he had left a bomb in the Chicago Civic Center which had not exploded. He said he had connections with the FLQ and a group of between fifteen and twenty members. He asked Demmerle to join him in an attack on U. S. Army trucks in New York City. Demmerle, who had been a paid informer since 1966, agreed to help; then he contacted the New York office of the FBI.

On November 11, Sam told Demmerle that the attack on the trucks would occur the next day. Demmerle again agreed to help and again contacted the FBI. That night bombs exploded at the Chase Manhattan Bank, the RCA building, and the General Motors building.

At 3 P.M. on Wednesday, November 12, Sam met Demmerle again. He told him that one bomb was already in place, set to go off at 9 P.M. He told Demmerle to go home, change into clothes "with big pockets," and meet Sam at 8 P.M. at an apartment Sam had rented on East 2nd Street. There they would set the bombs for the army trucks. Sam also told Demmerle that he planned to bomb New York City Police Headquarters and that he was preparing to pull off robberies to finance his group's activities.*

Demmerle contacted the FBI, changed clothes, and went to Sam's apartment on 2nd Street. They set the bombs, then went uptown by different routes. Carrying an Army duffel bag containing the bombs, Sam walked over to the B&H Deli, ate, then took a subway uptown. From the moment he left his apartment he was followed:

> Samuel Joseph MELVILLE was observed walking north on Second Avenue at Seventh Street, New York City, at approximately

---

connected to activity in the Midwest. Therefore, he never would have sought consensus from the New York collective, since he was no longer involved with them.

* JM: While FBI files are not definitive proof, Cohen nevertheless claims them as the source of his facts. I have read the FBI files on Demmerle and the dozens on my father. None of these disclosures are mentioned. Cohen's source for these facts is ambiguous. My guess is that, once again, he is relying on Jane Alpert, who, according to her 1981 memoir, was never in the room during these events.

9:35 P.M. carrying an olive drab bag which was slung over his right shoulder. MELVILLE was observed proceeding to the Astor Place station of the IRT Subway. During the ride from Astor Place to 23rd Street, MELVILLE was sitting with the olive drab satchel on his lap and he appeared to be humming a tune.

MELVILLE thereafter walked to Lexington Avenue and 26th Street, at which time he proceeded west on 26th Street. Several United States Army trucks were parked on the north side of the street, and MELVILLE was observed closely examining the trucks. He subsequently turned south and proceeded along Lexington Avenue to 25th Street.

He was observed engaged in conversation with GEORGE DEMMERLE for approximately three minutes and thereafter slowly walked north to 26th Street where he proceeded in the direction of the United States Army trucks.

Approximately 25 feet from the southeast corner of Park Avenue and 26th Street, MELVILLE stopped and noted the presence of Special Agent (SA) HODGENS and other agents in the area. At this point, SA HODGENS confronted MELVILLE at gunpoint, identified himself and advised MELVILLE to "Don't Move." MELVILLE immediately replied "Okay, you got me." MELVILLE was subsequently disarmed of the satchel he was carrying and a .38 caliber five shot revolver which he was carrying in a shoulder holster under his left arm. MELVILLE was further heard commenting that "The bombs are set for four o'clock."*

A few moments later Jane Alpert and David Hughey were arrested in Jane's 4th Street apartment.

In a memo to his lawyers Sam described what happened after his arrest:

> Undetermined number of agents held me against the wall. . . .
> My hands and face were against the wall. They took my revolver,
> pen knife, tear gas pen, and change and keys. My hands were
> handcuffed behind my back. Two agents took me to a car and
> drove me to 201 E. 69th. . . . We were met at the elevator by

---

* Cohen: This extract is taken from the FBI report on Sam's arrest.

several other agents, three of whom took me to . . . an interview room with a metal table and three chairs. My handcuffs were now removed and I was pushed face and hands up against the wall. All my clothing was taken off and carefully examined. My body was examined. I was given my clothes back piece by piece and allowed to redress. . . . For all of the above time I was calm and cooperative. Most of the agents, particularly those at the arrest and in the car, were extremely frightened. They spoke to me only to order me to assume a position. I spoke not at all. Now, in the office, with my clothing on and seated, the youngest of the three agents said in a friendly voice, "What is your name?" I said, "Sam Melville." He asked if that was my real name. I said yes. He asked, "Is it Samuel?" I said yes. He asked my address. I said 67 E. 2nd St. Another agent was writing this down. The third man was examining my telephone book and left with it at this time. The two remaining men then listed my possessions on an envelope and I was asked to sign the envelope which I did. The second agent was examining the tear gas pen and I cautioned him about handling it. I told him not to release the spring and to carefully unscrew the capsule. He did this with great care and I told him it was OK then; it would not fire . . . The first agent, a man about 30 years, said, "Sam, my name is Tom. Can I get you some coffee?" I said OK and also some water. He left. I asked the remaining agent if he was an FBI agent. He said yes and produced his credentials. He said I could call him Bob. He quickly became very friendly. He offered me a cigarette. I said I didn't smoke. He took one and said, "Well, Sam, you gave us quite a time." I nodded and half smiled. I was looking at him carefully wondering what was ahead and thinking this man was not capable of torture of any kind. I was thinking none of them were capable of it. He kept on with things like, "You were good," and "You had this office jumping for months." He was obviously trying to please me and win my confidence. I didn't say anything. He began to name some of the bombing targets and then interrupted himself saying, "You know that guy may die." I quickly said, "What guy?" He said, "The courthouse. You know, 100 Center St." I said, "Did it go? What do you mean about the guy dying?" Tom returned at this time with a container of coffee and immediately joined in with, "Yeah, he may lose his arm." I was concerned and sad.* They kept on about it and I said I never intended to hurt anyone. Tom said I must have known someone would be hurt when I put the bomb in the truck. I said I never put the bomb in the truck and wasn't going to. (The trucks were on the side of the street opposite the armory. There were private homes on that side. On four previous nights when I cased the job, the trucks were always on the curb immediately adjacent to the armory. I think the trucks were placed so it would appear that I cared little about people's safety. When I saw the trucks that night I decided I was not going to do it. When I was arrested I was in fact walking away from the trucks with the bombs still on my person.) They said, "What about the people at the bank building?" I said, "I never intended to hurt anyone." I then asked if I could see my lawyer. One of them said it was pretty late. They wouldn't be able to reach him before morning. They were both still very friendly and acted concerned. I asked about the man at 100 Center. They said he was seriously hurt and would probably lose his arm and maybe his life. I was very upset and they acted comfortingly but insisted on the course they had begun. Bob said I had gotten away with it for a long time but that I had to kill someone eventually. . . . Tom said, "This is strictly off the record, Sam. Did you intend to use the gun?" I laughed bitterly and said no. I wasn't even sure it would fire. It was very old and I had never fired it. Tom asked why I was carrying it. I said I didn't know. Maybe to impress people or myself. I would never use it, I said. . . . As we left the room I saw Jane and I thought all was lost. I was very discouraged and began to talk very freely. They asked if I wrote the press releases. I said yes. I said I did everything alone. Telephone calls, writing and placing of the bombs. . . . Bob then showed me a form which informed me of my rights. I read it but I don't remember what it said. I think it was in triplicate. I signed all of them. Tom asked me where I got the dynamite. He said, "We know you

---

* Cohen: As Jane noted, the story about this man's injury was a total fiction invented by the FBI interrogators in order to upset Sam, play on guilt, and make him talk.

got it in New York. Didn't you?" I said I wouldn't answer. Bob asked how many I had used at the Grace job [Marine Midland Grace Trust]. I said I wasn't sure, maybe 15 or 20 sticks. Tom then asked how many sticks I used on the average. I said on the United Fruit job I used a lot but little damage was done because the water (Hudson River) absorbed most of the blast. After that I always placed the bombs indoors and used about 12–15 sticks on each job. . . . Tom asked how I knew where to place the bombs so they would do so much damage. I said I used to work as a designer of mechanical systems. So I know where to look for shafts that ran thruout the buildings. . . . Tom asked if I travelled much. Had I ever left the country? I said no. I seldom left the city and I had never been out of the country. Tom asked me to think hard. Didn't I go to Mexico or Canada sometimes? I said no . . . Bob said he was going to read me a statement he had written. If I agreed with it, would I sign it? I said yes. He then read a two or three-page statement that listed all the jobs plus a couple I had never heard about . . . I said I wouldn't sign it. He then crossed out the two I said I hadn't done and again asked me to sign it. I looked it over and realized it was a confession. I said I wouldn't sign it . . . I said I wouldn't sign anything without seeing a lawyer . . . I said I wanted to see him then. They said that wasn't possible . . . Tom went to get a car and I was left with his partner. . . . We waited in silence for about 5 minutes. I asked about the man at 100 Center Street. He said he didn't know anything about it. Three new men came in and took me to the car. The lobby was very crowded with press and TV people. Coming down in the elevator, one man said to the other to go slow and watch the wires. I was to be held by two of them all the time.

The next morning the FBI searched Sam's apartment on 2nd Street. They claim to have found, among other items, one hand grenade, one 9 mm. Astra automatic, one .30 caliber M-l carbine, one 45 caliber semi-automatic, hundreds of rounds of ammunition, a high-powered scope, fifty-one blasting caps, handcuffs, tools, and a dozen books on demolition, riot control, and warfare.

Sam was first imprisoned in the Federal House of Detention on West Street in New York City.* Not prepared, ideologically or psychologically, for capture, he fell into a profound depression, imagining that his actions had at best been pointless and at worst insane. He told me that the seven white inmates in whose cell he had been placed felt very hostile to him, but when I asked him why, he said only that it was because he didn't brush his teeth. I assume that his cellies considered themselves patriotic Americans and hated Sam's politics. He had been in their cell only a few days when, during an argument over a game of cards, they all attacked him. He put his back to the bars, held on with his hands, kicked out his feet, and screamed. He was badly beaten.

He was moved to a cell by himself, and then to a tier dominated by Muslims. At West Street the Muslims wielded a certain power, because they were numerous and well organized. Because they were curious about Sam, they had requested that he be moved to their tier. Sam found the Muslims serious, well informed, disciplined, and dedicated. He came to like and admire them, and I gathered that they liked him. While he was on the Muslim tier he became a vegetarian. (He maintained a vegetarian diet for a year, until he was sent to Attica. Then, feeling that prison vegetables did not nourish him adequately, he again began eating meat.)

At West Street Sam tried to escape twice. During the winter he drew up plans for blasting his way through the prison's walls with dynamite, but the plans were discovered in a surprise shakedown. Then, in March, while at court, he was left alone with only one guard who was smaller than he, and unarmed. Sam overpowered him, tied his hands with his belt and ran down a flight of back stairs. He almost reached the street, but another guard cut him off and forced him to surrender at gunpoint. After his first escape attempt Sam was thrown into solitary; after the second he was transferred from West Street to the Tombs. This was partly a move to a more secure prison and partly punishment.

The Tombs is an inhumanly overcrowded and infamously brutal city prison. Men live and sleep not only in overcrowded cells but in corridors

---

* SF: Others who once were held at West Street through the years include Julius Rosenberg, Morton Sobell, Reverend Philip Berrigan, Martin Sostre, and hundreds of US draft resisters who refused to go to Vietnam. Among those once housed at the Tombs was Emma Goldman.

and on the floors, and are subjected to unlimited brutalities by a murderous staff. Dozens of men die there every year, in senseless fratricidal fights, in suicides, or as the result of beatings by guards. The Tombs is formed of a series of balconies surrounding a central well. In the center of the well is "the bridge," a platform visible from the surrounding cells. The guards use this bridge as a stage on which they beat prisoners—as punishment, as warning, as amusement. In this way while Sam was there guards fractured one man's skull.

At the Tombs Sam met Carlos Feliciano, a MIRA revolutionary;* Wood, a Weatherman;† two Chinese revolutionaries who had attempted to assassinate Chiang's heir; and several black revolutionaries. He became close to one Panther who, despite beatings and cruelties, had been organizing in prisons for years, and who expected to continue organizing until killed. It was his skull that was fractured on the bridge. Sam also met Herbert X. Blyden, whom he later worked with at Attica.

These men, by their example and conversation, helped Sam, and he pulled himself out of the despair that had oppressed him at West Street. From West Street he had written that his only options were "to become an expert in gin rummy or the Grand Master of postal chess," and he spoke of his fear of falling into "the incredible convict mentality of pettiness and stupid mind-destroying thinking about what hacks to beware of and how much

---

* DV: Feliciano was a prolific bomber, and the degrees of separation of political bombers in NYC at the time was limited. See "Suspect Charged with 35 Bombings," *New York Times*, May 18, 1970. One of the detectives who had been trailing Feliciano and who effected his arrest was Eddie Rodriguez, the same NYPD BOSSI (Bureau of Special Services and Investigations) detective who had infiltrated the "Cuban Power" campaign of more than a dozen bombings in 1968, which may very well have illustrated a template for Sam and the collective; their bombing campaign would look nearly identical to the Cuban Power campaign that dominated headlines less than a year before theirs (despite Cuban Power being radically *opposed* to Castro, in contrast to the left's devoted support of him at the time).

† JV: The Weatherman emerged as a faction within the New Left group Students for a Democratic Society (SDS) in June 1969, taking over the organization at its National Convention in Chicago. Initially, the Weatherman sought to build a "revolutionary youth movement" of working-class youth, who would engage in public battles with police. It soon abandoned SDS and formed into a smaller, clandestine armed struggle group seeking the overthrow of the US government. Changing its name in 1970 to the Weather Underground, it committed more than two dozen nonlethal bombings of military, law enforcement, political, and corporate targets. The group disbanded in 1977. Some former members turned themselves in to law enforcement while others continued armed struggle actions into the 1980s.

commissary I have this month." From the Tombs he wrote, "In the indifferent brutality, the incessant noise, the experimental chemistry of food, the ravings of lost hysterical men I can act with clarity and meaning. I am deliberate—sometimes even calculating—seldom employing histrionics except as a test of the reactions of others. I read much, exercise, talk to guards and inmates, feeling for the inevitable direction of my life." He was dealing with his own racism and changing personally: "One thing is certain: when I emerge to whatever sunlight is left in this world I won't be a honky any more."

Sam's reputation, his honesty, and his demeanor always frightened and angered prison hacks. Before he left the Tombs he had been placed in "ultimate security status." "I am in a cell alone (very rare here) and not permitted to leave except for counsel visit or shower twice weekly, and then I am accompanied by a captain. The light in my cell stays on throughout the night and a guard sits within ten feet. As has been amply demonstrated, his proximity is not for the purpose of doing me service."

In July, after he was sentenced, Sam was moved to Sing Sing prison. Upon arrival he was ordered to shave his face and cut his hair; in angry response he shaved his entire head. He received a stern reprimand, then spent a month in segregation. When he was let out into the general prison population, he walked in sunlight for the first time since his arrest; "I fondled one of the many cats on the grounds today. The contact of a live being responding to my touch blew my mind."

At Sing Sing, Sam began working toward prison reform, hoping to "reveal further the impotency of hypocritical liberalism." He did not relish this kind of work. He did not see himself as a "reformer" or as a strategist, and he hated courts and legalisms. He hadn't really gotten interested in his own trial. But he felt that "If I can be used to any advantage for the forces of social change I will feel much less oppressed by this environment."

Sing Sing is used as a temporary housing center where state prisoners wait, after sentencing, to be categorized and assigned to permanent prisons. Sam wanted to stay permanently at Sing Sing, which is near New York City, so his friends could visit easily. He asked his lawyer to fight for that, but in less than two months he was transferred to Attica. When he wrote to tell me of his transfer, he was depressed, "wearying of saying sieg heil," feeling that he had lost every battle.

At Attica Sam's "social worker" greeted him by saying, "Melville, the inmates here call Attica 'the end of the line.'" Sam quoted this to me glumly, almost fearfully. He was intimidated by the other inmates, and worried by their partition into racial groups which, he said, *never* mixed. He found the white population racist, reactionary and threatening. Fear of their response made him hesitate to mix with Blacks and Puerto Ricans, and he spoke pessimistically of the possibilities of organizing inside. He was wary of the guards, whom he found even more brutal than at the Tombs and who he was sure had a special eye for him because of his political reputation. He was treated as a security risk, despaired of escape (at that point no one had ever escaped from Attica), and for the first time began to think of the reality of serving eighteen years in jail. He was intensely depressed, and again spoke of insanity.

But Sam did not allow himself to stay down very long. He intensified his reading and studies, and set up a program of strenuous physical exercise in which he pushed his body to its limits. He became quite accomplished at yoga, and worked on strengthening exercises until he could do pushups standing only on his knuckles, feet straight up in the air. Three weeks after his arrival he was assigned to a job in the shoe shop, and, his depression dissipated, or at least controlled, he wrote a hilarious letter about the scene there.

Only a few weeks later Sam was transferred to the prison school, to teach mathematics. This job had several advantages, but Sam was most delighted to discover that it gave him the privilege of a garden plot. He talked almost gaily about what he hoped to grow, about the earth and the climate, and about an older prisoner who ran the prison greenhouse. He bought seeds and I sent him gardening books. But in February, when the hack who ran the school—who also censored incoming literature—denied Sam some periodicals he had ordered, Sam exploded at him with bitter fury. He was thrown out of the school, sentenced to keeplock (locked in his cell all day and deprived of privileges), and deprived of his garden.

Reading was an extremely important part of Sam's prison life. Before his arrest Sam had read mostly poetry and fiction. While at West Street he had read novelists, but he said that this was a retreat necessary to save him from madness. By the time he reached Attica he refused to look at poetry I sent him and read only political and historical works. To me it seemed that, since imprisonment was a consequence of his previous political commitment, Sam was redoubling that commitment in order to make prison less intolerable. Imprisonment would have been utterly intolerable for him if he had not been able to know that he was continuing the social struggle. Until he met other prison organizers and became accepted at Attica, that struggle could only take the form of study. By choosing to concentrate so intensely and exclusively on political and social study Sam was affirming that his previous choices had been meaningful and that his current life was still purposeful and meaningful, in the same way.

By the time he got to Attica he had developed extremely disciplined study habits—he once told me that while of course he wanted me to continue visiting him, my visits did disrupt his readings. I bought him a magnifying glass and he struggled through the fine print of the collected works of Lenin. He studied Marx, Engels, Trotsky, Deutscher, contemporary political theorists. He said that he used *The New York Times* "as a periscope," but he felt it was bad for him. He knew that it distorted events and selected news, and he felt it demoralized him. He begged for Left periodicals. He called *Monthly Review* "my only contact with reality."

The prison administration, of course, frowned on the literature Sam wanted, and they exploited his need for it as a vulnerability through which he could be harassed. They delayed the arrival of books, denied him several that were important to him, never allowed him to receive underground newspapers, forced him to use lawyers to get even *Ramparts*. When Sam exploded at the school hack, it was because he had denied Sam the right to receive *Monthly Review*. One result of this explosion, of course, was that even less literature got through.

Partly because of his need to study, Sam yearned for privacy and quiet. But during the winter he was located in D Block, where, according to him, there were many homosexuals, whose style of life he said was raucous and disturbing. Because D Block cells have only bars, not solid doors, he could not escape the noise. This oppressed him. Also, I think that the homosexuality itself upset Sam. We discussed prison homosexuality often—it upsets me too—and Sam told several horror stories of prison rapes. The one time I visited him when we were not separated by glass or wire, I embraced him enthusiastically; Sam kept his body rigid and his ass arched back, well away from me.

At Attica where you live is determined by where you work, so when Sam was fired from the school he was able to get himself moved to C Block, where cells have solid doors and are quiet. But by that time it was spring, and Sam had come to hate the guards with such bitter intensity that he could not enjoy the quiet. Now he felt that the cell was being used to keep him quiet. "A while back I saw a picture of an Israeli prison with Palestinians in a compound making barbed wire fences to be used against their own compatriots. I, too, am collaborating. I'm working in the mess hall so I can stay in the block with doors and quiet. We all have our price, I guess." So, predictably, he exploded at a hack in C Block, just as he had at the school, and lost his quietude.

Whatever acquiescence Sam had managed, however, could not have been too great. He always hated the prison's petty and cruel regulations, and he frequently refused to obey them:

> Sam's militancy as a prisoner was undisguised . . . The institution had been founded on lines of military discipline of the strictest type—only within very recent history were inmates allowed to speak, once out of their cells. [We] marched in uniform columns of twos, aligned symmetrically by height, everywhere . . . [One cold day] we were part way down the tunnel to D Block and the school when I heard [a] voice scream, "You there, get your hands out of those pockets!"
>
> I half turned and saw Sam fall out of line to face the guard. Sam's face was angry and his hands were still in his pockets. "I'm not a soldier in your army!" he shouted back. "My hands happen to be cold—that's why they're in my pockets!"*

As the months passed, Sam became increasingly stubborn and unsubmissive, and as a result was shuttled from job to job, cell block to cell block, from keeplock to the box (solitary). One inmate said he was

---

* Cohen: William Coons, "An Attica Graduate Tell His Story," *New York Times Magazine*, October 10, 1971.

"worked through every block in the prison, a circular trip, like a particle through a cyclotron."

While Sam was at West Street he had interpreted many events as part of a scheme to break him, to make him talk. When he was placed in solitary or moved about, even when his cellies beat him up, he told me "they" were trying to break him. There was some reason for him to suspect such a scheme; the FBI certainly did want to find out more about Sam's affiliations. But at Attica Sam never described his situation in those terms. His attitudes had changed utterly. In place of despair he felt determination; in place of the self-doubt that led him to see (probably) random events as a plot, he had a definite plan of his own and a growing self-respect. He was realistic, not paranoid, and he did not need self-aggrandizement.

Other inmates, however, say that the administration at Attica tried very hard to break Sam down. He was constantly at disciplinary tribunals, keeplocked, boxed, denied privileges. In his first three months at Attica he was keeplocked three times. In February when he was thrown out of the school he was keeplocked again; and at the end of April, when he was in C Block, he was keeplocked for five days. On May 12, in response to his protest over work assignment in C Block, he was sentenced to eight days keeplock. When this sentence ran out and he still refused his work assignment he was keeplocked again "pending interview with [the] deputy warden." That interview didn't take place until June 4, and then Vincent, the deputy warden, sentenced Sam to thirty days "punitive seg-regation"—solitary. While in solitary, on his way to the tiny exercise yard kept for men in solitary, he was ordered to fold his arms. He refused, and was sentenced to "fourteen days keeplock or until he conforms to rules." Thus he was not only boxed but denied all exercise. On June 24 he again refused to fold his arms, and four more days were added to his keeplock. On July 1 his earphones were taken away.*

But as the hacks' harassment of Sam intensified, his proud stubborn-ness only strengthened: "They've taken my earphones away—again for not folding my arms. Each time I leave the cell for shower, shave, meet the panel, I get another report for not folding arms. First they took away exercise yards, now earphones. Next it will be light bulb and newspapers

---

* Cohen: At Attica prisoners can listen to selected radio programs through earphones.

and books. I've decided not to leave my cell any more, which means they'll drag me, I guess." I visited Sam while he was in solitary. Though they were depriving him of his few "privileges" and harassing him—he did not tell me this, I found out only when I read his letters to his lawyers—he said that he did not find solitary too trying. To a degree he liked it, as he liked keeplock: it gave him solitude, which he treasured, and quiet to read and think. His only complaint was that he was suffering from recurrent headaches. They had begun in the late spring, and were occurring more and more frequently. When he went to the prison "doctor," he was given pills that gave him no relief. When he told the doctor that, he was thrown out and refused further treatment. He was beginning to worry about cancer. During the summer the headaches intensified until he suffered almost constantly, and had to stop reading and exercising.

The warden, Mancusi, threatened Sam with a second term in the box if he continued to refuse a work assignment in D Block, but Sam was determined to refuse even if it meant thirty days more solitary. Mancusi gave in. On July 11 he had Sam taken out of the box and transferred to the "idle company" on a special tier reserved—in Sam's words—"for madmen and incorrigibles," in A Block. Just as he had found pleasures in keeplock and solitary, Sam liked his new arrangements. He had more quiet, more yard time, more opportunity to talk with other prisoners, and he did not have to work at all.

The last punishment meted out to Sam before he was murdered was a fourteen-day keeplock in August, "for demanding human treatment" in the mess hall. He emerged from that on September 4, 1971, 368 days after he had arrived at Attica. In that year he had spent almost one out of every three days in keeplock or solitary. But he was far from a broken man. On the contrary, he was much stronger.

In the fall of 1970 Sam had written, "Tho I lack the double Y chromosome factor of most of my neighbors, I have managed to effect a significantly belligerent enough aspect to gain, if not the respect, at least the acquiescence of my fellow felons." Although he had been at various jails for almost a year, he still felt leery of other inmates, still held himself apart, still felt it necessary to feign toughness. Other inmates felt that Sam was "romantic" and unrealistic, and Blacks especially were wary of him because they thought him a "fanatic." This hurt Sam and fed his estrangement.*

But by the summer of 1971 Sam had worked through his fears and prejudices about the other prisoners, and had replaced his "romanticism" with a more realistic view of prison. His diffidence and distance were replaced by warmth and affection. Other inmates describe him as a "very gentle, very beautiful person" with a "willingness to help, to be of service, to give." His ability with his guitar and his lovely singing voice won him many friends: one prisoner became so attached to him that he "followed Sam around like a dog." His studies helped him become a clear, convincing, and useful adviser and speaker, and, most important, his proud refusal to submit to the hacks' harassment and intimidation won him widespread respect. At the outset it had seemed that he was simply "in for a rough trip"; but he turned the trip to his advantage. Each time he refused to submit, each time he stood up and spoke out, he increased the respect that other inmates felt for him. One inmate recalled, "Once when we were returning from lunch a hack coming in the opposite direction, all at once, with total and naked hostility, without any explanation, suddenly shouldered and shouted at about five of us who were not directly in back of those in front. . . . When he shouldered the man in front of Sam, then skipped Sam himself, Sam wheeled around and shouted at his back, 'What the hell do you think you're doing, Boyle!' Sam was the only one who made a reaction on the spot. I figured no one would back him, but by that afternoon he had a complaint written up with about fifteen signatures and was taking it to the desk."

---

* JM: Cohen's analysis of my father's psyche is an outright denial of other accounts, including the ones that Attica inmate leaders Herb Blyden and Jerry Rosenberg gave me when I interviewed them in 1991, as well as what was published in Warden Mancusi's "Muslim Reports" (referenced in the 1991 "Attica Brothers" civil trial). There my father is listed as a significant threat to prison order. This was seconded in Correction Commissioner Russell Oswald's memoir *Attica: My Story* (New York: Doubleday, 1972) and the state's McKay report. My father was extremely proactive within the inmate grievance committee and worked with several Black, White, and Hispanic leaders without friction. It was his talent for unification that made him dangerous to the prison administration (and a racist system) and what instigated his constant and sustained stays in keeplock. It's a shame (if not suspect) that Cohen, who has positioned himself as my father's "close friend," felt the need to marginalize his legacy in the introduction of a book honoring his achievements.

Sam turned the inmates' respect into support, and then he turned this support into power. As the inmates' support for Sam grew, the hacks became somewhat less willing to push him around. And the more the hacks backed off, the harder Sam pushed; because he was supported by the other men he could "give the guards more truck," as he put it. And because he gave the guards more truck, the inmates respected him more. It was a spiral of increasing power which Sam consciously created and maintained. By late spring some inmates held him in awe:

> I was walking with a curly-headed white kid wearing thick glasses, up on an assault rap, doing a "pound" (five years) as a result of a motorcycle-gang engagement. He put his hand on my shoulder and drew me aside. "Don't look right away, but look over there, at that table."
>
> I looked. I saw a large, strong-jawed, lean and bony- framed man with thinning hair, a set, stubborn expression on his face, hunched over the table, his hands folded together. There were curious round, dark protuberances on his knuckles. He wore glasses.
>
> "Who's that?" I asked.
>
> "The Mad Bomber."
>
> "What's his name?"
>
> "I don't know. They call him the Mad Bomber, is all." He gave me a sidelong look. "See those things on his knuckles?"
>
> "Yeah. What are they?"
>
> "Karate, I think."
>
> . . . There's no one more ultraright than the average biker, and this one was a Hell's Angels aspirant. . . . Here he was, pointing out Sam Melville, an ultra-leftist, professed Weatherman. . . . In my biker friend's voice was a mixture of awe, respect, and comical disdain. . . . He obviously had some respect for Sam as a heavy dude.*

---

* Cohen: Coons, "An Attica Graduate Tells His Story." Sam deliberately cultivated the calluses on his knuckles to give the impression that he knew karate, but he knew no karate and had little experience in fighting. And though he was thought of as a Weatherman at Attica, he was not.

Not only had Sam's relations with other inmates changed, but his perception of what was possible at Attica had changed. His first impression, that it would be impossible to organize at Attica, was wrong. Just one month prior to his arrival, at the beginning of August, 1970, about forty inmates had been transferred to Attica from Auburn, where they had been involved in a strong protest against prison conditions. This brought to Attica a large group of men of high consciousness and great commitment, who understood how to organize in prison and were willing to take the risks. Many of them were Five Percenters or Muslims. One was Richard Clark, a leader of the September '71 insurrection. On August 19, 1970, they helped stage a prison-wide strike which was extremely effective. Several small reforms were granted, but, more important, increasing numbers of inmates began to look upon themselves with new pride and self-respect. They shaved, dressed better, studied harder; they began to understand the value of organization and unity; their political consciousness increased. Thus when Sam arrived at Attica important organization had already been done.

Not only that, but Sam's original perception of race relations—that whites and Blacks were unalterably separated by racism—had also been wrong, or at least conditions changed very fast. When Tom Wicker left D Block only one year after Sam first entered it, he wrote of the "submergence of racial animosity in class solidarity," and of striking "racial harmony." To a significant degree Sam himself was responsible for that harmony. As one inmate has said, "Sam was a prince of war among imprisoned fighters. To Blacks he was that missing proof that 'white revolutionaries' deserve black respect. To whites he was like a shield against their own privilege-fed cowardice. He made whites believe in their own courage just by the way he walked down the halls or talked to the really pig hacks."

Sam gradually became very close to several black and Latino leaders, and in the spring both the Young Lords party and the Black Panther party invited him to attend their daily exercise and rap sessions in the yard, regularly, as a brother. Sam was pleased by these invitations, but he turned them down. To have accepted would have yoked him to only one group, while he wanted to remain mobile and in touch with many people. Also, he would have been unable to spend his time alone, and that was very important to him: he wanted to be able to lie alone and quiet in the sun when he felt the need. So he usually exercised alone, ran alone—he ran three miles daily—and joined a group rap session only when he felt he had something special to say.

In the spring Sam began to attend Fred LeShure's weekly sociology class at the prison school. Here, initially, about fifteen inmates concentrated on socioeconomic conditions at Attica: one of its products was Sam's "Anatomy of the Laundry" (which can be found in Section IV). Gradually, in part as a result of Sam's presence, the class turned into a Marxist-Leninist consciousness-raising session. Later it became one of the rare places where organizers from different blocks could get together to discuss strategy.

In the late spring, when Herbert Blyden returned from the Tombs— he had just gone through the prisoners' uprising there—he and Sam met in LeShure's class. They recognized each other—they had met at the Tombs—and Blyden showed Sam a list of demands that he wanted to present to the state bureau of corrections. Sam was very critical, but he took the idea back to his block to discuss with other men, and one week later he agreed to help. Out of these demands grew the twenty-seven demands which were mailed to corrections commissioner Oswald in July and then presented to him again, twice, in September. When Sam first spoke with Blyden, Blyden said that he thought Sam should organize whites; Blacks would organize Blacks, Latinos would organize Latinos. Sam disagreed with this, arguing that it would foster disunity and leave the whites very vulnerable; but Blyden convinced him.

The August 1970 strike had been organized and led by B Block, where political consciousness and organization were more advanced than in other blocks. In June 1971 B Block formed the Attica Liberation Front, which then expanded to include representatives from all the blocks—each of which had formed workers' coalitions—and from the Panthers, the Five Percenters, the Lords, People's Party 2, and the Muslims. Sam became the head of the white faction of A Block, chief of the A Block workers' coalition, and a vice-president of the ALF.

Sam developed great strength in A Block despite the fact that he did not arrive there until the middle of July. He had been there hardly a month when A Block called a "sick-in" to protest prison conditions. This was done without contacting the rest of the ALF, but it was extremely successful. Official figures, which at best are conservative, show that 190 men went to sick call that day. This was an extraordinary turnout. It reflected Sam's power and prestige, and it was the direct cause for Oswald's decision to visit Attica to confer with the prisoners on September 3.*

Sam had become a very effective organizer. Before his capture he had abhorred meetings and mocked suggestions that they were of much value. But at Attica he became a powerful and effective debater, driving, insistent and convincing. He tended to become angry when faced with someone whom he could not convince, but his raps were largely successful. One guard described Sam as the most well-read, articulate, and militant revolutionary in the prison, and said, after Sam's murder, that he had known that Sam would die for what he believed in.

In July Sam began to work with young whites, many of whom he described as "20yearoldnamvetheads," busted for dope, physically decrepit, confused, and depressed. To help them he gave up his yard-time freedom and solitude, and set up a group that exercised and rapped together regularly. When I saw Sam at the beginning of August he was very pleased with the progress of this group, saying that they were regaining physical health and were creating an understanding of the society which had drafted them, debilitated them, and then imprisoned them. The only drawback, he said, was that they never left him alone. But he felt that he was creating a coherent political group. After Sam's murder, one member of this group wrote, "Sam Melville is dead, Sam, who was and is my inspiration. I took, and our organization took, our strength and education from Sam."

In late July, again without consulting the ALF leadership, Sam began writing and distributing *The Iced Pig*, an underground newsletter which he handprinted, carbon-copied, and distributed secretly.† *The Iced Pig*

---

* SF: The "direct cause for Oswald's decision to visit Attica" was the concern caused by the unprecedented unity of the George Jackson memorial fast, the receipt of the manifesto, and the news stories by reporter Richard Roth. The mass "sick-call strike" on August 30 was because of the rumor that Oswald would be visiting that day and inmates thought they could see him. That was a false alarm, and he didn't arrive until September 2 and left September 3.

† SF: Why should Sam have "consult[ed] the ALF leadership" to put out a newsletter, whether under his own name or anonymously? That would have gone against every independent anarchist tendency Sam was known for.

described itself as "a continuing project . . . to help us to bring each other to an understanding of our place and role in neo-fascist Amerika & t American Auschwitz known as Attica, . . . to teach ourselves t truth of Amerika's myth. To forge ourselves into dedicated cadres committed to t construction of a society that will serve t needs of t people and make us into whole human beings at last." *The Iced Pig*'s message was, Refuse to be intimidated! Make your voices heard! Stay together: "Strength and Solidarity r t greatest weapons to gain dignity." Sam said that the newsletter was "a group project"; however it seems that he created and distributed it by himself. And took the risks by himself. He put out three issues before he was killed.

One week after the murder of George Jackson, on August 27, the ALF called a hunger strike to protest the murder and to honor their Soledad brother. At breakfast in one of Attica's two mess halls only thirteen men picked up their trays on the feed line; at lunch only seven men did. There was absolute silence. Even the guards, amazed and frightened, kept silent. During this protest Sam was in keeplock "for demanding human treatment," but after the memorial he began his last *Iced Pig* with, "U R beautiful brothers! Strength & Solidarity r t greatest weapons to gain dignity. Strength & Solidarity is what you showed on t 27th."

Toward the end of August Fred LeShure was boxed for sixty days for having "inflammatory literature" in his cell—Mancusi had discovered the nature of his sociology class. In one day the ALF collected 350 signatures on a petition demanding LeShure's release; Mancusi refused to listen. LeShure stayed in solitary, and his class was closed.

On September 3, Oswald arrived at Attica to discuss the ALF demands, which had been on his desk since July. When he met with Frank Lott, chairman of the ALF, he asked for more time. There was sharp disagreement within the ALF on how to respond to this request: many wanted to go on strike immediately. The final decision, however, was to give Oswald four to six weeks. Immediately after his departure, the ALF instituted a letter-writing campaign which sent from two to three hundred letters to senators, representatives, lawyers, and the press. At the same time they authorized Wayne Trimmer, a white inmate, representative of the C Block workers' coalition to the ALF, to speak to the press to discuss conditions and to air the twenty-seven demands. When Trimmers' interview was published Mancusi ordered him to solitary. The ALF protested, in Buffalo his mother spoke out in the press, and Mancusi was forced to back down; the next day Trimmer was released to his regular cell.

At the beginning of 1971, when Oswald took over the bureau of corrections, there had been a slight "liberalization" within the prison system.* At Attica inmates were granted one more hour of lights at night; censorship of mail to and from lawyers was ended; wages were raised slightly; penalties involving visiting rights were stopped; and, most important of all, inmates were allowed to gather in groups greater than three. But as the men organized and built their strength and solidarity, their increasing power frightened and angered the guards and the administration, and the prison atmosphere turned increasingly repressive. As early as April 18 Sam had written, "There are indications that the hacks are engaging in overt terrorism for a change. Conflicting reports have emerged but something's up for sure." On August 6 he wrote, "Rules about staying in line and talking in the corridors are being more strictly enforced." On August 20, "Political people in at least three blocks have been busted this week for petty shit." Then: "Pig Boyle still terrorizes the halls, only now his friends help out. . . . All rules are now *strictly* enforced. You're busted for dispensing lit, holding meetings, or staring at pigs. We are treated as dogs. . . . I was down to disciplinary court 2 weeks ago and there were more than 70 men waiting for a hearing. T old timers say it's beginning to look like t old days where u got KL for looking crosseyed at a pig." Nine days later the prisoners revolted.

Of course, like all prisoners, Sam thought about riots. In the last year of his life there were several riots in New York State alone, including major

---

* SF: Ultimately, Oswald announced reforms but took credit for changes that in fact were forced on him by the federal courts, in particular the right to uncensored attorney-client mail, which was due entirely to the *Sostre v. Rockefeller* decision. Many believed Oswald was sincere in wanting to make reforms and see inmates treated humanely—one of his stated goals was training for guards—but was hampered by lack of funds and racist guards and doctors he could not get rid of. However, on February 10, 1971, Oswald told the New York State legislature that prison conditions were "explosive" and "there is a new element which seeks to destroy the system rather than seeking better conditions." Charles R. Holcomb, "State's Correctional System Pleads for Expanded Program," *Niagara Falls Gazette*, February 11, 1971.

insurrections at the Tombs, the Queens House of Detention, and Auburn. By subjecting prisoners to total degradation—one inmate described Mancusi as "not a warden, but a concentration camp commandant to whom inmates are not even dogs, just numbers"—and by refusing the inmates any hope for significant change in prison conditions, the pigs created enough anger, frustration and despair to generate any number of riots. And by refusing the prisoners access to the media the pigs actually *encouraged* riots. As Sam wrote, "We are left with nothing except riots to bring our plight before the public." Most inmates, however, were afraid of riots, and in his histories and newsletters Sam frequently asserted that it was possible to protest in nonviolent ways. In July, while discussing the ineffectuality of a complaint he was filing against "pig Boyle," Sam himself commented on the impossibility of the use of force: "We have only one other alternative to meet their aggression, and at this time geography is against us—not to mention technology."

This is what Sam had said to me about riots—that they were futile and doomed to tragedy. Nevertheless, he expected that a riot would explode sometime somewhere he was imprisoned, and he knew he would be totally involved: he would have no choice.

However, it does not seem that Sam was dragged unwillingly into Attica's uprising; he may even have been the spark that ignited it. During the first battles, when the inmates seized almost all of the prison, Sam was in a position of strong leadership. This did not mean that he was able to control what was happening: he ordered that no hostages be taken, but was ignored.* But when the first leadership table was set up on September 9, Sam was one of the group who took control.

This group came together spontaneously, as the men had risen up spontaneously, and they were totally unprepared. No demands had been drawn up, no plans laid. It took several hours just to get a copy of the

---

* JM: This may have been a reasonable assumption at the time Cohen wrote this, but today we know otherwise. My father took twelve hostages from the metal shop and transported them down into D Yard. One was Ed Cunningham, who was killed during the assault by the state to retake the prison. From what I learned by talking to uprising leaders who survived, my father was not "ordering" anyone to do or not do anything in D Yard. This allegation (which might be a projection of Cohen's presumptions about Black inmates at Attica) places my father on a moral high ground above the prisoners of color who are presented as more violent than he.

ALF's twenty-seven demands, add on three more—the removal of Mancusi, the admission of observers, and transportation to a non-imperialist country for those prisoners who desired it*† (about 150 men still do)—and transmit them to deputy commissioner Dunbar.

Sam remained at the leadership table throughout the first day of the insurrection, helping organize the men, arranging for food, and getting tents set up in the yard. (Most men wanted to sleep outside under the stars rather than go back to the cells. Although it rained for two days during the rebellion, no one went back inside; staying outside had become a matter of principle, and was intended as a public statement.)‡

During the first hours of the insurrection, even after the inmates had it secured, D yard was in great confusion. Some men had raided the commissary, brought out all the ice cream, and now were fighting over it. A few men were raped. Whites of course were a small minority, and many, afraid that the uprising would turn toward anti-white vengeance, at first tended to group themselves closely together, separate from the other men. Sam reassured these whites of their safety and brought them into participation with the rest of the men. While he was at the leadership table Sam made only one speech. He said, You are beautiful, brothers. I know that some of you don't want to be here§, but we have it now. We must stay together. I know you will. These remarks took about thirty seconds.

---

* JM: A confessed Melville collaborator, Robin Palmer, ended up in D Yard during the uprising, after being convicted of a separate underground action in NYC. According to my talks with him, it was Palmer who suggested this demand. Other accounts disagree.

† SF: Palmer may have supported this demand, but every credible source credits L. D. Barkley. Rosenberg and Blyden called it "LD's brainchild," and New York State assemblyman Arthur Eve said Barkley "tried continually to whip up support for the demand." Stephen Bello, *Doing Life: The Extraordinary Saga of America's Greatest Jailhouse Lawyer*, 182–183; Donald Singleton, "Attica: Anatomy of a Tragedy," part 4, *New York Daily News*, October 7, 1971; Oswald, *Attica: My Story*, 24, 89–90, 114.

‡ JM: This is incomplete, bordering on inaccurate. Frank "Big Black" Smith was elected to the role of "head of security" in the yard and was not allowing inmates back inside the prison because some were trying to make deals with the troopers lingering just outside the inmate-controlled areas. Some inmates were beaten if they became insistent on returning to their cells to retrieve mementos or use the bathrooms. It was for this reason that my father saw the necessity for a latrine and organized (mostly White) inmates to dig a massive trench, first for waste and then ultimately as a defense against the troopers taking back the prison.

§ Cohen: Many men did not want to be involved in the insurrection. They were due for release soon and feared it would be denied as punishment, or they simply feared the police

Reports about Sam from this point on are vague and often conflict. It is clear that Sam left the leadership table on September 10. One man says there were too many men at the table, that Sam and others had to leave to cut the leadership to a workable number. Another reports that Sam gave his seat at the table to someone who had a greater knowledge of law. Another says that Sam felt himself increasingly out of tune with the general tendencies of the men, felt that what he had to say was not what they wanted to hear, and thus chose to leave the table. One of the leaders who was at the table with Sam, however, says that on September 10, when Oswald was inside D yard negotiating, one inmate publicly demanded that Oswald be taken hostage. Though this demand was not accepted, it caused such discord that the men decided to caucus by blocks to elect the new leadership. Sam was not selected.*

After this Sam apparently became a "non-table spokesman," a liaison between whites—especially A Block whites—and the leadership table. Several leaders have said that Sam was very effective in keeping the whites together, calming their fears of racism, dealing with problems, upsets, fights and freak-outs. During the four days the inmates controlled the yard, the men slept very little. There was constant excitement, pressure and anxiety. Many men were frightened by imagery of the police onslaught, and this imagery often swelled to terrorized obsession. At the same time there was a powerful desire among some men to express vengeance and hatred in the slaughter of hostages and other guards and police—even if this meant the destruction of negotiations and a bloodbath. Some occasionally dramatized this, as if to say to the others, This is our end—all the politics is superficial froth. Thus, in addition to fears of racism, police attack, and the expectable concerns of internal factionalism, there was a powerful strain of apocalyptic terror. In this atmosphere many men broke

---

response. On September 10 many men spent the day trying to get out of D Block by saying they were sick.

* JM: In speaking with Attica leaders and reading transcripts that surfaced during the civil trial of 1991, I was able to piece together a better understanding of why my father left the negotiating table: the direction of the leadership was becoming irretractable. Commissioner Oswald spoke to reporters on the second night of the uprising (September 10) and claimed (falsely) that hostages had been "mutilated." After that, the mood of the leadership shifted from collegiate to militant. My father gave up his seat to start making preparations for an assault prompted by the many troopers that could be seen gathering on the rooftops.

down, and Sam's work in calming them was of great importance. Certainly Sam must have been upset by the apolitical thrust for vengeance at any cost, and tried to direct energy instead toward organized, disciplined behavior struggling to raise consciousness, create solidarity, and achieve reform. One leader described Sam as "a servant of awareness"; another called him D yard's "prince of peace."

The last words of the last issue of *The Iced Pig* were, "On t day of Jackson's funeral t Weatherpeople bombed 3 offices of t California Correx Dept. Unfortunately, no one was hurt Get it together Weatherfolk!" But when the insurrection broke out Sam tried to prevent the taking of hostages, and protected them once taken. He was shocked by the proposal to hold Oswald, and vigorously opposed it. He was asked to build large explosive devices to be detonated if troopers tried to enter, but though he promised to, he never even began.*†‡ The press, which constantly lied about Sam, claims that he electrified certain gratings to

---

* JM: Sam did take at least twelve hostages from the metal shop; he spent at least some time in the line of Muslims who guarded the hostages from reprisals, which became known as "the hostage circle"; he oversaw the assembly of approximately three hundred dummy Molotov cocktails and a rocket launcher. By all accounts these weapons were part of his plan to combat the inevitable retaking. However, most of the bombs were made with cooking oil, which was not combustible.

† SF: Whether Sam did or didn't "run and carry four bombs" on Bloody Monday will continue to be debated. But Cohen is wrong in saying that "surely the inmates did not have the time or technology to produce small bombs." Surely they did. One direct source is Jameel Raheem, who told me that on Sunday night, September 12, he and his friend Willie West helped Sam fill small glass bottles on the ground in D Yard with an unknown liquid, apparently adding them to a stash already made. In Jameel's words, "We knew they wouldn't ignite, it was for show. We didn't know what was in 'em but we knew they wouldn't work. We did it for Sam." He did not know if any were ever thrown. About fifteen hours later, both Willie West and Sam would be dead. In testifying before the McKay Commission, Oswald cited five "factors" that he said "led him to conclude negotiations were doomed." One of the factors was "Intelligence reports that inmates were making more weapons, including an improvised mortar launcher, and were electrifying their barricades." Associated Press, "Why a Key Attica Aide Erred," *New York Post*, December 1, 1971. During the 1991–1992 Attica civil trial in Buffalo, Sam's rocket launcher was mentioned in court testimony by Franklin Davenport, a National Guard master sergeant weapons expert who was sent to D Yard as part of the backup force. He said he had found "a makeshift rocket launcher and some homemade bombs." Dan Herbeck, "Guardsman Backs Attica Inmates over Brutality," *Buffalo News*, November 8, 1991.

‡ SF: Sam's work in electrifying barricades has been confirmed by many credible sources, friend and foe alike.

hamper the troopers' entry; inmates say it was someone else. And in the yard, while almost everyone else carried some sort of weapon (knives, razors, clubs)—this was, after all, an army preparing to defend its last bit of territory—Sam refused to carry any weapon at all, and made a point of letting others know this.

However, while Sam opposed fatalistic vengeance, he felt quite fatalistic about himself. Even before the insurrection, he had told friends that he expected to die before leaving prison, and in the yard during the insurrection he told one man, "You know the beef I'm up for? If those troopers come over the wall, I'm dead." He was sure he would be picked out and executed. Still, this did not squelch his enthusiasm about the rebellion. Only hours before the police massacre, sitting with another inmate over a pre-dawn cup of coffee, Sam was excited by the men's determination. A few months before he had complained to the same man about the inmates' failure to organize and protect themselves. Now, however, he was delighted: "Man," he said, "we're finally *together*!"

The first press releases out of Attica after the police massacre included pictures of "Mad Bomber Melville" and the story that he had been shot by a police marksman while running across the yard with four homemade bombs in an attempt to blow up a fuel storage tank. On its face this story has several contradictions. *First*, a special gas was sprayed into the yard before the police opened fire. Rockefeller described the effects of this gas as "fantastic." Inmates said it was extremely powerful, sending men into convulsions. How could Sam have run purposefully through such gas? *Second*, how could he run and carry four bombs, unless they were quite small—and surely the inmates did not have the time or technology to produce small bombs (or any bombs) capable of penetrating steel tanks. *Third*, if Sam could have constructed bombs capable of penetrating steel, why would he choose to use them in such a dangerous and uncertain way? He had an hour's warning of the assault. If he had wanted to and had had the tools to blow up an oil tank, wouldn't he have done it so that he could have been more certain of success, and in a way that would not require such personal risk?

The story is clearly a concoction. As it turned out, although the press attributed it to Dunbar, it was actually offered by an unnamed guard who was leading pool reporters through the prison less than an hour after the massacre.* The story was simply taken down and distributed to other reporters, none of whom bothered to check its veracity. The press, like the prison administration and the state, felt a strong need to misrepresent and totally discredit Samuel Melville. I first heard about Sam's death on radio station WINS, which said, while "reporting" the massacre, "One prisoner who was killed no one will miss—Mad Bomber Melville."

The inmates' stories of Sam's death, however, are conflicting. Some say that just before the troopers came over the walls they saw Sam crouching behind some sandbags, seeking protection. One man says that he saw Sam stand up, as if to see what was happening, and that he was immediately shot in the neck or chest, fell back, bleeding profusely, and died. Five or six men say that they saw Sam shot by sniper fire.

Many more men, however, say that Sam was seen alive after the assault was over; that he was wounded in one leg but helped others who were more seriously wounded; that they saw him standing on one leg, leaning against a wall; that they saw him being carried away, alive, on a stretcher; and that he must have been executed afterward.

It is not hard to believe that Sam was executed. Investigators who have talked with survivors say that it is clear that some men were picked out

---

* SF: Cohen didn't have the benefit of reading Oswald's memoir; according to Oswald, the "unnamed guard who was leading pool reporters through the prison" was Robert Hulshoff (Oswald, *Attica: My Story*, 279). The only journalistic investigation of the alleged fuel tank Sam was attempting to blow up was done by the *Niagara Falls Gazette*, in "Attica— Monument to Despair" (October 24, 1971), which states that there was no such tank within or anywhere near D Yard. "The only large fuel tank known to exist within the prison is outside the cell block area," which was not occupied by inmates during the uprising. At a public forum on Attica in Buffalo two weeks after the assault, Assemblyman Arthur Eve described being present at "the twenty-four-man observer committee on a tour of the prison where Mr. [Walter] Dunbar described the knifings and the alleged mutilation of one [of the] hostages. 'The system was working together to fabricate a fantastic lie,' Eve charged." "Eve Says Official Circulated Report of Attica Knifing," *Buffalo Evening News*, September 28, 1971. Oswald later wrote that Dunbar "assumed they had died by having their throats cut," adding, "The reporters, for their part, did not check out these stories." (Oswald, *Attica: My Story*, 296). Walter Dunbar later acknowledged that he alone was the source of the "inaccurate reports," telling the McKay Commission they were not deliberate lies but were made because he "erred as a human being," a claim *Time* magazine called "inexcusable." "Dunbar Calls Attica Report of Slashings Honest Error," *Buffalo Evening News*, December 1, 1971.

to be executed, that some were executed by snipers and some by firing squads. The prison administration believed that the insurrection broke out in cell block A, company 5—Sam's company. Of the forty-five men in this company, fifteen were killed. That means that one-half of all the inmates who were killed came from this company.*

Certainly the prison administration had particular reason to want Sam out of their way. He was a powerful, effective, inspiring organizer; and that was clearly the way Mancusi saw him. Mancusi has said that the uprising was contrived and organized by "Maoists," militants and revolutionaries. He said that he could tell who they were by what they read and said. By these standards Sam had to be seen as a leading revolutionary spokesman; in fact, some guards have described him in just those words. By killing him the administration would remove a crucial man and a crucial image from the inmates' resistance, and would replace him with a lesson on what happens to those who stand up and resist.

Also, in addition to their own ordinary personal racism, the prison administrators felt a special racist hatred toward white inmates who conspicuously stepped across racial lines. Uniting white and black prisoners frightened them as administrators, for it created an infinitely more powerful inmate front. Clearly the administration wanted to avoid this.†‡ Just one week before the uprising they had taken direct action against Sam and two other inmates, LeShure and Trimmer, who had joined the struggle of

---

* JM: Here is what the Attica Brothers' attorney Elizabeth Fink told me in 1991: "There were forty inmates, including your father, housed in Five Company. It was Five Company that composed most of the so-called inmate ringleaders. And yet, seven of the twenty-nine prisoners killed—including your father—were members of Five Company." Five Company was where Warden Mancusi put many of the radical inmates.

† Cohen: The administration at Attica tried to keep prisoners divided in other ways also. In negotiations only four demands were categorically refused by the state: transportation to an anti-imperialist country (which the prisoners took very seriously), the removal of Mancusi, amnesty, and the demand that the four prison yards be united so that prisoners from the different blocks could mix. One of the greatest obstacles to effective organizing by the prisoners stemmed from the difficulties of communicating between blocks.

‡ SF: A couple of corrections are in order: (1) The only final demands rejected by the state were the removal of Mancusi and criminal amnesty. (2) Very few Brothers took the demand for travel a nonimperialist country seriously. However, it was Kunstler and Seale who stirred it up on the next-to-the-last day and created false hopes. Lynn Darling, "In Attica's Aftermath," *Newsday*, September 12, 1991, 1, 64–65.

black and Puerto Rican inmates. Several inmate leaders believe that Sam was pointed out for assassination because he had crossed racial lines.*

And the state police, of course, would have felt no objection to killing the Mad Bomber, Sam the Weatherman, Sam the Revolutionary. The state pigs are rabidly anti-communist, reactionary, and consistently politicized by the far Right, and in their assault they were led by a man with close connections to the secret service and the FBI. Before they charged into D yard troopers loaded their shotguns with .32 caliber "pellets"— the size of pistol slugs—especially chosen so that each pellet would have murderous effect. Snipers loaded their rifles with .270 Winchester .30 gr. expanding bullets. Ammunition boxes discarded outside the prison walls advertise "the exclusive Silvertip bullet with controlled expansion (and) soft-jacketed tip." In plain language, dum-dum bullets, which international law outlaws in warfare.

Thus there are three alternatives. Sam may have been hit by .32 caliber shotgun pellets which rabid troopers fired at random at niggers, crooks and commies; or he may have been deliberately identified in advance, picked out and assassinated by a sniper using dum-dum bullets; or he may have been executed by a firing squad after the assault was over. In any case he was murdered.†

---

* SF: It has always been my personal belief that Sam Melville was targeted for assassination on the first day of the uprising. Captain Henry Williams (an army counterintelligence officer for HUAC) led the assault force to retake Attica. It would appear Williams was more than just the boss of Vincent Tobia, the BCI inspector who took credit for killing Sam. A 1984 magazine story describes them socializing in bars together (Dan Herbeck, "Cops' Favorite Cop," *Buffalo Magazine*, August 26, 1984, 1, 18–19, 21–27, 30). Williams was promoted to colonel and made head of the seven-hundred-member BCI (Bello, *Doing Life*, 386).

† JM: I've spent years investigating such stories of a post-assault execution of my father. Aside from my father's autopsy and morgue photos, I've interviewed the pathologist who rendered them, looked at ballistics reports, and spoken to eyewitnesses. None of the post-assault theories hold up. My father was shot once in the shoulder with a zero-aught buckshot—a shotgun slug with pellets. His autopsy photo shows four entry wounds about two to three inches apart, in the upper left shoulder, each about the size of a quarter. He fell behind a barricade he was using as a perch, where he intended to throw Molotov cocktails at advancing troopers. His chance never came. The assault was over too quickly, and he collapsed after being hit and bled to death within minutes. Had the state police set up first aid stations in anticipation of the casualties, my father would probably have lived. However, there are many inconsistencies in the kill reports of Vincent Tobia, the trooper who shot

The original manuscript for this introduction was at the publisher's office when Jane's lawyer received her essay on Sam. In an accompanying note Jane suggested that her essay should be published in a magazine, but, even though the book was already past its deadline, Jane's essay clearly was best used to introduce Sam's letters. So I took my piece back, cut out most of my personal reminiscences—which largely duplicated Jane's—and concentrated instead on that period after Jane lost touch with Sam, when she went underground.

After Sam was transferred out of New York City, I visited him about two days every month. This is not much time, and two alienated men separated by wire, a month's absence, embarrassment, and the almost unbreachable fact that one is a prisoner inside and the other white middle-class outside, do not quickly flip into deep intimacy. We were getting to know each other better, nevertheless, and I know we came to love each other more; but Sam's two years in prison were a continuously intense experience through which he changed deeply and rapidly. What I have written about Sam's year at Attica, as that year progresses, comes more and more from others' reports of Sam, not from my experience of him. When the year culminates in the insurrection, *all* my knowledge of Sam comes from others' reports, very fragmentary ones at that.

Thus I don't know if I know very well the Sam who wandered through D Block yard during those last four days of his life. Obviously he was a very different man from the person I knew before he was jailed. But I think that in one essential way he remained the same. We discussed this subject many times. He himself summed it up best in a letter he wrote in early 1970. This letter is abstract and almost impersonal; but it is really introspective and accurate. It is a letter about the 1950's.

Sam talked a lot about the fifties. When he wanted to describe how difficult prison life was, he compared it to the fifties: "Imagine yourself having to go back to our lives of eight or ten years ago when the only break in the monotonous hypocrisy of society was to meet someone else, every once in a while, who felt your loneliness (which came out only as bitterness) . . . Prison is a microcosm of amerika circa 1950." The depressive

---

him—enough to support the notion that his death was not accidental. For more on this, see my memoir *American Time Bomb* (Chicago Review Press, 2021).

isolation and cynical despair of the fifties is ineradicable; it sticks in your memory as a terror and looms frightful whenever more hopeful perspectives seem about to crumble.

It is impossible to understand Sam without understanding this. His revolutionary fervor was a flight from despair: "We must move to a place beyond all known issues. It may be easier if there is a humanity to come—but that's not our motive. What we want is salvation from a meaningless annihilation. To not be cremated for coka-cola and plastic flags in waving simulation on the moon . . . Che was not fighting yanqui imperialism. He was desperate for meaning in a world of expediency."

Sam was seeking a sense of personal worth. Shortly after his arrest, in a brief, beautiful note to Jane, he said that he was proud of what he had done—I think he wrote, "At least we have not bent our knees to their false gods, or kissed their flag." Sam's goal was a sense of self-respect and dignity. Although in this sense his concern was individual and personal, he argued against any attempt to separate personal salvation from the struggle for social justice: "I don't think you can have inner peace without outer peace too . . . There is no individual change without social change . . ."

Sam *could not* turn inward: he suffered from such total alienation that he could not contact himself. After his bad acid trips I urged him to try to understand what they meant about him; he refused. His response was, flatly, that the acid was fucked up, and that was all. Once I asked him about his personal motivations for bombing; he absolutely refused to discuss them, and asked me to stop trying to discuss motivation. He said it was irrelevant.

For some people who are very alienated from themselves, self-understanding seems possible only in highly abstract forms. Sam was this way: he could be introspective only in abstractions. This is not peculiar to Sam; many of us can know ourselves only through abstractions. For many people like this, perhaps the only way to self-change and self-respect is through social action: definite action, understood abstractly, against a definite enemy, understood abstractly. When Sam wrote that "There is no personal change without social change," he was describing his own experience. He went from alienation, to abstraction, to social action.

But Sam seldom pretended he had a convincing social or political understanding. In one letter, when he summed up the arguments for his acts, he made it clear that he was aware of their fragility. "There are 4 views favoring paramilitarism: 1) It will snowball and bring down the PS [power structure]; 2) It aids 3rd World movements by diverting imperialism (2, 3, many Vietnams); 3) In a time when all action seems meaningless at least we won't be good Germans. 4) It's fun. It's not fashionable (yet?) to consider 4 and 3 offers little political meat. That leaves the snowball theory, which isn't working, and many Vietnams, which relies on the snowball." But even after he had demolished these arguments, he continued to argue for paramilitary action: "I could not live in Amerika without attacking it," he told me. Even as he argued for the creation of a Leninist national revolutionary party, he still said that he considered himself a Narodnik.*

It was argument 3 which was important to Sam. And it is important, in trying to understand Sam, to see that 3 is a negative formulation, that it rests on an uncertainty of one's own value: At least, if I have been nothing else, I will not have been a good German. Clearly this doesn't have much "political meat"; but that was not important to Sam. Though he was "desperate for meaning in a world of expediency," meaning did not come to him from analysis or theory. He could not tolerate the Movement's endless struggles toward an "analysis," which he felt as fearful rationalization meant to help avoid the risks of action. He once wrote, "In our blindness, the only relief from the chains of racism and an economy of constant expansion is 'action,' virtually any action." Another time he wrote, "Only the escalation of action to the point where our situation equals our philosophical desperation will bring whites into the revolution as committed as others have to be to merely survive." I think Sam comes through more clearly if I merge the quotes: In our blindness, only the escalation of action, virtually any action, will offer relief from the chains of our philosophical desperation.

---

* DV: The *Narodniki* (Russian: "populist") were members of a nineteenth-century socialist movement in Russia that believed political propaganda among the peasantry would lead to the awakening of the masses and, through their influence, to the liberalization of the czarist regime.

Political strategy remains obscure—even the results of action remain obscure—but at least the enemy is obvious. The forms of meaninglessness and futility—"coka-cola and plastic flags in waving simulation"—are also the forms of oppression and injustice. The only way to escape them is to attack them. That is the goal—escape from futility.

The knowledge that he personally had acted, even in the face of the Goliath state and possible failure, was essential. The agony of total alienation and total abstraction can only be relieved by concrete action. At his sentencing, when the judge tried to describe the "enormity" of Sam's acts by explaining that one of his attacks had cost the government ninety thousand dollars in damage, Sam said, "That's about two Viet Cong."* That was the only remark he made on his last day in court.

In part Sam's actions resulted from frustration and despair—frustration with the insignificance of protest in the face of America's enormous crimes, and despair of understanding a better way. Lack of understanding, however, caused Sam terrible anxiety after his capture: "Mostly, now, I feel that whatever I may have hoped to accomplish simply was a waste. Just one more nut who freaked out and took an O.D. or climbed up a tower and fruitlessly gunned down everything in sight." Sam's group also lacked a clear understanding. They argued, hesitated, and did not act, as Jane describes, until Sam finally acted alone. But this combination of his need to act and the group's weak understanding destroyed them all.

The group had unanimously decided he should not contact Demmerle, the informer. But Sam thought the group was wrong, and afraid; he did not have enough respect for them. Had there been a deeper understanding, a clearer strategy and stronger agreement, the group might have created enough discipline to control Sam. But Sam disregarded the group, went on his own impulse, and was captured.†

---

* Cohen: The US government was then estimating that it cost them about $35,000 to kill one Viet Cong guerrilla.

† JM: This is because by this time my father had abandoned "the group" and had begun working with other militants who were not mired in the philosophical meetings to which Cohen refers. It's true that my father lost patience (not respect) for them. He had little contact with the group after this and so never bothered to consult about Demmerle. Also, Cohen omits that he was aware Demmerle was already working with other group members before having ever met my father.

Sam told me that he had known he was being watched two days before his arrest, but that he went ahead with his attack on the trucks anyway. When I asked if one of his goals had been to get caught, he said yes. But it would be stupid and vicious to pretend to understand Sam's actions only in terms of suicide. Sam was suicidal; we all are suicidal. Sam was also a vital man, poet, musician, singer, athlete, successful engineer. Money and pleasure and even music, however, do not provide meaning; without meaning, self-respect is impossible; and without self-respect it is impossible to escape depression.

In one of his letters from prison Sam says, "If I can be used to any advantage for the forces of social change, I will feel much less oppressed by my environment." Each time I read that I feel that it pertains not only to Sam in prison, but to Sam in America; that Sam, with all his vitality and energy, was also deeply depressed. Depression is a result of misdirected anger: when one is afraid to turn one's anger against its real target, one turns it against oneself. The result is self-hate, depression. Shortly after he was captured, Sam said to me, "John, I have not been depressed once during the last year." He stared intently at me as he said this. It was of great importance to him.*

---

* JM: Earlier in this introduction Cohen claims that my father was "very depressed" during the periods of the bombings and the events leading up to them. I have many pictures of him, always smiling, always happy, even the candid ones. My mother has scoffed at Cohen's theory that her husband was depressed. After interacting intermediately with Cohen over the years, I'm of the mind that his opinions on Sam's "depression" are more the result of his own projections. Cohen may be trying to do his friend a service by psychoanalyzing/rationalizing Sam's bombings, to which Cohen objected, but I think history should be the ultimate judge of Sam Melville's mental state, and thankfully he has since attracted better historians.

LETTERS

by Samuel Melville

THE PERSONS TO WHOM SAM is writing and referring in these letters are:

JOHN COHEN, *a friend of Sam's from 1968 until Sam's death. All letters addressed to "My dear brother," "Dear brother," or to "Dear John," are to John Cohen.*

RUTH, *Sam's wife, had been separated from Sam for several years before his arrest.*

JOCKO, *Sam's son, was seven years old when Sam was captured. Ruth never told Jocko that Sam was in jail.*

RICHARD B. *Sometimes R.B. (changed to "Lenny" in the first edition), a friend.*

SHARON KREBS, *a friend of Sam's who visited him while he was held at the Federal House of Detention. She and Sam carried on an extensive correspondence, but all but one of his letters to her were confiscated by the New York City police in December 1970, when Sharon was arrested during an attempt to fire-bomb a Manhattan bank.*

BEATRICE, *a friend of Sam's with ties to Weather. Changed to "Charlene" in the first edition.*

JANE ALPERT, *referred to as "My lady," or "Jane," or "Juana," with whom Sam lived and who was charged with conspiring with Sam to destroy government property.*

BILL CRAIN, *Sam's lawyer, referred to as "Bill" or "Crain."*

JOYCE, *a young woman who knew Sam slightly and wrote him one or two letters. She was later arrested with Sharon in their attempted bombing of Chase Manhattan bank.*

Sam's spelling is atrocious, and I have corrected it. Otherwise I have left his writing style alone. Although in some letters Sam occasionally reverted to normal capitalization, he most often chose not to. In his letters to Jocko he always used standard style, perhaps because he did not want to confuse his son's education.

J. C.

NEW EDITION NOTE: All of Sam's letters have been reconstituted to the way he originally wrote them—punctuation, spelling errors, and all.

J.M.

I

FEDERAL HOUSE OF DETENTION, WEST STREET

November, 1969

My Dear Brother,

I've started several letters to you and wind up tearing them up thinking they might reflect a mood of despondency I'm not proud of. I'll say your letter and a visit from Sharon picked me up alot. But my prevailing mood must be called despair. Living among *our* people and taking from Amerika that amount I could stomach made me forget the vast waste of inhumanity that dominates this country. Here, I'm struck with the overwhelming insanity of popular opinion and taste without any relief! I don't know how long I'll be able to take prison life. Imagine yourself having to go back to our lives of eight or ten years ago when the only break in the monotonous hypocrisy of society was to meet someone else, every once in a while, who felt your loneliness (which came out only as bitterness). Couple this with a world *completely devoid of women!* Mostly, now I feel whatever I may have hoped to accomplish simply was a waste. Just one more nut who freaked out and took an O.D. or climbed up a tower and fruitlessly gunned down everything in sight. I know there is a Jane and a John and young brothers and sisters with another way, another music, another look, another *smell!* But it's all so unreal here. At first the shock of the arrest and the feeling of a common enemy made me groove on my cellmates, but after awhile I began to see so painfully the pettiness and hatred that is their "preferred" makeup. telling myself these are my fellow creatures just doesn't help for very long. I'm not Christ though i might like to think so sometimes.

My greatest fear is that my glib answer to the charge of insanity is totally wrong.*† I've always said that *insanity* was merely a malevolent society's way of dealing with an individual's action which threatens the functioning of that society. Now i'm beginning to realize there are creatures who, driven to despair at finding love, actually doubt their own reasoning apparatus, their own *needs.* I'm told by some that once i get to a bonafide prison, i'll be able to get almost any literature short of pornography and be able to have visits from anyone except co-defendents. It's a slender thread of consolation. My real options are (when i have the courage to face them): to become an expert in gin rummy or the grandmaster of postal chess. There really isn't much else. I haven't much hope of beating the rap. When i asked Crain whether i faced five years or fifty, he said with a frown, i'd better figure fifty. John, i don't think i'm strong enough. I think sometimes i have much love for some people and beliefs but i also know that my response to my environment is that of a pragmatic animal. I seek to satisfy my basic needs . . . not hunger or shelter from a hostile nature; but the soft voice of a woman, the laughter of a shared friend . . . *these* are my basic needs!

I watched the spectacle of the Army-Navy football game on TV today. The close-ups of the faces sent shudders through me. Strong,

---

* Cohen: Sam was not legally charged with insanity. There was some thought that his best course might be to plead insanity; but that was quickly rejected. He is referring here to remarks made by public figures, like Lindsay, police spokesmen, and newspaper editorial writers that the bombers were "madmen," "deranged," etc. Sam knew of course that these were simply attempts to deny his acts the meaning he intended; but in the intense depression he fell into after his arrest he worried—briefly—that he *was* insane.

† SF: An insanity plea would have led to "psychiatric evaluation," a favorite government tactic used against political defendants, and eventual psychiatric commitment. I am surprised that Sam was not sent to Bellevue for observation anyway, especially since his codefendant Dave Hughey was forced into three months of psychiatric observation for what the judge called living in "a world of fantasy." "Dave Hughey," *Rat*, October 6–27, 1970, 23.

crew-cut young men and obedient young women. Uniformed. Cheering. Mad. Completely mad. Camera cutouts of General Westermoreland.* It was a scene i lived twenty years ago. If my personal despair is reading the signs accurately, we're in for very rough times. Maybe we'll all be together soon. Somehow, i hope not.†

i love you

December, 1969

'mah frien john'

never never never apologize to me again! the most destructive weapons ever used against us were/are guilt & shame. lets not use them on each other. you are me and when your head is bowed i am in disgrace. the significant lesson the great teachers of the world taught was the incredible, inevitable quality of rebirth. whatever you may think about yourself the man i love is the impassioned fiery man that stood in front of an inert and bloodless people in the spring of '68 and demanded they be more than they were. you were called from among us and you didn't turn away. real issues weren't important. you screamed at a sleepy community that they were having a nightmare. and you kept screaming until it moved. for the past few months you were just resting your voice. ain't nothin to apologize for.

it's been years since i've written *anything* and this past month with letters, lawyers papers and random thoughts i bet i've written more than i ever have. i throw more than 90% away. it don't come out near what i want. in four tries on a letter to r.b. i still havn't sent him anything. tell him i'm trying. he's just not a person with whom one has verbal communication. i can tell him i love him but what else. r.b.'s just there, when you need him you go to him. he'll fix your bicycle,

---

* JV: General William Westmorland (1914–2005) was the commander of US military forces in Vietnam from 1964 to 1968 and a key architect of controversial strategies like massive aerial bombardments of North Vietnam. He was widely viewed as an antagonist by the anti–Vietnam War movement.
† SF: The "scene i lived twenty years ago" refers to the annual T-NT football games between archrivals Tonawanda and North Tonawanda, uninterrupted since 1896.

build your furniture, bury your dog. i say thank you in sign language! he's too beautiful and obvious to talk to.

on the multibiography of ours (the "white soul on ice" bill crain calls it) i'm afraid you and jane will have to do most of the work. i've tried but everything comes out sour and boring or else pretentious and stupid. i've rethought what i said at your last visit and i think you and sharon are right, there is a need for such a book and it might as well be us. i can contribute vague "facts" about what i remember of my past but not much more.*

item: i see my lady made the papers again, the [N.Y.] times briefly mentions the demo outside 100 centre for the panthers thurs.

item: in a retrial, Pierre Vallieres, an FLQ member, was given 2–15 years for involuntary manslaughter in a political bombing in montreal two years ago. the fact that defense established he wasn't even in the city at the time apparently didn't faze the john mitchell of canada.†

item: my french cellmate, who speaks no english, calls me 'boom boom.'

for my love, may i offer my left litisimus dorci—inexplicably becoming more developed than the right.

Sam Melville
#31882 C6-C max. max. max. max.

get me Harvey Wintson's address. i sent a letter to __ Regent st. and it was returned for insufficient address!

---

* Cohen: We had talked about Sam's writing an autobiographical/political book somewhat similar to Cleaver's *Soul on Ice*, thinking that it would help others to understand America and themselves better, and that it would help Sam tolerate prison. He thought about it for a while, then decided against it.

† DV: *White Niggers of America* (1968) is a vivid memoir by the FLQ's Pierre Vallières, largely written while he was held for four years in the same New York City Men's House for Detention ("the Tombs") where Sam Melville was later incarcerated.

January 6, 1970

Dear Ruth

i saw Harold [a lawyer hired by Sam's wife] yesterday and no doubt he has already spoken to you. if you do decide to see me, which i hope you do, we can perhaps straighten out any difficulties we may have regarding Jocko and the divorce.* you needn't be afraid, we'll be separated by glass and we'll have to speak thru telephones.†

i'm only allowed one visit each week so let me know a week in advance if you are coming. personally i'm looking forward to seeing you. my remembrances of you are not *all* unpleasant.

Sam Melville
#31882 69377-158
C6-c max.

Tuesday, January 20, 1970

dear brother:

the letter schedule has improved 300%! i just got your sunday note and what timing! with tomorrow's hearing (and possible decision on bail) i need all the support i can muster. by the time you read this, whether or not i will be released at all will have been decided. i hope you can just tear this up but i'm preparing for the worst. when i say that i can really mean it now. i'm much stronger. the court scenes with all the folks behind us—i can feel the strength of our numbers and determination swelling my body. also, bill crain's coming around as he did has certainly helped much. he was outasight yesterday [in court]! for so long i was troubled about how we could make a political thing without accusations and egg-throwing. but i'm beginning to see now.

---

* Cohen: Sam and Ruth agreed to get a divorce as quickly as possible. Sam wanted to marry Jane Alpert, in order that Jane would be able to visit him in prison. They never were married: Jane went underground rather than go to jail.

† JM: There was never any history of violence in our family. My mother always described Sam as a gentle man. I think this comment about being "afraid" was sarcasm, which my father was fond of.

absolutely *any* front we attack will be vulnerable politically because virtually all of existence in amerika today is a political confrontation. i said once to you and sharon every man behind bars in this country is a political prisoner.* i didn't realize how i might be able to make it stick. when the pig cross-examines tomorrow i hope i get a chance and am together enough to prove it.

monday in court i was running a high fever and right now my head weighs about 200 lbs. it set in nose and throat sunday night and of course the treatment here ain't exactly mount sinai. but i'll hit (or at least swing) with both fists tomorrow.

i'm worried about my lady so much. she thinks me distant and unsure of her. i can't possibly tell or show her how i feel. i'm so confused also about "protection" and "male chauvinism" and fears about what the pigs might be able to do to her. the new indictment carries a possible 35-year max for her. i'm too old now to throw off my feeling of obligation to stand between her and our enemies. i feel she is stronger than i ever can be and i think the coming times will prove that out. but for now i do what i do. try to explain to her how one can't be a weatherman at 34 yet still know which way the wind blows. you might remind her that nobody could ever compete with the slutty ways she demonstrates *her* love anyway.

love & power!

Sam Melville

#69377 (C6-c max.)

---

* SF: The idea that "every man behind bars in this country is a political prisoner" has been debated for years. Inmate leader Richard X. Clark disputed that: "We're not political prisoners, we're slaves." Richard X. Clark, "The Aftermath," in *The Sound Before the Fury* (New York: Consolidated Color Press, 1992), 18. Likewise the word "revolutionary," which got thrown around a lot back then. In a long letter about Attica from the box at Clinton Correctional Facility, Martin Sostre stated flatly, "The only one to my knowledge who was a revolutionary before he went to prison as well as in was Sam Melville." Martin Sostre to Sharon Fischer, January 9, 1975, 4.

Friday, January 23, 1970

dear brother,

after a solid week of courtroom drama all that's changed is the addition of some 60 pieces of evidence from janes apt (including love notes
between pam & david [friends]). super pig [the judge] wants to interview
our secret bail backer in chambers. he didn't impress me as a dirty old
man at first. and today jane pulled a nice move—the gov't requested a
sealed testimony as evidence from canada and jane insisted it be open so
folks can see some of the inner pen of our porcine officials. sandy [Sanford
Katz, Jane's lawyer] said to "the court" that counsel had no objections to
the gov't request (thereby retaining X exam rights), i'm not sure what the
outcome is but doyle [the assistant US attorney who prosecuted Sam] was
clearly disappointed, oinking for assistance from the bench.

i read what i'm told is j.p.'s article in rat [on Sam's case]. it's pretty
good but the picture is one of my favorites. the best part is cut out though.
if you could see my whole right arm you would also see it snuggly nestled
between the fine mammary development of my lady. and if her face
weren't in such shadow you could see the elicit promise in her features.

i didn't get to read anything else though and i want to read the
excerpt from J.R.'s [Jerry Rubin's] book, so when you next visit (tuesday, i hope) bring it to read to me.*

the times carried a very small piece on the montreal trial of Pierre
Vallieres.† i'm very confused about his proceedings at this point but
in any event he's been in prison since '66 and at his last court appearance this past week he got another six months for shouting that he
was a political prisoner. Daniel Cohn-Bendit‡ was at the courtroom

---

* SF: The excerpt Sam wanted to read in Jerry Rubin's book was undoubtedly Rubin's analysis of George Demmerle. It mentions Sam twice, in lists of names, but devotes six pages and
a photo to Demmerle. Jerry Rubin, *We Are Everywhere* (New York: Harper & Row, 1971),
57, 142–143, 146, 215–218. Sam finally got Rubin's book at Attica—slipped through the
cracks somehow, as it was still on the media review committee's banned list when he died.
Sam's comments about Rubin's book appear in his letter herein dated August 30, 1971,
although he does not mention Demmerle.

† JM: FLQ organizer. This is significant because Sam was trying to assert that he was a
"political prisoner" as part of his defense. He would learn, as he states in his letter of February 12, 1970, that under US law no such defense is possible.

‡ JV: Daniel Cohn-Bendit (1945–) was a charismatic leader of the "March 22 Movement"
of university radicals in Paris and a major figure in the student-worker rebellions of May

and maybe he's doing some stomping. he probably won't be able to get in the USA but if he does try and see him.

i still haven't got any more books and we may have some truck from the parole office but send them as soon as you can and we'll see. i would also dig pictures of all the folks and the dogs [Sam and Jane had two young dogs] when somebody gets a chance.

see you soon. love

Sam Melville
#69377
C6-c max.

January 26, 1970

dear brother

finally got two more books: "revolution in the revolution" [by Regis Debray]* and a collection of MR [*Monthly Review*] essays on latin american revolution. debray is a heavy but great writer. i find i can't skip one sentence. there's so much! a few months ago i read the part on the politics of armed self-defense which he's very critical of. not that he says it isn't a useful stage in revolutionary struggle but that the inherently defensive posture doesn't move to a politically sound stand. to expect to just defend your own while the state power structure remains apart from you just won't work. thats very oversimplified of course. debray spends 20 crowded pages arguing from every possible viewpoint. in those terms, asserting every possible position and one by one destroying them, he reminds me of the swiss writer friedrich durrenmatt. i read a novel of his (i think "the visit") years ago and was overwhelmed with that style.

reading solid revolutionary thought really helps pull my head together. without it i can see myself hopelessly falling into the incredible convict mentality of pettiness and stupid mind destroying thinking

---

1968 that nearly toppled the French state. He had been born in France to German Jewish parents who had fled Nazism. He was a beloved figure on the student left in France and worldwide.

* DV: Debray's *Revolution in the Revolution?* (1967) was well known and frequently cited among New Left activists and radicals during the '60s and '70s.

about what hacks to beware of or how much commissary i have left this month. and while it's time-passing to read the *times* daily i can easily see how it can distort my hopes and destroy morale. It would be a big help if the letters—yours and joyce and sharon—could include passages or condensates of stuff from the good underground rags.

jane told me the original batch of books from grove was selected and sent by r.m. [Robin Morgan].* except for malcolm's story, they were all depressing trash.†‡ if she wanted some measure of revenge against male chauvinism she succeeded. receiving those books has made the prison administration wary of letting others through. (it draws mice you know.)

i heard i may be moved tomorrow [to another cell]. it's got to be an improvement so i'm looking forward to it, but constantly having to adjust to new people is not always pleasant—or safe.

see you soon—love

Sam Melville
#69377

---

* JV: Robin Morgan (1941–) is an activist and author who became a leader of the "Second Wave" feminism of the 1960s and '70s. She spearheaded the protest of the Miss America Pageant in 1968 and in the 1970s published the edited volume *Sisterhood Is Powerful*, which helped ignite feminism worldwide. Highly critical of the male-dominated American left, she grew in close contact with Jane Alpert while the latter was underground. Morgan influenced Alpert's 1974 essay "Mother Right: A New Feminist Theory." In the controversial piece, Alpert sharply criticized Sam Melville for his alleged sexism and even disavowed the rebel inmates at Attica as "male supremacists."

† JM: Joyce and Sharon were allegedly part of an offshoot of the Melville Collective. Their central link was another confessed Melville collaborator, Robin Palmer, who was incarcerated at Attica after being apprehended with them for the attempted bombing of Chase Manhattan Bank in 1970. Robin Morgan was Jane's mentor and shaped much of her post-arrest thinking and career moves. According to Jane's memoir, Morgan was a heavy influence in Jane's decision to fathom the bombing of Standard Oil on Veteran's Day 1969, without Sam's help. This would ultimately be the bombing that led the FBI to their door in two days.

‡ SF: This obviously refers to Malcolm X, presumably the *Autobiography*. Eight months after Sam wrote this, he would be serving time at Attica with one of Malcolm's killers. Thomas Hagan (a.k.a. Talmadge X Hayer) was in D Yard with Sam and survived the assault. In 2000 he was awarded $6,500 in the federal court lawsuit against the state for his injuries. Testimony of Thomas Hagan, Decision and Order of August 28, 2000, US District Court, Rochester, 39.

January 27, 1970

My dear Jocko,

It has been a long time since I have seen you but you have been in my mind and heart always. I remember the good times we had together walking the streets and singing with you high up on my shoulders. I have a picture of you taken last Easter in Riverside Park. It is a beautiful picture and I keep it with me all the time.* I hope you will send me more. Your Mommy has sent me your latest school reports which are excellent and I am very pleased. You are a very bright boy and I know you will always do well.

I am sorry I have not written to you before this but I promise I will write to you often from now on. If I am not around to help you when you need me you must always remember I love you very much and I carry you in my heart always.

Write to me soon.

All my love,
Daddy

January 27, 1970

dear ruth,

i got your letter but didn't find it too depressing. If that's as bad as they're going to get you can keep them coming. i wrote jocko what i felt was a sincere letter which i hope helps him, and you. i don't put much credence in schools or their reports but i'm glad you sent them just the same. he's a bright boy and won't have any trouble in that respect.

it's hopeless to anticipate getting bail release no matter how hard people work. this country is approaching a computerized fascism that must make examples of any who refuse to obey its commandments of war and racism. i only regret they will probably deny me a death by firing squad.

---

* JM: Although I can never know for sure, Sam must've hated this picture he references. An eight-year-old me dressed in a brown three-piece suit must've reinforced the fact that he had very little control over his child's conventional and bougie upbringing from prison. He attempted to compensate with his letters to me.

Harold [Ruth's divorce lawyer] has not been to see me and i will throw him out if he does come. i hope you can accomplish everything without me but i will cooperate with anything you may require.

tell our supporters at your office that i love them and all who say *no* to this dying system.* remind them that they cannot rely on leaders anymore. every man and woman must fight for their rights and needs to build a just and happy society freed from greed and power and private lives of alienation.

please don't sign "with much affection." i love you still.

Sam

January 29, 1970

dear brother

yesterday i was moved back to my original cell and everythings cool. except for one, the old gang has been shipped out to real grown-up places like atlanta & leavenworth [federal prisons]. of course i have my old privileges, like a sneak peek at the ice-covered hudson and art films on saturday.

don't call philly. i received a letter last night with a couple of pictures. everythings the same with them apparently. nixon, shmixon . . . it's all same.

you mention the upsetting experience at the film benefit—some people are speaking in glorifying terms of the [Charles] manson thing.† i'm not sure of this but i think much of the mania is due to our lack of a unifying voice. in other movements, not internationalist in scope,

---

* JM: Ruth worked for the Metropolitan Life Insurance Company. Its skyscraper on East Twenty-Third Street (next to the Flatiron Building) was thought to match the corporate profile of the collective's other targets. This letter is in response to my mother's plea that Sam relay to Weather that her building was off-limits.

† JV: Charles Manson (1934–2017) was a cult leader who led a group of runaways and drifters in a series of gruesome murders in Southern California in the summer of 1969. Manson's victims included the (pregnant) Hollywood actress Sharon Tate. Manson was convicted for multiple murders in 1971 and served the rest of his life in prison. His cult, the "Manson Family," embraced the drug use and sexual license of the '60s counterculture and was widely seen as a dark extreme of the hippie phenomenon.

there seems always to be a party or some sort of spokesman to claim the alleigence of most of the activists. our movement is leaderless by both choice and necessity. any together group that attempts a vangard position cannot cope with the diverse needs of its constituency nor the repressive actions of the gov't. witness the cp [Communist Party] of '30's and '50's and the bpp [Black Panther Party] today.

while che may be an internationalist revolutionary his thoughts were always anchored to latin needs of liberation from yankee imperialism. his political line was "humanist" only after it was socialist. che never dealt with a post-industrial society, not that I heard of. and surely there are enough movement people schooled in marxism-leninism who, if they could, would have come up with some answers from those two thinkers that could deal with the particular problems we face in the US today.

in our blindness, the only relief from the chains of racism and an economy of constant expansion is "action," virtually any action. action is energy. energy is the life force which is both good and evil. panthers and yippies as yet haven't answered the needs of enough of the people to gain hegemony over that energy. ultimately, increasing repression will unify folks and the direction of action will become clearer as the face of the ruling power is unmasked.

on rereading, all this seems very glib. but here, removed somewhat, things begin to lose the grayness and the extremes seem more vivid. much thoughts on women's lib coming soon, stay tuned.

Sam Melville #69377

February 5, 1970

dear brother,

excuse this quickie. i just spent myself on a longer one to sk [Sharon Krebs].*

malraux is certainly a fine writer but i wonder how a chinaman would have written about the affair [the Chinese Revolution. Sam refers

---

* JM: An alleged collective member arrested months later for a conspiracy to firebomb Chase Manhattan Bank. There are numerous references in other letters by Sam to this case.

to *Man's Fate*]. the judaic-hellenic tradition i think will pale next to the cosmic consciousness of the easterns—even in our eyes, eventually.

in the dictionary you sent me: the first word i looked up was *perpiccacity* [*sic.*; Sam's spelling was atrocious]*. it wasn't listed.

send me the lyric to "i am a lonesome hobo" from dylan's john wesly harding.

dave dellinger[†] is in jail as of yesterday. it's not an unfamiliar place to him of course. that will be true of many of us soon i fear. i love maryann weissman![‡§]

you too!

Sam

---

* SF: It is surprising to me that "Sam's spelling was atrocious," because he was the product of a very good public school system and, according to lists regularly published in the *Tonawanda Evening News,* he was often on the honor roll.

† JM: Dave Dellinger was one of the Chicago Eight as well as part of the "Action Faction" of the Columbia takeover of 1968.

‡ Cohen: Maryann Weissman had stood up while a spectator in court during the trial of the Panther 21 and denounced Judge Murtagh's "racism." She was sentenced to thirty days for contempt of court. Sam never knew her personally, but often voiced his appreciation of her, especially of her efforts on behalf of prisoners.

§ SF: Maryann Nigro Weissman was born and raised in Buffalo and joined the Workers World Party when it was formed there in 1959. In 1962 she became national chair of its youth group Youth Against War & Fascism (YAWF); she has also been active in WWP groups Committee for G.I. Rights, American Servicemen's Union, Prisoners Solidarity Committee, Women United for Action, and others. In 1967, while organizing support for an antiwar soldier's court-martial, Maryann Weissman was almost lynched by a Lawton, Oklahoma, mob, and she served six months in jail there for trespassing. When I knew Maryann she was a warm, cheerful, tiny bundle of energy, always fearless in standing up for the rights of others. Andy Stapp, *Up Against the Brass* (New York: Simon and Schuster, 1970), 65, 86; see also Mike McKeating, "Workers World Fronts Have Varied Missions," *Buffalo Evening News,* June 16, 1976.

February 10, 1970

dear ruth,

Harold was in to see me on friday (2-6) but due to some incredible misunderstanding i thought i wasn't to sign the documents [divorce papers]. so i told him i would await further word from you. today, at a meeting with my co-defendants, i was advised to proceed as quickly as possible on the divorce. we may be forced to go to trial in mid-march and after that, in prison, it will be very difficult to get things done. i will write harold and tell him to come in again and i'll sign whatever has to be signed. let's get moving on this as soon as possible.

i got the letters from you and jocko this evening and they really cheered me. if he's responsible for just 20% of that letter he's way ahead of what you led me to believe in terms of spelling and syntax. the only trouble i have reading that beautiful scrawl is with this strange water that floods my eyes when i look at it.

yes, william crain is my lawyer and he is on the "panther 21" case, which is the reason there's a hassle about the trial date. the fascists want to execute us in mid-march but the panther trial may go on till may or even later. we don't know yet what will happen. they conceivably could force us to trial with new (court appointed) lawyers. in such event you may expect proceedings similar to what happened to bobby seale at the chicago conspiracy kangaroo trial.

i asked harold to renew my daily times sub for another 3 months but i'm not sure he'll do it—i was pretty nasty to him. he's such a creep!

i will write to jocko very soon, i want to get this out to you tonite.

love,
Sam

February 11, 1970

Dear Jocko,

I got your letter and was very happy to hear from you. You certainly are a good speller even though mommy helped you a little bit.

I am glad to learn you are studying Hebrew and enjoying it. It's very hard to learn another language when you don't get a chance to speak it too much. I think nana can speak Hebrew so you should try to practice with her whenever you see her.

If I were able to see you I could explain some things about eating food which I have come to understand. Talk about this with your mother and perhaps she can help you understand. I am a vegetarian. That means that I don't eat meat. I know mommy and nana have told you that meat is very healthy and you must eat it, but they are not clear on their understanding of the whole subject. Now it's true that most meat does contain high amounts of protein. Protein is a necessary ingredient to good health. But there are other foods which contain high amounts of protein but do not have the fat content that meat does. This fat content is responsible for much heart disease and other diseases that can be very bad for the body and the mind. But besides the question of health, meat is the flesh of other living animals. Every time you eat a hamburger you are eating part of a cow. The cow must be killed to provide you with that hamburger. When you go to the zoo and look at the cow, can you imagine having to kill that beautiful beast just so you can eat a stupid hamburger that isn't healthy for you anyway? And when you eat pork chops or jello you're really eating parts of a pig. When you're eating lamb chops you're really eating part of a beautiful sheep, maybe the sister of the sheep right in the Central Park Zoo.

I will write more about this to you and mommy. But you should remind both mommy and nana about this whenever they try to force you to eat meat.

Tell mommy to send me pictures.

I love you,
Daddy

February 12, 1970

[To Richard]
dear brother,

i received a batch of books yesterday. i'm especially pleased with the inclusion of R.D. Laing's book "politics of experience." i've been wanting to read it for more than a year. also the alan watts book i'm looking forward to very much.

you've no doubt heard of the great escape.* it still remains the main topic of conversation here. feds are trying to track down leads with the inmates but so far no success.

as the conspiracy trial in chicago winds up and 7 of the [Washington] d.c. 9 are carted off to prison and with the panther 13† farce developing i'm sure the courts will have a well-developed technique for handling these affairs by the time we come up. i don't have much hope of a so-called "political trial." i'm not sure i ever did. folks are either beyond needing that kind of education or it will never move them anyway. that's not to imply i'm discouraged. i'm just getting realistic. with repression getting heavier folks have got to move beyond the kangaroos. i find it laughable that we can still have papers printing info on [Molotov] cocktails and other things.

anyway, i hope the home fires keep burning.
i love you much.

Sam

February 12, 1970

dear brother,

i've put in a letter to Mr. Shade telling him you'd be in next week to speak to him about the pictures and the de Sade book. i

---

* Cohen: About nine prisoners escaped from the West Street House of Detention at the beginning of February.
† DV: The Panther 13 and the Panther 21 are the same case. Initially, twenty-one Panthers were arrested. Ultimately, only thirteen were tried. By the time the case went to trial it was more often referred to as "Panther 13."

thought it might be better if he were prepared. i think they might start to get up tight about all the books i've requested and anyway i'm not gonna be able to deal with them all at once so i'll ask you to cancel everything you haven't ordered so far and just get the bakunin* and some lenin stuff and we'll wait on the rest. the same goes for the stuff from monthly review except for the subscription.

i'm deep into laing's book, but i understand very little of it. after several pages of what must be heavy psychological jargon he'll break into vietnam or national defense, and by examples he makes some real good points. but i wish i could handle all of it.

the newspaper accounts of the d.c. 9 trial were very discouraging. the legal technicalities in a courtroom simply don't recognize such a thing as a political prisoner. of course i've never held much faith in trials anyway. by the time our thing comes up the kangaroos will be able to handle those kind of things anyway. i've seen it happening at the panther trial. i wrote to richard saying folks are either beyond political education (by the courts) or nothing can move them anyway. in amerika, a crime is a crime and that's all there is to it. in other countries there's some courtesy to people whose actions are beyond personal gain. amerika hasn't even time for dignity—forget about justice. the gavel goes thump thump—"50 years. next case."

something just triggered a chain of thought which led me to yeats' "second coming."

> the best lack all conviction, while the worst
> are full of passionate intensity

one wonders what is left for anarchy to save. Then comes a sarcastic remark with the word "surely." out west people use "surely" with a negative response. "have you got any bananas?" "i surely don't."

---

* SF: Two of the Attica Brothers who first met Sam in the Tombs told me that a Bakunin book was covertly passed around there until confiscated by guards. It may have been this book that Sam was trying to get again. Michael Bakunin spent eight years in brutal czarist dungeons, where he nearly died of scurvy, and inmates related to his prison suffering as well as to his theories. One of his most famous sayings would have appealed to Sam: "Every command slaps liberty in the face."

surely some revelation is at hand.
surely the second coming is at hand.

i'm not on the court list for tomorrow (friday the 13th). i guess the bail is out. no matter.

i love you much

Sam

March 1, 1970

dear ruth

jocko's valentine was great. the spelling might be improved upon, unless the kids are into some new language we're not hip to.

harold came (can you imagine that!) and i think i signed all papers required. i haven't pushed on this because i thought i had plenty of time, but with the break in the panther trial i could be forced to trial *very* quickly.*

i get a funny feeling you're holding out on the vegetarian business to jocko. now i have fought many battles with you and your androphagous mater and lost most of the time but i could usually get in my word. all i ask is for you to present him with it. let him

---

* DV: The Panther 13/21 case would ultimately be the longest, and the costliest, trial in New York City history up to that point in time. Every one of the defendants was cleared of every single charge; the NYPD, however, was the subject of tremendous criticism as a result of the case. The Panther inner circle had been entirely infiltrated by NYPD Bureau of Special Services undercover detectives. The press, the public, and even the jurors had come to believe that the undercover detectives were more guilty of breaking laws (including violating civil liberties of the Panthers and potentially creating the plots they then charged the Panthers with) than the Panthers themselves. The landmark *Handschu v. Special Services* class action lawsuit emerged immediately after the case concluded, and the result was the dramatic restraint on NYPD undercover and political spying operations that had resulted in millions of dossiers on purely political and legal activity, as well as investigations into those like the Panthers, Sam Melville, and other political activists and bombers of the time including Cuban Power, the Jewish Defense League, the Minutemen, and others. Incidentally, Robert Collier— the ringleader of the plot to bomb the Statue of Liberty in 1965 that was supported by members of the FLQ, who had been arrested due to the work of an NYPD BOSSI undercover operative—had been recently released from prison and was one of the Panther 13 defendants.

make the choice. and in the immortal words of edmond muskie, "let us have dialogue."*

love,

sam

March 1, 1970

Dear Jocko,

The valentine card you made for me was just beautiful. Some of the other people here received cards too but they were bought from a store. Yours was so much better because you made it.

Maybe you have been hearing some things about *pollution* and care of the *environment*. When your mother and I were going to school we didn't learn anything about this subject. We were taught only how to use the *environment*. We didn't know about protecting it and caring for it. Now, for you and your friends, and all the living creatures of the world, it is the *most important* part of your education. *Pollution* means to poison and to make unpure. *Environment* means all that is around us including the air, the water and the earth. New York City is your *environment*. The air you breath in New York City is very different from the air in some other places. It's dirtier, thicker and doesn't smell so good. It is even poisonous to some people and many kinds of animals. It is *polluted*. Mainly it is *polluted* because of gasoline engines in automobiles and buses and all the many factories like Con Ed that send up smoke into the air. If your school teachers are not teaching you anything about this you must begin to ask them questions about it. Ask mommy and talk about it with your friends. If you don't learn about *pollution* and how you can correct it, soon the air will be so bad that nobody will be able to be healthy.

---

* JM: Mom never edited my father's letters, other than to cut off the bottom, which had the point-of-origin credentials. I remember asking her about what a vegetarian was. She always tried to paint Sam in a good light, despite their differences.

What I told you about not eating meat is also important to this subject. The animals you eat are part of the *environment*. You must think of them as your fellow creatures to share the earth with.

I still have not received any pictures of you. Please tell mommy to take some and send them to me. I am very lonely and I would like to be able to be reminded of you and the pictures would help.

When you write to me, ask me questions about the *pollution* and *environment* and *vegetarianism* (not eating meat) and anything you have been thinking about.*

I miss you and I love you,

Daddy.

March, 1970

[To Sharon]
dear sister

please know that no matter what i may say i must continue to grow and change and however much i may seem shattered by some concepts of male ego and man-woman relationships, i want the criticism. i must be a part of the people of tomorrow and to be that i will have to be pulled now. on the outside i could see and gauge people's thinking and move with them. now, in here, i tend to cling to safe, secure ways of thinking. i'm not really as obdurate as i appear often. i know you love me and will always try to help.

my love for you and all my sisters.

Sam

---

* JM: What is so sad is that the one thing I really wanted him to talk about was when we would be able to see each other, and this was the one subject that my mother demanded that he avoid. He finally gave in with a hybrid answer in my favorite of his letters to me, dated June 24, 1970.

March, 1970

dear brother,

i am beginning to know the meaning of the revolution. it is the desire for ecstasy and i think only desperation can produce it. those who are willing to yield every last privilege, who drive themselves to the limits of desperation, will make the revolution. the problem with the "power of love" is that despite its once hip notions, it's tied to traditional definitions of brotherhood and pantheism. i don't speak for that definition as it applied in the past, though i very much suspect it. we must move to a place beyond all known issues. for us, now, it is a terrifying plunge. it may be easier if there is a humanity to come—but that's not our motive. what we want is salvation from a meaningless annihilation. to not be cremated for coka cola and plastic flags in waving simulation on the moon. to want that today in amerika is to be very desperate. menken and miller could laugh at amerika 30 years ago. sardonicism sometimes passes being a bourgeois pastime. it is in "the field of criminology." can you imagine even lenny bruce today?

it's not insignificant that the only issue the white left has come up with is a regeneration of occultism. it's the hallmark of our desperation. that's why che and mao are our heroes. che was not fighting yanqui imperialism. he was desperate for meaning in a world of expediency. i don't mean to say 3rd world issues can't provide clues to salvation. to the extent that they strive for a *definite morality* and the dignity of the human relationship to labor they *are* salvation. the venceremos brigade would have been far less popular if instead of cutting sugar the folks were asked to program computers, no matter what the product of those computers might be.

prison life—light

the irony of the amerikan prison system is that it *is* rehabilitating. of course for just the opposite reasons its promoters endorse. for the first time since i was a small boy i have no money and no keys in my pockets. you can't imagine the rehabilitating effect of that! from the muslims i am learning to fast and control my own body. from reading thoreau and some of the eastern teachings i can live on much less than even prison allows. i drive my body to extreme exercises till my temples pound. and i am tripping all the time. not with the frenzy of acid but with the confidence of my liberation from superficialities.

prison life—dark

prison is a microcosm of amerika circa 1950. as i have told you, the real punishment prison represents to me is this frustration of having to start all over again, to forget the moments of genuine communion i felt in the past couple of years. i have returned to old solitary thoughts. faulkner and thoreau are my confidants. it's a matter of survival.

i have been informed i am placed in isolation after my escape try because i made statements to the effect that i would kill myself. i don't know if any statements got around but i assure all the only thing i know that's killing itself is the good old amerikan way of life. and many of us are preparing a great celebration of that event.

give my love to all and i'll write next week.

Sam Melville
#69377

March 14, 1970

richard:

it's been a helluva week bro. at this moment the saccharine sounds of an ad for bell systems is floating to my ears. i'm grinning from ear to temple.* as i said to bro j.c. [John Cohen] only the escalation of action to the point where our situation equals our philosophical desperation will bring whites into the revolution as committed as

---

* Cohen: In the week Sam is referring to, Ralph Featherstone was killed when a bomb exploded in the car he was riding in, Rap Brown went underground, the courthouse where Rap was to be tried was bombed, and a townhouse in Manhattan was demolished in an accidental dynamite explosion which killed several Weatherwomen and men. But Sam says he is "grinning" because just after the townhouse exploded the Manhattan offices of three large war-profiteering corporations were demolished in three simultaneous explosions.

the others have to be to merely survive. (if that last seems unclear it's because it's in code. use the last 3 pages of grimm's edition of the upanashads to decode.)

i'm still in isolation of course. they're afraid if they let me on the roof i'll do some yoga breathing and kill myself from the pollution. the nixon boys couldn't cope with ecological martyrdom right now.

as you may guess my depression and defeat of last week [the aborted escape attempt] has abetted and i'm in good spirits once more.

getting my body adjusted to my new food habits has a lot to do with it. i eat oranges, apples and milk—twice a day. unfortunately the fruit must be purchased from commissary. the $10 j.c. left me last month is about depleted. next time you come leave some bread. also send the dylan lyric in a letter.

you better suspend the book shipments for awhile till we see if bill can get a court order to get them thru. also make sure my n.y. *times* sub has been picked up. its been two weeks since i've gotten one.

it's estimated a prisoner costs the feds $1400 per annum. i have some comforts.

love, Sam

March 16, 1970

dear brother,

power to the great brothers who offed the bomb ship to cambodia! the very last day is surely near. with the armed services in forceful mutiny, the people forming guerrilla bands, even the mobe [National Mobilization Against the War] advocating open civil disobedience—it's coming my brother, it's surely coming. law and order is sweeping the land. the law of the inevitability of an idea whose time is come. the order of folks gathering to the discipline necessary to bring that idea to birth. all the pig repression cannot stop it. folks will get frightened and protective but our desperation is multiplying by the minute. it won't be long now.

March 18, 1970

dear my divorced wife,

you must consider the bread you lost in mexico [obtaining a divorce] as reparations for all that yanqui imperialism has raped from them. the few pennies they manage to get from slumming gringos is not to be questioned.

your cyst is very unfortunate. Tho you were sometimes reluctant to use those parts you invariably took much pleasure when you did. at least my male ego remembers it that way.

perhaps if you ate the proper foods (no meat) and used that thing the way it was meant to be used (more meat) you would not be suffering today—tho you might have other ailments. really, how serious is it? if surgery is the answer don't wait. those things don't usually go away. in another few months, when you begin to enter middle age, things in that region are potentially dangerous.

regarding jocko: i'll admit i'm sometimes a bit paranoid about what you do & don't say to him. but i believe you read my letters to him entirely. if he's into saving them he'll pin you to the wall when he's older. you mentioned he requested a map of mexico. if he digs geography i'll be happy to rap about that with him. i've got any number of "lessons" for him.*

they're not lessons of course. i rap like that to everybody. that's partly how i wound up here. as for us identifying with an eight-year-old—i don't have the slightest remembrance of being eight. I have trouble remembering being fourteen. the letter about pollution was the only thing that can be said about camping anymore. i loved camping but i gave it up 4 years ago because anywhere i went the struggle with beer cans and throw-away bottles and shitty streams and joe-loves-mary-painted-on-impossible-to-get-to-rock-faces and dead squirrels shot for sport and motels offering the great bourgeois fantasy to the weary hiker got to be too much for me. (pages of illustrations).

---

* JM: When I was eight, many of his concepts confused me. I complained to Mom as to why he was "giving lessons." If memory serves, I may have even complained to him in one of my letters. Mom asked him to "lighten up" on the politics.

what's with the divorce? do i get my papers or something? am i free to marry tricia nixon?

love,

dear your divorced husband

it does sound pretty funny.

March 18, 1970

Dear Jocko,

It's so good to read your letters and the pictures mommy sent are a true delight.

I'm sorry if I seem to be giving a lesson in my letters to you. When people say or write something it is usually an abstraction. Since I don't say things which are unimportant to me it seems my abstractions become, as you say, lessons. Because if one is going to be forced to abstractions it might as well have some significance or else it is a waste of time. Besides, it would not seem like a lesson if you helped me with it. You would see what a good thing it would be if you told me some of the problems and situations in your life and we could discuss them in our letters. I feel that the things we take into our bodies become us and influence everything we do, so I want to talk about that to everyone. I also feel that the study and care of the environment is a very important subject to all people. Do you talk about the environment in school or with mommy or your friends? If not, you should. And I want to be among those you talk to about all the things that affect your life. If I could be with you it would be different.

March 22, 1970

[To Richard]
dear brother,

your letter of "14 Marzo" finally arrived. i guess the [postal] strike messed things up. they wouldn't let the song thru probably because it didn't come from the publisher. it doesn't matter. the lyric was all i wanted, it's really a great song, as is most of that album.

you're right about the bombings all over endangering the country. i guess it is a very serious problem. too bad.

my thought of being placed at lewisburg [federal penitentiary] is evidently wrong. lewisburg, by reputation for the gentler souls, is for 10-year stretches or less, usually. although morton sobel was there and he was on a 30-year bit. the parole officer says i'll probably go to leavenworth or atlanta—particularly after my alleged escape attempt. they're rough places i'm warned. but the inmates say "jail is jail, man." the lawyers say now the judge will rule i not be permitted to see my lady in court meetings anymore. i will miss those furtive moments. i draw so much strength from her. even 10 minutes in a room with her presence charges me with new blood & life.

i hope you're giving your great new banjo a workout. if i can get out maybe you & i can be the flatts & scruggs of the twenty-fourth century. because, believe it brother, we're going to live forever.

love, Sam

P.S. if you can, please leave a few dollars when you come next.

April 2, 1970

dear john,

the parole officer, Mr. shade, has just told me i would be permitted to have 5 books at a time in my cell. after reading those i would return them and could get 5 more. these would be from the approved list that [assistant US attorney] doyle (evidently) reviewed. i don't remember the books on the list (i never saw the list really) but i'm sure it contains the things we mentioned at our visits. so, go ahead and order 5 volumes which will include 1. the complete bakunin, 2. a selection of lenin, 3. a selection of marx-engels, 4. the new collegiate dictionary (latest printing), and any other related volume on the list.

my lawyer, whoever that will be, will be permitted to bring in Rat and Ramparts,* which i will be able to read in the office (not in my cell).

i was also told that if any more of my letters are printed my correspondence privileges will be stopped.†‡

see you soon,
love to all.

Sam

April 2, 1970

ruth

i'm not permitted (by my lawyer) to discuss the alleged escape attempt. if they want to bother it means another 10 years (5 for escape, 5 for assault). that brings my total indictment charges to 370 years. the irony of it is, as it occurred, crain was dickering with the d.a. for a settlement of something like 15 yrs to a guilty plea. 15 years means i could be eligible for parole in about 5 to 7 years. i'm not down about it though—the system won't last even that long.

bill told me you'd called & said you are very concerned & willing to cooperate any way possible. well thanks, i was sure you would but i don't see how right now but maybe . . .

we had to get a court order to get books sent into me. it's finally come tho and i'll be getting some heavy stuff soon i hope. i'll be able

---

* JV: *Ramparts* was a California-based radical magazine popular among the New Left of the 1960s. It featured left-wing commentary, investigative journalism, and reportage about the Vietnam War and the era's protest movements.

† Cohen: Two of Sam's letters were printed in *Rat* in March.

‡ SF: After two of Sam's letters appeared in *Rat*, he was threatened with denial of all "correspondence privileges" if it happened again. This reminds me of the famous quote of Ruchell Magee, the codefendant of Angela Davis: "What terrible crimes has the oligarchy committed that they fear the voice of one man?" Although Sam had confessed, he had not yet entered a guilty plea and so retained the presumption of innocence. Correspondence "privileges" should have been his constitutional right.

to read underground press things in the parole office but not in my cell. i'm told there's a letter of mine along with a picture of me in the Rat of a couple of weeks ago. call Rat and ask them to send you a copy if you want. i was told if any more were printed my correspondence "privileges" would be discontinued.

if you've been following the papers you know they've been linking me and others to all the shit [political bombings in New York]* that's been going down recently. the trial delay was probably due to that! apparently there is now an official, revolutionary underground in the mother country and folks are getting things together at last. it means times will get rougher & tougher from both sides, but that's what this country's needed for many years. i can't offer you any advice because your circumstances are so compromised. just don't get too scared when the fan starts turning in all directions.

i don't know why but my name is on the court list for tomorrow. maybe i'll be freed for lack of evidence or something.

i'll write jocko soon. the pix were nice.

love, sam

---

* DV: The political bombings that Sam is talking about in this letter are in fact historic in nature. Just months after Sam wrote this letter, in the summer of 1970, then commissioner of the NYPD Howard Leary testified before the US Senate that bombings in New York City in the previous eighteen months (including, of course, the Melville bombings) had reached "gigantic proportions," greatly exceeding anything before. The wave of "terrorism" in New York City exceeds—in sheer number of incidents and in the variety of political actors employing it—any other such period or place of similar violence in all of American history. In the few years both before and after the actions of the Melville Collective in New York City, political bombings—terrorism, by many definitions—had spread to virtually every point on the political spectrum. The long list of political actors to engage in what many call terrorism during these few years in NYC includes the Statue of Liberty plotters previously mentioned; the Melville Collective; virulent anticommunists like the Minutemen and the John Birch Society; political-religious actors like the Jewish Defense League; and nationalists from as near as Cuba, Puerto Rico, and Montreal and as far away as Croatia.

April 3, 1970

[To Richard]
dear brother,

i just ate my first bean pie. it was delicious! bean pie is one of the muslim triumphs over the federal bureau of prisons regulations. they are made by the shabazz bakeries (a chain of many bakeries throughout the country where muslims have developed a community) under strict supervision of officials of the nation of islam. needless to say, they are very nutricious as well.

this week a new fed indictment (the 4th) will be given to the grand jury. also, the state indictment will probably be handed down. the fed trial is scheduled to begin 4/29 and bill crain expects there will be no further delays despite the addition of one john grell as co-conspirator in the forthcoming indictment. several folks are trying to find out grell's present situation: we hear he was released on bail in albuquerque but bill doesn't believe it; the feds were trying to extradite him to new york; his parents are trying to get him committed for psychiatric examination; there are rumors he is wanted for questioning by the japanese federal authorities for smuggling samuri pocket-knives into a buddist temple in okinawa.

keep writing. your letters help keep me in touch with a reality which is rapidly slipping away.

love, sam

II

THE TOMBS

April 15, 1970

Dear Jocko,

I'm sorry if it seems I haven't written to you in a while. I've been very busy lately. By the time you read this you will be 8 years old. That's getting to be close to a young man already. If you had a good birthday party please tell me about it. I'm sorry I can't send you a present from here but they don't have anything suitable for you. I hope you will consider the gift from mommy as being from me too—unless it's one of those new pollution toys that give off smoke or something. In that case I don't want any part of it. Perhaps in a while you'll understand how perverse the hunger for money can make some people. Meanwhile, I hope you have a happy birthday.*

Love, Daddy

---

* JM: The "gift from mommy" that year was a detective kit. It came with a plastic badge and fake nickel-plated revolver that was so realistic that the toy was outlawed in New York. I have always wondered if this present, bought by Mom, carried a touch of spite. I never asked for such a gift and never told Sam about it.

April 20, 1970

dear brother,

in "pilgrims progress," Mr. valiant-for-truth says he will keep his scars as a witness that he has fought his battles. my new residence [the Tombs] i take to be just new scars. since i'm not allowed to write about the institution and i can't have my books or newspapers there's very little i have to say. not that there isn't a wealth of valuable experiences here. if folks outside could see the conditions under which amerika forces its misfits to exist i'm sure many would be able to realize the brutal indifference that exists all the way up thru the system.

if its true "you are what you eat," i will emerge from here a test tube. the comestibles are under contract to dupont i'm sure. it's expedient and it saves the taxpayer oodles of money.

see what you can do to save the bread spent on all those subs. i should be back in federal prison in 4 to 6 months. we can renew then.

give my love to all.

Sam

bill hasn't been in since last monday. i had a state court appearance friday and he didn't show. the fed trial begins next week. what's happening? please *answer soon.*

April 20, 1970

dear ruth

i had hoped i would have seen you by now. my lawyer promised he would tell you the day they moved me over (4-11) [to the Tombs]. you're the only one i'm allowed to visit and it would break the monotony so much. you're allowed 1/2 hour visits monday thru friday 6:30 to 8:30 PM. you can come more than once. i don't get papers any more so watch the news for me. *please please* come soon. 125 white st.*

Sam

---

* JM: My mother would visit Sam at least once a week. He had few visitors at this time and, according to my mother, claimed that his other visitors were not able to bring him things.

May 16, 1970

dear brother,

i think the combination of age & a greater coming together is responsible for the speed of the passing time. it's six months now [since Sam's arrest] & i can tell you truthfully few periods in my life have passed as quickly. i am in excellent physical & emotional health. there are doubtless subtle surprises ahead but i feel secure & ready.

as lovers will contrast their emotions in times of crisis so am i dealing with my environment. in the indifferent brutality, the incessant noise, the experimental chemistry of food, the ravings of lost hysterical men i can act with clarity & meaning. i am deliberate—sometimes even calculating—seldom employing histrionics except as a test of the reactions of others. i read much, exercise, talk to guards & inmates, feeling for the inevitable direction of my life.

despite by & large a better education & intelligence, the federal prisoners are quite inferior to the state prisoners at chess play. federal inmates have more privileges (diversions) so they don't play as much. but there's more to it. federal crimes are things like mail theft, forgery, drug smuggling, bank robbery—usually non-violent crimes. whereas state offences often involve assault, even murder & usually include a deadly weapon. state inmates are direct, bold individuals living in a not-so-quiet state of desperation. in chess, contrary to popular thinking, the bold aggressive stroke, the brilliant sacrifice will almost invariably triumph over the devious, prudent maneuver. great regis! a lesson for the revolution?

on monday night (5-11) at about 11 PM the unmistakable blast of dynamite jolted the sleepy inmates. whistles, power calls & right-ons kept us up a long while. it took a full 12-15 minutes for police & fire engines to respond. we learned from a guard the next day it was a garage housing vehicles of city or gov't employees. what i saw of the media carried nothing on it. little damage was done although i'm sure it was a large charge & evidently placed in an automobile.

just 2 cells away are the two young taiwanese who allegedly attempted to assassinate Chaing's heir at the waldorf a couple of weeks ago. they are good, together people & although we are on different walk schedules we have had long harangues about nationalism & the international revolution. i like them very much. with them & two others we make up the intelligentsia of our block. perhaps not a formidable accomplishment but we do what we can. the other two are: a black actor charged with a shotgun slaying of a viet marine hero in greenwich village in 1967 (he got a hung jury & the case is still pending after 3 years imprisonment); a frail, impossibly hassidic jew charged with (get ready for this) a knife duel killing of a puerto rican over the favors of a prostitute. moishe is a characature of the brooklyn sect. surely tomorrow is the very last day.

i have little to say regarding our last court appearance & its possible effect.* i just don't think folks need further demonstrations of the court's bankruptcy. for the few who were looking forward to some antics there is little revolutionary future. i may be overlooking something & please tell me if i am but in a strict sense pollack [the judge in Sam's case] was right: our's is not a political case. we aren't testing the letter or the intent of the law. the *law* is our enemy. with one's enemy it is sometimes expedient to make deals. but to be forced to acknowledge their procedure & rhetoric without denying their authority would be treachery. there are other reasons of course but none the lawyers have been able to comprehend. i leave that to minds with greater tolerance than mine. the panther trials are quite different though. i'm sure you see that.

love to all

S

P.S. special love to flotsam & brood, beatrice, richard, jetsam. address your stuff to my cell:8UA5
watch the parking meters
state sentence: June 5
fed sentence: June 19
predicted total time: 15 yrs (they haven't got it to give)

---

* Cohen: On May 8, the day his trial was supposed to start, Sam pleaded guilty.

May 28, 1970

dear brother,

i haven't seen bill in some time so if there's been some arrangement regarding where i'll finally be located, i don't know it. in any event it should only be 3 more weeks before i find out.

here at the tombs, since my arrival, the area known as "administrative segregation" has become the political prisoner wing. we've got the taiwanese nationalists who tried to assassinate Chaing's heir; we've got the mira [a Puerto Rican revolutionary organization] revolutionist carlos filiciano; a black panther (can't mention his name); and me. several others, whose crimes may have been motivated by let's say extra-political reasons, are certainly now considered political because of their obvious awareness. i've been having good rap sessions with the panther and the two taiwanese (one of whom was bailed yesterday). as with most good issues more questions were raised than answered but there's a clear revolutionary direction in all our various positions. the man from mira doesn't communicate well in english but i sense his power and he seems very together.

it's inevitable that i get to know nechayev [a nineteenth-century Russian terrorist] so you might start to pick out some of his stuff for me to order when i get to prison.*

2 days later

"Wood" was just brought in. he is a reputed weatherman who, with his pregnant wife, was captured on 103rd st. friday nite. he is 3 cells away and we have talked briefly. strange.

the panther (Kato) was set upon by the goon squad and he is now in bellevue with a fractured skull. we don't know how serious it is. in our brief acquaintance i've grown very fond of him. things are *very* tense here. the hacks act with impunity. i have previously underestimated their willingness to use brutality. i have given them more truck than the Kato, but they are apparently reluctant to mess with a federal prisoner.

---

* DV: Sam articulates that he was not familiar with Sergey Nechayev. Perhaps without knowing it at the time, Sam and the other members of the collective had mimicked much of the approach to symbolic, political violence that Nechayev and other Russian revolutionaries (and terrorists) like Narodnaya Volya had trail-blazed in the nineteenth century, including the use of dynamite, clandestine cell structure, and propaganda of the deed.

i don't know what recourse we prisoners have of dealing with them. the inmates are too frightened or untrusting of each other to form alliances. the hacks demand and get instant obedience & they expect a good attitude as well. dignity is a bourgeois luxury here; survival is where most of us are at.

your story of the washington (state) affair [a yippie happening] is beautiful of course but i'm sure much more serious things will be happening soon. (praise mao!)

i enclose two succinct clippings from our own n.y. times for your delectation.

i received a warm letter from r.b. i don't write to him as often as i might. be sure to give him my love and of course share my letters with him.

to avoid the tombs stupid censor i'm having this mailed out without their seeing it.

my love to all fighting bros & siss.

S

June 6, 1970

dear bill,

i gave carlos [Feliciano, the MIRA bomber who was in the Tombs with Sam]* your address for advice. his wife & family have been very harrassed by authorities apparently with his lawyer's knowledge.† his

---

* SF: Carlos Feliciano was a member of the Nationalist Party of Puerto Rico and served time there with Don Pedro Albizu Campos. In 1956 he moved with his family to New York to escape constant FBI harassment and worked as a cabinetmaker for fourteen years. On May 16, 1970, he was arrested in the South Bronx for possession of a bomb in his car that was supposedly hidden in a loaf of bread, charged with bombing thirty-five buildings, and even accused of being a Cuban agent. He also was accused of being a member of the underground group MIRA, which he denied but which Sam stated that he was. In 1970 he was tried in the Bronx on twenty phony bombing charges and acquitted; in 1972 he was tried on the same charges in Manhattan, convicted, and sentenced to four years in prison. Committee to Defend Carlos Feliciano, *Carlos Feliciano: History & Repression* (New York: Committee to Defend Carlos Feliciano, 1973).

† SF: Carlos Feliciano was represented by Bill Kunstler, although this may refer to another lawyer.

lawyer did not accompany carlos' wife to an 8-hour interrogation tho he knew in advance. he was to get some strong lawyers from Puerto Rico but nothing came of it. *please* help him.

i got the papers [newspapers] for 3 days after you spoke to cunningham* but they've stopped again. must give him another call and remind him.

i've not been able to see wood [the Weatherman].†

i was told sentencing was set for 19th in the state. you say 16th, which?

Sam

June 18, 1970

bros JC, rb, sister beatrice;

as i may have told you before i am to do state prison time rather than federal—for reasons crain cannot or will not explain.‡ my queries of inmates indicates this is very unfortunate. the brutality & lack of

---

* SF: On September 9, Cunningham was in the metal shop when, according to Oswald, fifteen to eighteen inmates broke through: "Leading the invaders was Sam Melville, the 'Mad Bomber,' Sam Melville ordered the hostages to strip." When Sergeant Cunningham resisted, Sam told him, "Cunningham, you're mine now!" (Oswald, *Attica: My Story*, 64–65). Cunningham will be remembered for his September 12 televised plea to the governor to come to Attica: "If Rockefeller doesn't come, I'm a dead man" (Wicker, *A Time to Die*, 239, 258, 284). Inmate leader Roger Champen called Cunningham "the toughest fuckin' sarg't on the job. He put more guys in keep-lock than any 40 hacks around" (Wicker, 237), and Jerry Rosenberg called Cunningham "probably the most hated man in the whole institution. A real tyrant. The only sergeant I ever seen who carried a bit. And he used it. . . .This bastard Cunningham tormented me for six years straight. I lost my visits from my mother. My packages. No mail of any kind. But when that riot jumped off, fuckin' Cunningham was . . . the first one killed by the assault force when they came over the wall. Shot by his own kind . . . and I was glad" (Bello, *Doing Life*, 168–171).

† SF: Lee Wood was the alias of Raymond Heidi, an alleged Weatherman (there were doubts). He and his wife Patricia Wood (Bonnie Heidi) faced serious charges in California and after ten months were extradited back there.

‡ RK: Without access to the indictment(s) and transcripts of the other proceedings, it sounds as if the federal prosecutors decided to hand this off to the NY County district attorney. I am guessing that the feds had input into the plea agreement, and that the charges Sam plead to, and the sentence he received, satisfied federal interest in the case. Hence, Sam did not face a federal indictment, trial, or plea.

privileges when compared to federal institutions is an endless lament among prisoners. while my loins are not ungirded my prevailing view is jail is jail, man, & i wanna be with my people.

some changes here in the political wing of the tombs: one of the formosans was bailed. he is an architect & we have several acquaintances between us; carlos (from mira) has had all but two charges dropped. the pigs have no evidence. he expects a bail reduction soon. lee wood (heidi), the alleged weatherman, was here for two days but was moved to the 7th floor. yesterday i got a new "celly"—a fidelista! a 38-yr-old cuban who fought with che & fidel in 1958. he left cuba in '64 to "see the world." he was busted for h sale [heroin]. it's a little disappointing. he's not very together. no politics at all but a good man never-the-less.

when you read this i will have been sentenced. crain is optimistic. doing state time has at least the advantage of possibility of parole sooner. the state prisons are quite crowded so they try to get some out a bit earlier. with me it's a question mark. i've mellowed alot since coming to the tombs so maybe i can get out with 5 years. alot depends on the state. i still have much unchecked fury but when i see so many black men in circumstances far worse than mine i try to relate to that & come out okay. one thing is certain: in spite of the high racial tension (or perhaps because of it) when i emerge to whatever sunlight is left in this world i will not be a honky anymore.

you must give my special love to beatrice. she wrote another beautiful cheering letter this week. i doubt they'll let her hortatory thru upstate & i'll miss her words alot. her family seems to be making waves (she says because there were none). she's strong & she'll weather (man) the storm.

the paper's coming thru just about every day now. maybe we'll have more difficulties when i move, which will probably be next week. i got some books from the "cherry pie series" of chelsea house publishers. "dynamite: a study of class violence in amerika" is outasite. it was written in '34 but is still very instructive. the way author adamic tells it the wobblies came oh so close and it's discouraging to see their failure.*

---

* SF: "the wobblies came oh so close" refers to the Industrial Workers of the World (the IWW or the Wobblies), a revolutionary trade union. Founded in Chicago in 1905 to unite the American working class and create "one big worldwide labor union," they embraced Blacks, immigrants, and unskilled workers. Their membership spread to other countries

it makes our struggle seem so far off. but then I realize our struggle is not the same as unionism and its bourgeois goals. have you ever noticed the beautiful potency of words beginning with "d"? decimate, detonate, destroy, dynamite, dicnixon.

my schedule is: sing singaround the end of the month; then auburn, clinton, attica, or another of their "correctional institutions for rehabilitation." man! am i getting rehabilitated!

Love & power to all

Sam

June 24, 1970

Dear Jocko,*

I got your pictures and they were very nice, especially the one of you and Mommy in Riverside Park.

I realize you are probably a very busy man these days—traveling as much as you do and making arrangements for camps, etc. So I really don't expect you to write all that much and you need not be sorry.

You ask what kind of job I have. Well, I am a temporarily retired social reformer. If you don't understand that I will explain sometime in the future. Perhaps Mommy can tell you, but she is not a specialist, you must remember, and she might explain it differently than I would. Until recently I was part of a demolition company but we went out of business. In the immediate future I think I'll be making license plates just to get some ready cash and perhaps some useful experience. But

---

and grew to over fifty thousand strong. Some members were poets, artists, and musicians, which would have appealed to Sam, and they printed their own songbooks. The government considered the Wobblies anarchists and jailed over a hundred of their leaders during World War I. Other members were framed and killed, including the legendary Joe Hill, whose famous last letter to Bill Haywood said, "I'll die like a true-blue rebel. Don't waste any time mourning. Organize." Over thirty thousand workers attended his funeral. Today a few small IWW chapters remain in the United States and Canada. Joyce L. Kornbluh, *Rebel Voices: An I.W.W. Anthology* (Ann Arbor: University of Michigan Press, 1972); Wallace Stegner, *Joe Hill* (New York: Doubleday, 1950), 326.

* JM: Of the six letters my father wrote to me from prison, none capture his humor more than this one. I reread this letter many times over the years.

you must realize that social reforming is a very addictive occupation and once you've become an S.R. it's very hard to give up. It's also a little dangerous but the rewards sometimes make up for that.

Don't worry about writing me, just think about learning and understanding everything that happens to you at camp and school.

Love,
Daddy

June 24, 1970

my dear brother,

i am still at the tombs awaiting john mitchell's signature to okay the running of the sentences together. if he does not we will withdraw the pleas and go to trial—an unlikely event. he will probably sign within the next 2 weeks and i will be shipped out promptly.

the ordinary procedure (which may not apply) is 2 to 3 weeks at sing sing, which is now a "reception" center. then i will be sent to prison proper. in my case it will probably be attica (about 60 miles this side of buffalo). attica is the oldest maximum security prison in new york.* in the main it is reserved for men who are no longer young and doing a great deal of time. my time may or may not be a great deal but my prison record thus far is not favorable and judging by their actions recently the authorities will not take any chances with me.

Since returning from court friday i have been put in ultimate security status. i am in a cell alone (very rare here) and not permitted to leave except for counsel visit or shower twice weekly, and then i am accompanied by a captain. the light in my cell stays on throughout the night, and a guard sits within 10 feet. as has been amply demonstrated, his proximity is not for the purpose of doing me service. as you may imagine i am not unanxious to split upstate.

visiting priviledges at most of the prisons is table visit. that is, inmates and visitors sit across a table in a large room with others under observation. you can visit all day (6–7 hours) once monthly.

---

* SF: In fact, Auburn, built in 1816, was the oldest. Attica was built in 1932 and dedicated by Governor Franklin Delano Roosevelt.

persons on the inmate's mailing list are able to sent food packages weekly. it will be good to receive shabazz bean pies and some health food stuffs sometimes.

unless there are objections i am going to put you and r.b. as my visitors. but i will need a *home* address for you i think. tell me what to put down. consistent with this nation's god-fearing policies, i will not be permitted female visitors outside of my immediate family, which in my case means none.

please save all underground press news about reaction to our case, particularly regarding the cop-out [his guilty plea]. no editing! i want the good and bad. bring them with you on your first visit which should be within three months. bill mentioned a letter alledgedly by j. a. [Jane Alpert] in a recent rat. bring that.

i'll want my guitar of course but i'll have to get permission first.

weird as it sounds some prisoners are permitted to have pets! if i am one i'll take one of your family [of puppies] if you can part with one.

Love to all.

S

address to new cell, 8LAI

June 26, 1970

dear brothers,

the optimum bullshit conditions that began last friday still prevail. bill was here wednesday & today but he still doesn't know how long i'll be here. it all seems to depend on the federal marshalls releasing me, which they say depends on when mitchell signs this agreement. meanwhile i'm still a federal prisoner. and dig this kick in the balls: the time i've served so far, at least the 5 months at west st. and maybe the 3 months here, doesn't count! since i'm to serve state time it doesn't officially start until i'm turned over to the state authorities. it may not really make any difference since i'm not likely to be paroled on my first few visits to the board anyway. but it will definitely mean i won't see the board for the first time until i'm in state custody for the full 1/3 time which, from what i can figure out, is 54 months.

i've just reread "soul on ice,"* and realized i must have been asleep
the first time. it's an enormous work! an inevitable book! to combine
such incredible vision of the socio-psycho-sexual make-up of amerika
with such poetry of force and humanity! by no standards can i be
called a well-read man. not counting technical stuff, i've read more in
the past 8 months than in all of my former life. but i'm certain there
are few writings as potent and visionary as cleaver's, one strange and
sad thing to note tho: altho "soul on ice" (and "die, nigger, die!") has
evidently been well circulated here and at rikers island [another city
jail], few of the men who read it are influenced very profoundly by it.
i think much has to do with the fact that because of lack of education,
even rudimentary, much is lost on them. they respond to the anger,
such as in the part "Allegory of the black eunuchs," but find completely
uncomprehensible the brilliant following essay "the primeval mitosis."
by the way, none of the dictionaries here lists mitosis or "ofay," which
i take to be western black argot for white society, none here use or
know the term.

excuse the abrupt ending, but the last mail pick-up of the week is
here—

S.

P.S. the times sub has run out. don't renew till i'm settled upstate.

---

* DV: Eldridge Cleaver's seminal work, which he wrote while imprisoned in California
during the 1960s.

III

SING SING

July 13, 1970

Dear John,

I arrived here at Sing Sing on Thur 7/9.* The last several weeks at the Tombs were not pleasant and I lost too much weight. It's much better here; the air is cleaner, the food much better and some sunshine. But best of all: quiet! The noise at the Tombs was its most oppressing aspect.

It's not likely I'll stay here, although I might. In any event I would like my guitar brought up soon so if I am moved I can take it with me. Also, could you renew the Times subscription and get a sub for Monthly Review.† I asked so many times for that, but it hasn't come through. I'm sure the prison authorities will let it in here. They gave me all my books except the Rap Brown. The Lenin volumes, which I saw for the first time Friday, are very tome-ish in several ways.

I want to have you and Richard visit me but there's a catch: you must be fingerprinted. Of course I won't hold you & R.B. to coming if you want to avoid the indignity of the ink. If you can find someone

---

* JV: Operating since 1826, Sing Sing Correctional Facility was a maximum security prison outside of New York City, notorious for its brutal conditions.
† JV: Founded during the McCarthy Red Scare, *Monthly Review* is an independent journal of socialist thought best known for Marxist analyses of political economy. It remained Marxist in the 1960s but grew critical of the Soviet Union and its version of communism.

who is willing I would very much appreciate it. If you do come you must do so Mon thru Fri the first time. Thereafter, any day is okay. Visiting hours are 9 to 3 with a lunch break. You can stay the whole 6 hours. We would sit at a table in a room (with others). No phones or glass. We might even shake hands!

I'm permitted to receive one fifteen-pound food package each month. If there's anything in our defense fund, I would like some natural honey, wheatgerm, good peanut butter and dried fruit & nuts. If you can find the Muslim bakery in New York include some Shabazz Bean Pies. I'm really hung on them. Wait until 4 days after July 9th before you send anything or before visiting.

For whatever it means tell Bill Crain where I am. He told me to keep him posted.

Give my love to everyone. I hope we can meet soon.

Sam Melville
#146-410

July 26, 1970

Dear Bill,

Refer to the Rule Book "Revised Sept. 1, 1968" (check if that's the latest). Start drawing up court proceedings regarding the following rules: numbers 6, 21, 47 thru 52, 54, 56, 59, 60 & 63. Also the following:

Literature forbidden on grounds other than obscenity. (Rap Brown's book was not allowed. My request to receive Rat & Guardian will be denied.)

Hair length. I was obliged to shave & cut my hair upon entering Sing-Sing. When I subsequently shaved my head completely I was told if I did it again I would be placed in keeplock.

My request to sleep on the cell floor was denied! [The bed springs sag, creating a health hazard.] With respect to Mess Hall rules: while there is nothing apparently objectionable about them, the conditions we eat under make it difficult to maintain the civility demanded in rules 29 & 30. I will explain when we next meet.

I realize the Correction Dept, may have an out claiming their "little blue book" is not a legal document. But if it isn't, I want to force them to reveal the one that is—if it exists.

The basis for Judge Motley's decision in the Sostre suit was that convicts still retain constitutional rights & the violation of these rights constitutes cruel & unusual punishment.* What we must do, in the words of V.I. Ulyanov [Lenin],† is to "move the contradiction to a higher level." The end we must keep in mind is forcing the state to reveal the mercurial nature between the avowed raison d'etre of their "Correctional/Rehabilitation Facilities" and the written & unwritten regulations which maintain in the Correction Dept.

---

* SF: Judge Motley's decision in the Sostre suit was a landmark federal court decision granting some of the most sweeping prison reforms in US history. The judge called Sostre's 372 days in solitary "cruel and unusual punishment," which violated his constitutional rights; she limited solitary confinement to fifteen days, and only after a hearing at which he could have counsel, question witnesses, and have a written record. She further ruled that prison officials could not censor or deny communication between Sostre and any attorney or public official and could not deny him political literature or freedom of expression. And, in an unprecedented finding, she awarded him $13,020 in damages for pain and suffering. "$13,020 Damages Awarded Convict," *New York Times*, May 14, 1970. It was because of *Sostre v. Rockefeller* that the Brothers in D Yard wanted Constance Baker Motley to sign the injunction (she declined as it was not her jurisdiction), and also why they asked for Tom Wicker, who had written a column praising the decision. After the assault to retake the prison, officials blamed the uprising on the federal courts and this decision in particular. Mancusi told the House Select Committee on Crime of "federal court interference in state prisons without responsibility for the results." William Ringle, "Attica Chief Claims Letters Plotted Revolt," *Niagara Falls Gazette*, November 30, 1971. Oswald told a group of Attica guards' wives, "It's not easy to administer a prison when some judge tells you every other day what you can do. You used to be able to run prisons without interference from the courts and the liberal segment of society." Bob Buyer, "Corrections Chief Assails Interference by Judiciary," *Buffalo Evening News*, December 11, 1971. An important analysis of the Attica rebellion came from Sostre, who had spent four years in the box there and from it waged the fight that forced the courts to recognize Islam as a bona fide religion. He wrote in part, "The Attica Rebellion not only was the direct consequence of [the] systematic denial of our basic human rights, but of [the] adamant refusal to accord us the civilized treatment ordered by Federal Courts in *Sostre v. McGinnis, Sostre v. Rockefeller, Sostre v. Otis*, and in many other decisions." Randy Tennen, "Martin Sostre: One Man's Drive for Prisoners' Rights," *Commentator*, November 17, 1971, 4, 11.

† JV: Vladimir Ilyich Lenin (1870–1924) was the principal leader of the Russian Revolution and later the head of the Soviet state. A master tactician, Lenin worked out both a theory and practice for communists to make revolution and seize state power. His legacy includes the creation of innumerable "Marxist-Leninist" political parties throughout the world, including in the United States.

I'm aware of the arguments for the state in claiming that altering their rules would not produce a rehabilitated citizen; e.g. Rap Brown's book creates rebels, etc. But it isn't difficult to counter every objection they can raise—even on their own terms. We must go into every aspect of prison life, if possible, and reveal further the impotency of hypocritical liberalism—force them to acknowledge what their prisons really are. They can respond in only limited ways. And any of those ways will further our cause. Incidently, I think the Correction Dept, appealed the Motley decision. Check the results. Also, of course, we'll use what gains your people made in the Panthers vs. Correction Dept, if applicable.

In view of the recent exposes in establishment journals regarding prison conditions the sooner we proceed the better. (In addition to the Times & News stuff, the Village Voice of July 16, 1970, contraband here, by the way, featured no less than three separate articles on prisons, plus an announcement of a symposium on prison reforms.) Talk this over with your brothers & sisters at the commune to see if this rates any priority. In any event, let me know immediately this reaches you. Include the date you receive it. You needn't respond to the body of the letter. I only want to know if it reaches you intact.

Other news—my advice to you is to get out of the mess between rock capitalists and "the hip community." The days for that bullshit are certainly numbered if not over. "The hip community" should be into more aggressive ways of raising funds and getting our people back.

I've received no mail for two months. Ask J.C./R.B. if they intend to write and/or visit.

Sam Melville #146-410

August 2, 1970

Dear Richard,

Wrote to John 3 weeks ago but his P.O. box is evidently screwed up. I put you and him on the visiting & correspondence list.

We are permitted to receive 15 lbs of food per month.

I need protein! No meat or meat products. You can mail it or bring it if and when you come.

If you're not into visiting write and let me know. It's been over 3
months since I've heard from anyone.*

Sam Melville
#146-410

August 10, 1970

dear brother,

go to oak publishers (ask at the folklore center). have them send
me 1 or 2 volumes of *advanced* finger picking styles (regular musical
notation or guitar tablature). Last summer oak had released the first,
and possibly the second, volume of a proposed 4 volume set of many
southern styles—blind [*illegible*], john hurt, mance lipscom and others.
by now the entire set may be out. Thoes will do very well. If you can't
get that, happy tavern's book (with john hurts' incredible fingers on
the cover) will be a good second. That's also published by oak.

i was let into population on friday. got some sun, a little exercise
and the guitar. the yield of a slattern, some panamanian erythrism
[Panamanian Red—super grass] and zap! it's 1968—was there ever
such a year? for sheer survival, and to avoid an obviously developing
misanthropy, i have made some alliances. it turns out they are not
unwelcome. believe it or not there are freaks at sing-sing. or rather,
ex-freaks, since the former nomenclature seems inappropriate without
the usual hirsute development and other accompanying accouterments.
They are 4. Young and not inarticulate. One is a YSA [Young Socialist Alliance][†] member. two say they know me from the street but that
seems doubtful. my resemblance to the sam of a year ago i think is
very remote. Anyway, they help the time pass less unpleasantly. and
with the relative freedom of movement, i can feel my body shaking
out the kinks of 9 months lock-up.

---

* Cohen: Letters to and from Sam sometimes took months to arrive. It seemed that they
were analyzed by the New York police, the FBI, and the prison authorities before being
delivered.
† JV: The Young Socialist Alliance was a youth organization of the Trotskyist Socialist
Workers Party, active in antiwar and other protest movements in the 1960s.

the food package arrived sunday, and none too soon judging from the intense dialogue the figs and soybeans and i got into. the vitamins alas, are not permissible.

i fondled one of the many cats on the grounds today. the contact of a live being responding to my touch blew my mind.

let me know when you're coming again.

Sam Melville

#146-410

Aug. 23, 1970

dear brother,

your letter came thru stamped twice in red "advise writer to sign name and address." for all the correction dept knows it could be from anyone whose name begins with J and of course that won't do.

i am negociating with the authorities to receive Kate Millet's new book [*Sexual Politics*] but it looks doubtful. either word of the title is anathema here so you may imagine their consternation at seeing the juxtaposition of the two. i'll know the decision after Sept. 1st. however, i don't think they'll have objections to the recent random house issue "history and human survival" by robt. jay lipton. if the surf board of directors grants us a decent discount off the $8.95 (for just 400 pages!) have them send me a copy.

in the next food pack send only the soy beans. you know i'm working now so i'll be able to pay my way. i earn $0.10 every day. do you think i should stay with dreyfus or switch to loeb?

give my love to all.

Sam Melville

#146-410

Aug. 27, 1970

dear brother,

   i'm moving up in the world, tomorrow i assume my new position as second trombonist in the band. quite a leap from chapel porter. a prerequisite accruing with the new job is that i am not required to go to lunch—which represents a great relief to me.

   i'm tempted to ask for a thesaurus, but an inexpensive thesaurus is worse than none at all (fealty to roget's subject categories is thrown to the winds by editors hard pressed to put out popular editions) and i don't want you to spend any bread that might be sorely needed elsewhere for what is clearly a luxury.

   hope to see you soon.

Sam Melville
#146-410

Aug. 31, 1970

dear brother,

   i'm being transferred tomorrow to the big A. it's about 60 miles east of buffalo i think. if you sent anything to sing-sing i'm told it will get to me, but not to hold my breath. attica does not have a "good" reputation among inmates but i am "in omnia parratus."*

   some determination must have been made in david's situation by now. *please* let me know.† i do not want anything to do with crain anymore. the more i think about all that i've let him do the more i am

---

* SF: Asking for Sing Sing was naive. Requesting a specific prison, unless as part of an informant's deal, is usually time wasted: (1) if you state a preference they will usually do the opposite; (2) if they do make a promise they usually break it; and (3) they wanted Sam to be isolated, so sending him to Clinton or Attica was probably inevitable. Since Sam had already tried to escape twice prior to sentencing, and Attica was supposed to be escape-proof, that undoubtedly is why the state chose Attica. Craig R. Whitney, "Suspect in Bombing Conspiracy Foiled in an Attempt to Escape," *New York Times*, March 12, 1970.

† Cohen: David Hughey, convicted of having conspired with Sam and sentenced to four to six years in a federal penitentiary. Sam is asking about David's sentence.

depressed about all that's gone down. i realize how eclectic my politics has always been, and to have been saddled with the likes of him only served to magnify the debacle. being sent to attica represents his last defeat at our expense.* the recent insurrection at the tombs makes me even more convinced that good political mileage can be had from exploiting liberal hypocrisy toward the prison system. while i am not overly enthusiastic regarding my own participation in this particular matter, if i can be used to any advantage for the forces of social change i will feel much less oppressed by this environment. so if someone can be found to work with us in this have him or her contact me as my prospective attorney.

if you are denied permission to visit me or you do not hear from me for more than 5 or 6 weeks it will mean i have been "boxed" [put in solitary]—not an uncommon occurance if one shows signs of wearying of saying sieg heil.

my love to all.

Sam Melville
#146-410

---

* Cohen: Sam had asked Crain to arrange for him to stay at Sing Sing, closer to New York City.

IV

ATTICA

September 6, 1970

Dear John,

Attica, formerly the hunting grounds of the Seneca tribe of the Iroquois nation, now the adjurant, parasitic landscape of the Bethlehem [!] Steel cartel,* is now my home. The architecture is best described as expedient Byzantine. The population is predominantly tacit porcine. It snows alot.

We are not permitted to write about the prison nor to solicit funds or packages—for excellent reasons.

Put the following down on your list for immediate action:

1. Subscribe to the daily [not Sunday] N.Y. Times;†
2. Subscribe to Monthly Review and Trans-Action (Irving Louis Horowitz's magazine);‡

---

* JM: The bracketed exclamation point, though formatted like an editorial insertion, is in fact part of the text of Sam's original letter.

† JM: The bracketed note "[not Sunday]" likewise appears in the original letter.

‡ JM: Irving Louis Horowitz (1929–2012) was author of more than two dozen books and over several decades worked to develop a sociological theory that measured state-sanctioned violence. Sam knew Horowitz as a teenager and was best friends with his son-in-law. My mother claimed Horowitz had a strong influence over him, even more so than Sam's own father, who himself was an organizer in the labor movement. Horowitz was an influential American sociologist, author, and college professor who was key to introducing the phrase "Third World" into social research.

3. Transfer about $20 from the Defense Fund to me here via *postal* money order;

4. Get a lawyer. I intend to fight before going insane.*

Write soon.

Sam Melville
#26124

September 13, 1970

Dear John,

Come get the guitar. They won't permit me to have it.
Send the following:
　　Sub to the N.Y. Times
　　Unabridged Oxford Dictionary
You may forget all other requests i've made. If you need money for the dictionary sell the guitar.

If you are unable to write, have Crain or John Mitchell or somebody tell me what's become of David.†

Sam Melville
#26124

September 20, 1970

[To John Cohen]

Actually it's been only about a month since i last heard from you but Attica represented such a cultural shock to me it seems much longer. I'm becoming somewhat acclimated now & tho i lack the

---

* Cohen: The longer Sam stayed in prison the more strongly he suspected that his lawyer had been inept and had accepted a longer sentence for Sam than necessary. At Attica, Sam became convinced that the whole deal Crain made with the government had been a mistake, and he was considering withdrawing his guilty plea and going to trial.

† JM: John David Hughey III, Sam's codefendant.

double Y chromosome factor of most of my neighbors, i have managed to effect a significantly belligerant enough aspect to gain, if not the respect, at least the acquiescence of my fellow felons.

Owing to my extensive experience in pipe design & music the authorities have assigned me to the Shoe Shop, where i have moved quickly into the ranking group of checker players. Penitentiary checkers, which i hope you may never have occasion to play, is somewhat different than the virginal pastime you may have learned as a boy. This, i think, is owing to the overwhelming ebony influence. The board & pieces are the same but the non-kings are obliged to jump both front & back if the opportunity exists & the kings may jump the entire eight squares or any part of the diagonal. It's a little more subtle than your other checkers but somehow i don't envisage becoming passionate about it. The penalties for losing range from 10 to 50 push-ups or 3 "hootchy-cootchies." A hootchy-cootchy consists of placing the hands on the hips and suggestively moving that part of the anatomy the repudiation & shame of which, Freud has submitted, is responsible for the malaise of western civilization. Hootchy-cootchy by the way, i suspect, has some etymological consanguinity* with the word the Iroquois used for home-made liquor: hootcheney.

I'm taking steps to be transferred to the school program but as yet i'm termed a security risk; which, at Attica, is an absurdity Camus would have difficulty explaining.

Make tracks to get a sub to the Times (not Sunday). There's not exactly a plethora of news reports in the Niagara purlieu. Please treat my request for the Oxford English Dictionary & a good thesaurus as a spurious whim. These are to have priority over every other requests i've made including food, money, books, or even visits. Should books be easily available by all means have them sent. Any non-fiction title is welcome. I'm especially anxious to read Robt. Jay Lifton's recent Random House pub. & Kate Millet's book which will be permitted here.

I can't expect you to visit up here tho i would like to see your beautiful head again but *please*! write at least a note every 3–4 weeks. I've no word of David & i'm sure his situation is altered since June. I'm not completely free of insecurity & your lack of response sometimes makes me think i'm imposing. Circumstances change folks so quickly now i can't be sure where you're at. Forgive me if that seems lack of fealty. Be assured it is not.

My love to you & our brothers & sisters.

*If i had an O.E.D. you might not be burdened with such constructions.

Sam Melville
#26124

P.S. We are now allowed instruments. My psychic stock rose 100%. Have you sent those music books & strings?

October 3, 1970

Dear John,

Here is a list of publications I want for the present:

—Unabridged dictionary [Random House fine]*
—Deutscher Trotsky biography 3 vols.
—Kate Millet
—Lenin Selected Works Vol. I *only*

& of course the Times, M.R., Transaction & the Liberated Guardian.

Since your visit i've come across a Random House catalog on Social Science publications 1969. Dig, I want many of the titles in the Political Science section and several in the Anthropology. Send what you can but for now the above list has priority, especially the Deutscher & the dictionary. Also, *please*! those advanced finger picking books from Oak publishers.

In the next package send 2 sets of guitar strings and the reading glass or that magnifying sheet you mentioned.

Love to all.

Sam Melville
#26124

---

* JM: Bracketed in original letter.

October 11, 1970

Dear John,

The Times began arriving Thursday—at last. I'm still pining for the dictionary and the literature I've asked for.
Don't send any more food until I ask. But do send the reading glass (they've given approval) and the guitar strings—tout de suite.
Some far out news reports recently.
Love to all.

Sam Melville
#26124

Send up a 6″ slide rule. Pickett metal preferable K&E bamboo okay.

October 16, 1970

Dear Brother John,

Vestigial puritanism? I think not. Vestigial misogyny—only not so vestigial. Every state needs laws. From alexander on laws have been passed to protect men from the influence of women. La femme is forbidden for correspondence or visiting. Quarantine is perhaps a better word.

So—i got your letter & telegram. Evidently you haven't gotten my recent mail. Everything you ask about i've already told you. No more food for a while. A reading glass, guitar strings & slide rule are what i need. No books have come as yet tho i still harbor hopes you may remember them. Yes, the [N.Y.] times has started to arrive.

Since your visit i've been transferred to the school. Logarithms & binomial expansion are recalcitrantly returning. Under the guidance of a very paranoid state of new york, i am an instructor in mathematics. Tho it beats repairing shoes i miss playing checkers.

Send love to all.

Sam Melville
#26124

December 11, 1970

Dear Brother,

Don't concern yourself with letters or packages or visits until you gain some equanimity. I will continue to write, mainly to practice organizing my thoughts but also, hopefully, to give you some idea of the understanding that I think I am gaining.

My love and strength to all those in need.*

Your brother,
Sam Melville
#26124
39-23

December 25, 1970

Dear John et al,

Misc.

The Times stopped Dec. 14. I wrote them to ask if the sub expired & if so to renew & send you the bill. Nothing yet. Please check.

Received the package most gratefully. Dates & nuts is real funky food. I wasn't allowed to see the letter in the pack. You should know by now anything that's logical & direct is against the rules.

Got your news of Bea [Beatrice]. She's beautiful. About receiving Good Times—send it. Send anything. Send everything! Something will get thru. Prison teaches some skills in this regard.

Just after your last visit a bunch of "adventurists" [including Sharon] were busted in Lindsayville. I haven't heard anything since. Let me know. Also, what's the denouement of the Seattle conspiracy?

I'm in keeplock for the third time in as many months. This will be a 10-day stretch, maybe more. It's better now tho; I'm in C block with a door & window. It's quiet & I can control the heat. The "food" that's passed thru the door I relay on to the weird creatures who gather

---

* Cohen: Sam's friends Sharon and Joyce had just been arrested in the act of trying to firebomb a bank.

at the windowsill. They're the mangiest critters you ever saw. About half the size of crows, brownish-gray. The snow is deep & it's really cold & they shiver so pathetically. Maybe they're a special genus who exist only around prisons. It's for sure they couldn't survive without inmates feeding them.

I sort of welcome the keeplock. The school was getting to be a drag. Now I'm working hard on Spanish & reading Trotsky* (I copped the one volume at the library). I'm really getting good at Spanish. The feed-up man is puertoricano & we rap thru the slot in the door. Before I moved, I worked out almost everyday with the latins in D block. They are fine, generous hermanos y muy aplicados. I used to study with a lady [Jane]. She was very good but she had this soft way of slurring syllables I found distracting. It wasn't her fault. She spoke english the same way. Even when she spoke Greek she said the same things. It had nothing whatever to do with verbs & nouns.

Naturally, I'm spending time with my body. It's not surnuf yoga but the control I'm gaining gives me much confidence. Sometimes my knees & ankles absolutely refuse any cooperation. But I keep right on them, cursing & forcing them to make love with my back muscles. With a lot of imagination, I can even get a little turned on tucking my nose into the scrotum.

It seems to me that the trouble with yoga is that you can get so spaced out you don't care about things like justice or injustice. You have to separate yourself so much from your fellows. I don't think you can have inner peace without outer peace too. Or do you think we're too concerned with justice anyway, Hamlet?

I work the guitar some. Not hearing the good sounds or playing with others is very limiting. I'm going to write the folk center & ask Izzy to send some stuff & bill you. Okay?

---

* JV: Leon Trotsky (1879–1940) was a leader of Russia's October Revolution of 1917, a major figure in the Communist Party, and an important official in the early Soviet state. In the 1920s he led a failed opposition to Joseph Stalin, leading to his expulsion from the Communist Party in 1927 and exile from the Soviet Union in 1929. He was killed in Mexico in 1940 by agents of the Soviet state. Trotsky inspired a global movement of communists and socialists who opposed Stalinism and largely broke with the Soviet Union. An American Trotskyist movement took hold in 1928, inspiring various left parties over the next decades, including the Socialist Workers Party and Workers World.

"The spirit is of no avail against the sword, but the spirit together with the sword will always win out against the sword alone ... And I am tempted to tell you that it so happens that we are fighting for fine distinctions, but the kind of distinctions that are as important as man himself. We are fighting for the distinction *between sacrifice & mysticism* (outasight!), between energy & violence, between strength & cruelty, for that even finer distinction between the true & the false, between the men of the future & the cowardly gods you revere."

Camus: Letters to a German Friend. 1944

Love to all

Sam Melville
#26124

merry christmas   happy tet

I wanna be exchanged for POW's too.*

January 1, 1971

Dear Bill,

Your efforts to have the time at West Street included are successful. My new release date is November 11, 1987.

Two books have been withheld so far, Rap Brown's and Bobby Seale's. There will be others soon. What can you do to help?

Good luck in the present trial [of the Panther 21].

Sam Melville
#26124

---

* SF: When the Paris Peace Talks began between the Nixon administration and the National Liberation Front of North Vietnam, one hope was that prisoners of war would be exchanged. Sam refers to the belief of US draft resisters and others imprisoned for antiwar activity that they, too, were prisoners of war.

January 8, 1971

Dear John,

I hope you get a chance to come up soon; there are several things we must talk about. Our last letters evidently crossed. The *times* is coming thru again. The music books I want are all published by Oak. Please send the books.
Will write again soon.
Love to all.

Sam Melville
#26124

January 17, 1971

[To John Cohen]
Dear Hamlet,

In situ: For 3 hours every Saturday night WBUF gives its FM band to the Spanish community. Mucha musica y conversación buena. Mostly UB [University of Buffalo] students but often non-students. It's the best show we get. How's this for a sign off (en ingles) "The airwaves belong to the people." I am, dig, bilingual. Reading Nabokov's lubricious "Ada," Trotsky's "Stalin Falsifies History," and some popular short stories en español. None of the following package is approved yet: 10 copies "Greening of America"; 2 copies "Seize the Time"; 3 copies "Empire & Revolution"; 12 "History of Russia"; 11 "Latin American Radicalism"; 6 "In a Time of Revolution"; 7 copies of "Sisterhood Is Powerful";* 9 "Roots of Modern American Empire"; 4 "History of Human Survival"; 1 copy of "Violence In America." Huh?†

Coprophagous: Most cess pools are in two parts. The first absorbs the turbulence of the incoming sewer and permits the raw sludge to

---

* JM: "Sisterhood Is Powerful," compiled by feminist activist Robin Morgan. Although Morgan was never connected to the Melville Collective, Jane Alpert claims in her 1981 memoir that Morgan was an adviser and confidant to her during the time of the bombings.
† Cohen: After months of frustrated attempts to get a package of books sent from this publisher to Sam, a computer freaked out and sent multiple copies of each.

settle. When the level rises to the top of the separating partition, the lighter sewage oozes over a weir and into the second part and then into the leeching pipes and disbursed in an area deemed safe.

In recent issues of Rolling Stone and The Whole Earth Catalog it's clear that, after salaaming to "frugality" & "humility," the great American youth is intent upon a concupisceint chase after the same whore their fathers wasted over. They've changed the prophylactic but the effect will be equally disastrous. Master Nixon has reordered our priorities. Oh-see-the-new-priorities-dick-has-ordered: SST, so our leeching time is hastened; the Alaskan pipe line to power machines to manufacture machines to fuel machines which we are assured will be extinct in '76; the cross-Florida canal (to cut shipping time???) to let the light sludge of the Atlantic to ooze into and hopefully extinguish the inferno that was the Gulf of Mexico. And oh yes, the great adult Disneyland annex amid the recalcitrant sequoias will be announced in the heat of the '72 campaign, coinciding with the final Vietnam withdrawal (leaving a skeleton corps of 300,000 to continue the necessarily increased bombing sorties and the ever efficacious helicopter crop runs). The homecoming boys with their smiling girls and free bhang (being now legalized) will be treated to the gala opening in the once effulgent California sunshine. Others have reordered priorities too. The petulant Miss Dohrn [Bernadine Dohrn, of the Weather Underground] says to go back to the campuses & organize. Other vixens, dropping their mercurial foals at all-day all-time care centers, speed off to consciousness raising sessions. Being an obdurate turd I never made it over the weir to the second partition. I use the N.Y. Times as a periscope to see the leeching area. I'm iracund but I love some much. I hope you come soon.

Sam Melville
#26124
39-16

January 30, 1971

Dear Bill,

After some confusion I have your letters of Dec. 18, 31 and Jan 25. There should not be any difficulty in the future. My jail time has been adjusted; thank you. My health is good and my spirit more afloat than a few months ago. There's no indoor recreation here and the weather now prohibits the yard. So, being locked up I've been reading a lot. I received multiple copies of 10 different titles from Random House Jan. 11th. So far they've let me have 7 single copies and threatened to not allow one or two but I don't think they will.

I do want to prepare a law suit to test their stupid brutal regulations but a personal interview with you would be necessary. I don't think you should try to come up before April though. The roads are closed frequently because of snow. In view of the recent federal ruling deny-ing the Berrigans the right to petition we really can't be optimistic.* But it will be a way to make people more conscious of what's going on behind the wall.

Those of us who haven't made a life for ourselves inside feel so incredibly cut off. No matter how accurately I could describe it, I don't think you can realize the total isolation of prison life. Each day is exactly like the one before and one has no sense of the immediacy of the revolution in the world. I know that's true of many outside as well but there's some awareness however subtle. In here one deals only with unrelieved violent male tension. Very unconducive to spreading seeds and growing plants.

J.C. says he's ordered Ramparts quite a while back but nothing's come yet. Will you see if you can push it. We need tangible evidence

---

* SF: The "recent federal ruling denying the Berrigans" refers to *Berrigan v. Norton*, a 1970 federal lawsuit filed in Hartford, Connecticut, by Dan and Phil Berrigan of the Catonsville Nine. They sued for the right to write for publication, to disseminate sermons, and to write freely to the news media without censorship. Judge Clarie threw out the suit as a class action and ruled that there was no First Amendment right to write for publication. In his prison journal, Phil Berrigan was discouraged, citing "Constance Baker Motley's Martin Sostre decision" as a "rare exception," and adding about the lawyers, "devoted to us though they are, energetic and competent—they are still lawyers [who] believe entirely too much in the law and in the courts" (Berrigan, 74–75).

for a law suit and based on the past they will disallow it. Dig: the Village Voice is contraband. The Village Voice.

Keep in touch.

Sam Melville
#26124
39-16

February 9, 1971

Dear brother,

I really dig our visits & especially the last one. It screws up my reading schedule but the spur i get from seeing you drives me even harder. Remember i asked you to see if you can help a friend find a job. Well he needs a letter stating that he has the promise of a job before he can get out. He's due to see the board soon so if you can, please move on this. Send me a name for him to write to requesting employment. The answer to that will be fine.

Here's the book list. Keep it impaled to your body until all the squares are checked.

Author	Title	Publisher	Ordered	Mailed	Unavailable (explain!)
Lenin	Selected Works (Vol. I only)	International			
Engels	Origin of Family	"			
Deutscher	Biography of Trotsky (3 vols.)	Vintage 1965			
"	Stalin	Oxford University Press 1967			

Trotsky	Permanent Revolution, Results, Prospects	Pioneer 1967	
	Selected Works in Marxist Philosophy	International	
Marcuse	Essay on Liberation		
Lessing	The Four Gated City	?	
Melville	Quiero a Juana		Probably temporarily out of stock
	Unabridged Dictionary	Random House	

how do you spell forigated—what does it mean?

I've thought much of S[haron]. She's a beautiful sister & whatever changes she goes thru she comes out just fine. I read an article recently about migrating geese; why they fly in that "V" formation and keep honking. It seems the formation creates a semi-vacuum by the large air movement making it possible to fly long distances without tiring. They honk because they are rooting, cajoling, scolding each other to keep up and pumping so the group can make it. Yeah.

Honk! Honk!

Sam Melville
#26124
39-16

P.S. Get me on NACLA's [North American Congress on Latin America] mailing list and a catalog from International Publishers. Also the addresses for Trans-action, Ramparts & Disent. I'll order them from here.

You're right. Ebullient is i-bul'-yent. I didn't even realize there was an i in the mother.

Dear Bill,

Please send up the pictures I believe are still in your possession.

Sam Melville

#26124

39-16

March 1, 1971

Dear Brother,

Got the package last week. Good stuff. They wouldn't let the raisins thru. (We can make booze!) Also word of your architectural plans. The stone house sounds great. Don't worry about permanence; a stone house, if unelaborate, is an organic and ephemeral feature of the landscape. Insulation may be a problem but hardly insurmountable. See Architectural Design by Seelye published by Wiley & Sons for good advice.

I'm really anxious for the subscriptions to Dissent, Transaction & Ramparts. Please stick to it. If there's a money problem tell them the cause and if they're still recusant perhaps a hex is in order. The mags will help put all the history and herstory I'm absorbing in a perspective I could benefit from. If you have any contact with David Horowitz (Ramparts) tell him I'm very grateful for his "Empire & Revolution." It's a fine book and taught me so much.

Also, I expected to hear about my friend's job opportunity by now. You know, it need not be permanent. The point is to get out, then, if need be he can look on his own. But as long as he's inside he's trapped.

I have a garden plot. There's been a break in the weather and if it doesn't snow next week I'll put down some manure. The soil's very tired and you have to coax everything up. I think it'll be a lot of fun.

I wrote Crain last week about sending up those pix I had at West Street. He took them to his office when I was transferred to the Tombs. Push him on that if you can reach him.

Quiero a Juana y todos mis hermana y hermanos.

Sam Melville
#26124
39-16

If Paul S. want to visit—write I have to get permission and for that I need his address.

March 12, 1971

Dear Bill,

Although 6 previous copies of *Monthly Review* were approved, the Feb. issue was not. Nor will any future copies of MR be allowed. I am expecting the same for *Dissent* and *Ramparts*. This is clearly because of an argument I had with the education supervisor, who is the censor.

I ask you please to move as *quickly* as possible to get a court order approving these publications.

Here are names you may require:

Vincent Mancusi, Supt.

?   Vincent, Act. Supt.

William Dickinson, Education Supt.

Also, can you find out if mail to attorneys can be censored in view of the recent Federal Appeals decision re Sostre.*

---

* SF: The "recent Federal Appeals decision re Sostre" was a rare en banc sitting of the entire court "because of its significance" (i.e., the enormous political pressure brought by the state). Most of what was won for prisoners' rights was overturned: limits on solitary, the right to counsel at a hearing, the right for a written record of disciplinary proceedings; Rockefeller was held not responsible, so the defendant became McGinnis (Oswald's predecessor); Sostre's damages were reduced to $9,000, of which he got nothing because the warden died. But inmates retained the right to political expression, the right to sue prison officials, and the right to send and receive uncensored attorney correspondence. Arnold H. Lubasch, "Court Extends Convicts' Rights," *New York Times*, February 25, 1971.

Let me know *immediately* what action you're taking & how long to expect results. I'm very anxious about these magazines. MR is my one firm attachment to reality.

Sam Melville
#26124
35-28

March 18, 1971

My Jocko

I know it's been a long time since I wrote and I have certainly neglected you. But I do not like to write letters. I have to work very hard at relating to your life now. The small boy I remember is not you anymore—nor am I the same person I once was. Your mother tells me beautiful things about you and what you are doing and I am very glad and happy for you. But to participate so remotely in your life is not easy.

Really, to think of you, I want to be with you and part of your existence—share your experiences, and *see* you grow and change. That's the only real excitement and meaning between people no matter if they are father and son or whatever. I read your mother's words and wonder is she just saying things that don't have a reality—it's hard to imagine you thinking about me at all now. Soon perhaps, your mother will tell you some things about me and then I will not have to feel so dishonest when I try to write to you.

You see I'm in a very strange position: I could write to you and make comments about your activities, perhaps attempt some instruction here and there and sound just like the fool I would be if I did so; or, if you understood my circumstances, I could try to relate my life honestly to you—and then I would have much to tell you. I don't know how much of it you would benefit from but at least it would be honest and you could pick and choose as you like. It's not that I'm not interested in your activities; I'm more than interested; I'm envious! A nine-year-old youth with so many interests and accomplishments!! Judo, music, biblical history, geography, science, magic. . . . ! ! Instead of an absentee father you need several fulltime secretaries.

About your opening move in our chess game: P-Q4 is a very aggressive beginning. (Your mother says it's a *yellow* belt you're trying for, not a *black* one.) Well, alright, let's see if you know this response: I move P-KN3.*

I've been working on "small space exercises" and maybe you'd be interested in this one (if you're ever in a small space): Kneel on the floor, sit back on the bottoms of your feet, hands on stomach and touch your head to the floor *behind* you. If this is too easy try putting your arms folded across your *back* and do it.

I don't know Hebrew at all but if you ever get into Spanish maybe I can be of some help. Spanish is a good language to know these days, especially in Nueva York.

Keep working and studying and growing.

I love you much.

Dad

Sam Melville

#26124

35-28

March 19, 1971

Dear John,

I told you last time that I could pay for the Times sub. Well, that will probably be true in the future but not just yet. I expect the sub to expire sometime soon, possibly next week. Could you please renew it for me and consider that my package for the month. I was thrown out of the school in February for arguing with the sponsor, so I didn't earn anything for some time. I got another keeplock behind it as well. The supervisor is the creature who approves literature too and he promptly decreed Monthly Review no longer acceptable. I wrote Crain last week

---

* JM: My father taught me to play chess when I was three. I never really took to the game, but years later when I complained to Mom that I could not understand my father's prison letters, she in turn suggested that we play a game of correspondence chess. This letter was his first counter to my opening move. The uprising occurred only days after he received my response.

to ask him to get a court order for MR, Dissent and Ramparts. See if he got my letter and what plans he has.

I thought Dissent is the publication at the YSA but I read recently Irving Howe is the editor and somehow that doesn't jell. Which is the YSA publication?

I hope you write soon and let me know about the books and mags.

Sam Melville
#26124
35-28

P.S. Don't send anymore fruit. Oat cereal & nuts only

March 21, 1971
La Primavera

Dear brother John,

Misc: No books yet except for "Organic Gardening"—a cruel irony since i was dismissed from the school for insubordination and of course blew the garden. I still guard my seed tho.—sent a letter to Ramparts. Dissent coming. Nothing from Transaction or Goodtimes. Izzy Young sent a very good book—Monthly Review was censored but i wrote to Crain to get a court order. You should pressure him. I know you don't like him much, but i need help and you & he represent my entire arsenal. If the RH dictionary (unabridged) is unavailable may i have the desk edition? The unabridged has a good Spanish diet which i wanted too. John, it's been 8 months I've wanted the dictionary.

Ratiocination perhaps: There is no individual change without social change, and there is no social change without *political* revolution. The USA notwithstanding, Marxism-Leninism remains the watchword of world revolution because it presents an analysis that deals with reality that has meaning *and salvation* for at least most of the world's individuals. Even modern bourgeois sociologists are now taking without question an underpinning of Marx: that individual behavior (and consciousness) is determined by society (economic relations between classes). Those who are frightened by the cataclysm political revolution presents (Krishnamurti, Charles Reich, R. J. Lifton, J. Cohen?) or who fear the power of repressive status quo have the choice of either being swept under by the maelstrom of social upheaval or using their acumen (gleaned from the sufferings of others) to guide us to an understanding of our present political reality (not our individual insecurities) so that we may pass to our next evolutionary stage, unforeseeable from our present, narrow, *class* perspective.

More familiarly: my studies and prison experience have led me to rely on what seems to be the most consistent explanation of reality. Again: to maintain a dialogue between my irrational, confused desires and my communicative apparatus it is necessary that i develop an overview of my personal circumstances, past and present. The unavoidable conclusion i arrive at is that i was not born in a vacuum; that i see my reflexion in many, many faces. Now, it follows that if i am a sociological phenomenon and i suffer a sociological disease i must have a sociological prognosis. It's here that our manifest viewpoints part. You want to care for each tender shoot that springs from the earth while (seemingly) not acknowledging the entire forest is violently aflame. I am presently seeking answers that may tell us either to put out the fire and repair what we can or help the fire along and hope its end will leave the soil fertile enough to grow anew. These viewpoints are a microcosm of the left now. (A still smaller view is the glaring contradiction between the entente of my irrational desires and communicative apparatus on the one hand & my extraordinary maunderings and behavior on the other. More about that when i see you.)

Horowitz: haven't read the article* but i suspect Mr. H considers himself *the* Leninist theoretician now that Deutscher's gone and he's taking his cue from Lenin's attack on "spontaneity." To spend time and valuable media space in the most successful commercial leftist journal on the vices of paramilitarism is indulging academicism. At its present development & projecting it to any conceivable maximum, paramilitarism represents no meaningful threat to power (that's the classic argument i believe. You know my position) without an accompanying political awareness among large segments of the population, viz. the middle classes and the armed forces. Judging from the popular media,

---

* Cohen: By David Horowitz, on Weatherman, in *Ramparts*.

paramilitarism has not radically alienated anybody. Furthermore, the strong arm of repression has not been set in motion by bombers (for all the publicity) as much as by the spread of ghetto crimes & mentality to the middle class.

There are 4 views favoring paramilitarism: (1) It will snowball and bring down the PS [power structure]; (2) It aids 3rd World movements by diverting imperialism (2, 3, many Vietnams); (3) In a time when all action seems meaningless at least we won't be good germans; (4) It's fun. It's not fashionable (yet?) to consider (4) and (3) offers little political meat. That leaves the snowball theory, which isn't working, and "many Vietnams" which relies on the snowball. Tell me how H and others address this. It's evidently going to be a while before i can get that lit.

—S: i offer my love and ask that she (and you) consider anew the prospects of winning. In forging a new vision the price of bypassing the complex in favor of what *seems* direct results often in personal political suicide. In the present circumstances, it is, to use your words (but in another sense) accepting the gov't definition of ourselves. Yes, we are well acquainted with guilt & shame and any relief seems welcome. But in the advancing vision of what victory means, guilt & shame become very small dragons indeed. Revolutions function by the laws of "conditional determinism." You cannot assume an action that does not lie within the range of possibilities, nor can you wait for others to determine the conditions.—Quiero a Juana mucho. Damn it! I can't stop reliving that year.

Sam Melville
#26124
35-28

April 1, 1971

[To Ruth]
My oppressed sister

Got your last missive not unhappily. I have snowed myself under
with political & historical literature (such that is permitted) and an
occasional letter brings me back to the real, if not ephemeral, world.

A seemingly off-hand phrase you used touched some thoughts about
my circumstances. You refer to my "anger at the world." It's true I
have much anger, but to say I am angry at the world not only misses
the point but casts much doubt about any of the constructive energy
my anger has generated.* I think sometimes you think of me as a foolish misanthrope whose frustrations drove him to extremes of social
behavior. Surely you have learned some things about the malaise of this
country and the epiphenomenon I and others represent. At another
point you say it is not like me to be ungiving, indicating the ambiguous thought-feelings you have always had towards me.

A recent issue of Time magazine coos seductively that Amerika is
"cooling off," that the violent convulsions of '69, '70 have passed and
that sober reflexion about this country's destiny shows we are a good
people who sometimes go astray but generally tread the virtuous path.
If you want to believe a man who is often very angry but nevertheless
sometimes possesses a remarkable ear, I tell you we are living in the eye
of the hurricane. That the violent and irrepressible winds of change are
swirling round us throughout a world that will no longer pay the bill of
our government's rapine appetite. And that soon the tremors of the last
couple of years will be as a sleeping lion lazily swatting a fly with his tail.

Incidentally, it would be more than foolish if you thought you and
our boy can escape to a nirvana in California or Israel. (Israel?! ! !)
Our world is smaller today than Jonah's when he tried to flee the judg-
ment of his god. And the thing you would be attempting to flee makes
Jonah's god seem like a small-time Ellery Queen.

Sam Melville
#26124

---

* JM: If any single phrase could capture the ideological dynamic between my mother and
father, this would be it.

April 7, 1971

Dearest brother John,

This is just another brief note, i'm sorry, i liked your last 2 letters much. Of course send Liberation and the YSA pub. I haven't gotten my books yet but they're screwing me around a little. I don't mind the keeplocks at all; i need the time alone desperately sometimes. the big disadvantage about being keeplocked is that it goes on your record and when you come up for parole they sock it to you. i can receive visits so don't worry about coming up in vain.

A while back i saw a picture of an Israeli prison with Palestinians in a compound making barbed wire fences to be used against their own compatriots. I too am collaborating. I'm working in the Mess Hall so i can stay in the block with doors and quiet. We all have our price i guess.

Write soon and tell me which books you sent. It could be important. And *do* keep after Bill. He hasn't answered my cry of nearly a month ago.

Love to all.

Sam Melville
#26124
35-28

Bring up 2, 3 white X-large tee-shirts & gray or white sweatshirt when you come.

April 17, 1971

Dear Bill,

You haven't answered my cry of last month so I'm assuming you didn't get it. I'll repeat: the warden or his assistant has decided to prohibit some publications, namely, Monthly Review and "Seize the Time." They also have in their possession (although not officially banned yet) 4 issues of Socialist Revolution, "Selected Works of Lenin," "Permanent Revolution," and others unknown to me. Six previous copies of MR were approved, then, suddenly, with February's issue, the periodical was banned. Please get a court order as you did at West St. to have these admitted. I'm not anxious about "Sieze the Time" but I do want the others. MR represents clearly scientific approaches to problems otherwise only dealt with viscerally. The same for Socialist Revolution, a quarterly out of San Francisco. It seems whenever these cretins see the word Revolution they instinctively pull out their black stamp. Please help me with this or advise me what to do. We are permitted to send and receive unopened mail from attorneys now so if you were before, you needn't be inhibited now.

Write soon.

Sam

If you need names:
Supt. (Warden) Vincent Mancusi (Cretin)
Educational Supt. William Dickinson (Neanderthal)

April 18, 1971

[To John Cohen]

The news and moves from China are really great! Remember the Moysiev dance troupe and the result that had? Perhaps now we can divide the world up for keeps between US, USSR and the Peoples Republic of Mao. I hope your ping pong game is in shape.

Nothing new happening here of course. Met a man who looks about 50 but says he's 31. Says he refuses to count the jail time. Also another friend (?), anyway, someone I can argue with over political abstractions. He's a terrible cynic but well read and tremendous powers of description. The more than a little touch of bathos in his aspect makes him very funny and when i'm not lamenting his cynicism, my sides are splitting over his incessant characterizations of people and events.

There are indications the hacks are engaging in overt terrorism for a change. Conflicting reports have emerged but something's up for sure. They're all pretty pissed about the great man Sullivan and that

Good Friday morn. I'm writing a song about the affair—sort of like the Stagolee ballad or Jesse James.*†

I hope your country plans work out. You make it sound very confusing. What book are you indexing? And what kind of stuff are you doing on guitar-banjo?

Some books came this week. Lenin & Trotsky, I think, also Socialist Revolution magazine. I haven't seen anything yet because they haven't passed the censor. I'm sure there'll be trouble and I'm relying on Crain to get the court order. I still haven't heard from him you know. My friend has a term for lawyers. It's said very quickly so it comes out one word—lawyerliarleech.

I'm sorry if some of this is illegible. I wrote it off the top and I don't really have much to say, evidently.

Hope to see you soon.

Sam Melville
#26124

The nuts came. Thank you much. Inexplicably they won't let the cereal in tho they have in the past.

---

* Cohen: A prisoner named Sullivan escaped from Attica—the first one ever.
† SF: Attica was supposed to be escape-proof, but thirty-two-year-old Joseph "Mad Dog" Sullivan proved that wrong. Sullivan was a colorful character from Rockaway Beach serving a twenty- to thirty-year sentence for a hold-up slaying. He escaped on Good Friday, April 9, 1971, hidden inside a flour sack on a truck while four accomplices distracted the driver by playing a guitar. He was captured forty days later in Greenwich Village, having gotten married while on the lam. He managed to make parole in 1975 with the help of Ramsey Clark but was sent back for life for committing several more murders. (The FBI thought he was a "contract killer" for the Gambino crime family.) A movie was planned about his life, *Tears After Tiers* starring Jon Voight, but was never made. It is not known if Sam's song about "the great man Sullivan" was ever finished, but given Sam's musical talent and Sullivan's fascinating story, that would have been some song. "Attica Escape in a Sack?," *New York Post*, October 15, 1971.

May 7, 1971

[To his lawyers]
Dear People,

Man, it was certainly relieving to hear from you. J.C. told me you had written to [Warden] Mancusi. I think that's what got my books thru so quickly. I will deal with the eight points in your letter of May 6, 1971.

(1)   To this date i have received all literature that i know for sure has been sent to me except Seale's "Seize the Time." There was a long delay for the Feb. Monthly Review but i got it last week. They had written a form attached to my correspondence folder banning MR but your weight changed that.

(2)   I cannot possibly remember the "details of each and every disciplinary proceeding" in the time i've been here. Nor is it germane to the direction of your energies. The mickey mouse bullshit they pull on individuals will fall away once we successfully attack the fundamental question of prisoners' rights. If you're intimate with the Appeals' decision of the Sostre case you know that really we lost (potentially) much more than we gained.* But so you know what i'm talking about, here are some of the things they've busted me for:

Walking with hands in pockets; Refusing to go to the messhall because i wasn't hungry; Refusal to line up according to height; wearing a white shirt rather than grey to tribunal proceedings;

---

* SF: Sam's comment about the "Sostre case" shows he had read this decision. Although Sam Melville and Martin Sostre never met, they had a mutual admiration and respect for one another as reflected in their letters. Although they were from vastly different backgrounds, the similarities in their lives are astounding. Among the many ironies about these men, in 1967, while Sostre was awaiting trial on a vicious COINTELPRO frame-up, a "liberal" Buffalo law firm "bungled the case and then abandoned it" due to political pressure (and, in my opinion, racism). He was forced to trial and received a forty-one-year sentence. Years later, the same "liberal" law firm hired a lawyer, Vincent Tobia, who as a New York State trooper claimed he was the shooter of Sam Melville. *Bar Association of Erie County 1997–1998 Pictorial Directory* (Lake Helen, FL: 1998), 75; Martin Sostre, *Letters from Prison* (Buffalo: Martin Sostre Defense Committee, 1968), 35–40; Vincent Copeland, *The Crime of Martin Sostre* (New York: McGraw-Hill, 1970), 25–27, 141–142; Bob McCubbin, ed., *Martin Sostre in Court* (Buffalo: Martin Sostre Defense Committee, 1969), 7, 23.

Wearing a sweatshirt to the messhall; taking a day off from a 7-day work week in the messhall.

All of these things are written in the report each officer fills out but the charge you're penalized for is disobeying an officer, or some "rational" shit like that. I'm not sure of the exact figure but i've accumulated something around 20 days keeplock so far. I don't mind the K.L. personally; i get a lot done. But the hanger is that every 3 days K.L. equals 1 day off your "good time." So your "conditional release" is always being pushed further away.

(3)   See number (2).

(4)   Clearly, withholding literature that is available at any bookstore is a restriction on my social or political beliefs. Being keeplocked effectively prohibits me from communicating these social/political beliefs to my brothers. Another rule says that literature approved for one inmate will be confiscated if found in the possession of another. This last i have never seen enforced but it is punishable and has certainly dampened communal feelings to some extent.

(5)   I had an interview with my parole officer shortly after i got here. (A monomaniacal penchant for swatting flies. He had two varieties of swatters and insisted upon demonstrating his technique. A neanderthal pig yahoo.) He told me my conditional release date and when i would be eligible to see the parole board (April 1976). Other than that, nothing.

(6)   Most of us have difficulty with the oldliners; those pigs who can't get used to not being able to bust heads when somebody doesn't jump when they belch. The younger hacks are easier. They can't seem to remember the rules themselves most of the time.

(7)   H. Whalen, hall officer of D block; W. Dickinson, educational supervisor; Lennox, package room officer. These 3 seem to go out of their way to fuck me.*

---

* SF: William C. Dickinson, deputy superintendent of program services at Attica, was the subject of many inmate complaints. Among other things, they felt he thwarted their hopes for an education by rejecting offers from area colleges to teach free courses to them at Attica. He also acted as censor for Mancusi and denied inmates many items to which they legally were entitled. The removal of Dickinson was added to the ongoing demand for the removal of Mancusi and Dr. Williams. "Inmates' Demands at Attica Include Dismissal of Three," *Buffalo Evening News*, December 3, 1971.

(8)   There are many men here who have been either victim or witness to "systematic mistreatment." Three who will definitely testify should it come to that are ————— and ————— of the Young Lords Party here at Attica and ————— of the Panthers. Of course there are doubtless many others but as i write this i am in K.L. I was transferred from C block without requesting it. So i'm locking my door until they move me back.

I'm not sure i understand fully what you mean by a "full scale 'legal political'" attack; but, other than the petty indecencies all inmates must live with, the following are some of those that most of us feel must be changed:

Above all is *access to the media*. Several media representatives have filed a show cause in behalf of 3 boxed prisoners here who took part in the Auburn rebellion last year. We don't know the outcome yet. N.Y. State is one of the few states (if not the only state) in the east that doesn't permit prisoner contact with the press. We do not have the right to petition among ourselves and we have very adumbrated rights to assembly. We are left with nothing except riots to bring our plight before the public. The authorities are very frightened of publicity. They enforce barbaric regulations that 18th-century Italians would be ashamed of. Their experience has been: every exposure has proved costly. They have to dig into their treasury, spend money that might otherwise be graft; they have to recondition their piglettes as well as hire more of them. And further up the ladder of course are the political ramifications. Prison authorities and parole board members are political appointees. If unfavorable publicity regarding prisons can affect a gubernatorial election the whole system gets shook-up.

The *parole system must be attacked*. Most men in prison are violators. The conditions of parole are so degrading that many men stay in prison and max out. For this, as well as most of the things here, i refer you to the Fortune Society. Ex-cons turned liberals. I don't know how much headway they've made but they have a lot of information you might otherwise spend much time gathering. They have an office in Greenwich Village, i think.

There are several men here who have been offered "conditional release." That is, they have done 2/3 of their maximum sentence and have accumulated the rest as "good time." However, the state now demands that they sign a statement saying in effect that they will live under the conditions of parole. If you sign the form and go home and later violate, you come back to prison and all the time you spent on the street doesn't count. E.g., there is a man here who is finishing up a 12-year bit for a crime he committed 16 years ago!

Unlimited correspondence and non-censorship of mail goes without saying. And, incidentally, if you think this letter will not be read by the pigs, guess again. When we are in the yard or messhall they shake down our cells. Men who they are sure have outside help with legal matters have the legal papers and correspondence rifled.

If prisoners are obliged to work, the state should be obliged to pay comparable street *salaries*. Otherwise, let the state tap the vast unemployment ranks and not have inmates feel like collaborators.

As far as *rehabilitation* is concerned, some of the chief officers have openly admitted to me (in some of my many "court" appearances) they don't believe in it. The physical aspect of the *education plant* here at Attica cannot accommodate more than 1/10 of the inmate population. Those that work in *industry* (some 30%) are shown a simple two or three-step task and day after day, year after year, repeat those two or three steps. They are handsomely rewarded with between 35¢ and 80¢ per diem. The state machinery is self-supporting and many inmates who should know say a good profit is turned to boot. The rest of us mop floors, clean windows, mow lawns, etc.

Of course most of the inmate population is black. But in my several outside visits with J.C. seldom have i seen a black man with his loved ones. Many of the men come from NYC and their families simply cannot afford to visit. Nor are they likely to find lodging once they get here. We want either the *state to provide the transportation and lodging or put us in prisons close to our homes.*

The list is endless: conjugal visits, commissary prices, less pork in the diet, access to viewing TV, Puerto Rican recognition, guards representative of the ethnic population (there are *no*, repeat *no* black guards at Attica and one, count him, one Puerto Rican). Let me say while i recognize the importance of all this to me personally, and to some extent acknowledge it as a valid political endeavor, i consider it peripheral to my political education and potential. Having correspondence with a lawyer certainly makes the pigs more wary of leaning on a man and for that of course i want you to keep in touch. But there are men here, good, articulate people who have for years been trying to effect meaningful reform, with whom you could probably get more mileage with than me.

The sentences of Sharon, Robin, et al. were certainly a rotten deal.* I hope they are planning to appeal. From my perspective of the N.Y. Times the Panther denoument is not entirely bleak. I pray that's true.

I enclose two ominous onion skins [warrants pertaining to Sam's case]. I ignored them when i got them at Sing Sing, but recently i asked the chief clerk to see if i had any outstanding warrants. Indeed i do. Please see what they mean and let me know as soon as possible. Also, see if it is recorded anywhere that my sentence for federal is running concurrently with the state.

Certain friends have advised me to withdraw my plea and threaten to go to trial. They say i will probably be offered a reduced sentence. What do you think?

Write soon. Give my love to all.

Sam

I have a carbon on this. Should you need to, refer to page number. This is not paranoia. It's good old bourgeois efficiency.

May 15, 1971

Dear Bill,

I offer the following report. As of this date I remain K.L. until either I hear from you or they capitulate and restore my former assignment. I can only guess at Mancusi's reasons. What an irrational wounded beast will do is not always analyzable. Under no circumstances will I accept any other [work] assignment so don't write and say you're trying to straighten things out and until then I should cooperate. Should you find it necessary to come up, see J.C. about a place to stay.

---

* Cohen: They got from four to six years for the firebombing.

I am in good spirits and on the threshhold of becoming a Marxist, shedding all the mysticism that determined so much of my past. We just got word of the Panther acquittal. Great, great news!

Sam

Report

Since December 1970, I have been trying to get assigned as a C block porter. I was told by other inmates that if I worked a while in the messhall I would probably get it. Although the messhall work is long hard hours and 7 days per week, you lock in C block and that's where you have to be to get a C block porter assignment. On March 10, I moved to C block assigned to the messhall. I worked hard and cooperated in every way, without incident or report until April 30. When I was returning from work at 5:30 I stopped to chat briefly with a friend who locks a few doors away. Virtually all inmates do this every night until the officer on duty rings the bell to lock in.

As I prepared to leave for work the next morning I found I was keeplocked. This was Saturday May 1. Since the disciplinary tribunal does not meet on weekends I had to wait until Monday to know the charges against me. The charges read to me in "court" Monday said I refused to lock in when told to by the officer on duty and also that I made a contemptuous gesture to the officer. I of course denied the charge. The charge was signed by an officer Brown. The chief officer Mulrooney then asked me who locked in 36-5 cell, that I felt compelled to speak to every night. I said I didn't see how that was relevant. Mulrooney said he didn't care what I thought was relevant and insisted I answer his question. I said if he wanted to know so badly he could easily look it up. He then sentenced me to 5 days K.L. with 2 days served (the Saturday & Sunday preceding my "court" appearance).*

---

* SF: The "chief officer Mulrooney" (some sources say "Maroney") who sent Sam to keep-lock played a key role in events leading to Sam's death, too. Most sources say a "misunderstanding" occurred in A Yard when Black inmate Leroy Dewer and White inmate Ray Lamorie were practicing football plays and Mulrooney thought that they were fighting. An altercation ensued and, as the New York Times wrote, "Lieut. Richard Mulrooney, a seasoned correctional officer . . . ordered Dewar out of the yard—to 'the box,' or segregation. . . . A rumor that the two inmates had been beaten . . . began spreading through A block's 12 galleries." Joseph Lelyveld et al. "The Attica Revolt," New York Times, October 4, 1971.

On Wednesday May 5, I was released and reported back to the messhall. The next day I was told to pack up, I was moving. I asked where to and was told one flight downstairs to the C block porters company. Naturally I was glad. I reported to work after moving my things and was told I was an extra, that I would be assigned in a few days.

On Tuesday May 11, I was called in to the desk and told I was moving to D block to be assigned to the State shop (where incoming inmates are fitted for clothing). Normally you are not moved from one block to another unless you request it. I protested I had made no request to move and did not want to move. The officers said they would have to move me if I refused. They suggested I lock in at my new location and I would go to "court" the next day. I did. At court the chief officer said he didn't know why I was moved and that I should put in a request to see the Deputy Warden and he could explain. He further suggested I report to work as assigned to avoid further difficulties. I did as instructed. The next day, Thursday May 13, I was called to the administration block for an interview with Mr. Pheil, the assistant deputy warden.* I asked him why I was moved. He replied Mr. Mancusi had instructed it, that I was a security risk and could better be supervised in D block. I asked in what way was D block any more secure than C block. He replied he was only following orders and if I wanted to see the warden I should put in an interview request.

I returned to my cell and informed the officer on duty I was refusing any further cooperation. I was immediately K.L. On the next morning, Friday, May 14, I appeared once more before the disciplinary tribunal. I told them I was refusing any further assignment until either I spoke with my attorney or they restored my former assignment as C block porter. They said the warden had ordered the change and they had not the power to move me back. They gave me 7 days K.L. for refusing work.

---

* SF: Karl Pfeil became an important part of Attica history on February 4, 1992, when a federal court jury in Buffalo found him guilty of cruel and unusual punishment against the Attica inmates after a three-month trial. Pfeil was held liable for the reprisals because, as deputy superintendent, he supervised the inmates' "re-housing" on September 13 and did nothing to stop the beatings and the torture. Later that night, he took part personally in more inmate beatings, particularly of Rosenberg and Blyden, while they were locked inside their cells. Dan Herbeck, "Riot Leader Accuses Top Attica Chief," *Buffalo News*, October 31, 1991.

History of the Attica Strike*

Sometime in the spring of 1970, a group of inmates in "B" block drew up a petition asking for higher wages and lower commissary prices. ("B" block, with 500 inmates, is immediately attached to the industrial plant. Most of those who lock in "B" work in the metal shop, producing state-used material, *sold* to other state institutions.) The petitioners gathered around 125 names on the petition and presented it to Warden Mancusi. The administration selected from the list of names those they thought were responsible and immediately "boxed" them (put in punitive segregation). Subsequently, most of "B" block locked their doors and refused to work. The administration had *all* of "B" block lock in and kept it locked for about two weeks. Most of the "leaders" who had been boxed were shipped out to other institutions. Things returned to normal with the administration saying it was considering some salary changes (and they reduced commissary immediately).

In the fall, a directive from Albany came listing the various jobs and grouping them, attaching a wage scale to each group. *All* salaries were raised considerably, e.g.; metal shop workers jumped from 15¢/day to 55¢ to $1.00/day; school instructors from 15¢ to 55¢ to 85¢/day; etc.

Since the initial commissary price drop, prices have been raised *monthly* to a point now where every item has increased over the original price prior to the reduction. Sometimes this had been done by changing the unit price, e.g., prior to the strike, a 20 oz. jar of wheat germ cost 54¢, presently, a 12 oz. jar of wheat germ costs 48¢

An Anatomy of the Laundry†‡

Because of the Pig-santioned Right to capitalize on the needs of other inmates, and the accompanying fear of losing their lucrative

---

* Cohen: This is Sam's brief history of the August 19, 1970, strike which he learned about and which is referred to in my introduction. His sources are different from mine, and so are some of his facts.

† Cohen: "An Anatomy of the Laundry" grew out of Fred LeShure's weekly sociology class, which Sam began to attend in the spring.

‡ SF: Edward T. "Fred" LeShure was a disc jockey from Corning who was in Attica for selling heroin. It was his "sociology" class that enabled inmates from all four blocks to meet and discuss strategy and make plans. When guards found out, the class was shut down and LeShure was put in the box. In addition to politics, LeShure and Sam shared a love of music, and both had folk guitars they played at Attica. Brian B. King, "Attica Revisited," *New York*

Jobs, our brothers who work in the Laundry have become docile slaves, House Niggers, and therefore, an impediment to our Liberation.

These Laundry slaves, who, for the most part, are some well-meaning and intelligent individuals, have been so thoroughly indoctrinated and duped by this Dog-eat-Dog system that they don't even realize that they have become House-Niggers and instruments of their own oppression.

How does the Pig exploit the Laundry slave? How does the Pig profit? Like so: The average wage of a unionized Dry Laundry Worker on the outside is 3.50 per hour, whereas, the average wage of a Laundry slave here is 25¢ per day. The Laundry slave works 3 1/2 hours per day for 25¢; an outside unionized worker would earn $10.50 for the same work. Projected to a monthly basis, the slave gets $5.50, while an outsider gets $231.00. There are 40 slaves in the Laundry for a monthly payroll of $220.00. If the State were forced to pay union wages, the payroll would be $9,240.00. Yearly, it's $2,640.00 as compared to $110,880.00 (Dig). Our active support of this saves the State $108,240.00 annually.

HOW?

The slaves are allowed three Laundry contracts at one carton (33.50) per month. So the slaves *real* salary is $10.50 per month, plus the $5.50. Who pays this? WE DO! We pay the slave $3.50 for four work days a month, work which he completes in no time at all. The Pig pays the slave $5.00 for 22 days *hard work*! Thus, the State gets 18 more days of labor than we do, for our $3.50, and the State only pays the slave $1.50 more. Now, I ask you, is that ignorant slave with the crease in his

---

Post Daily Magazine, June 5, 1972, 25. Another inmate teacher who worked with Sam was William Coons. Paroled just before the rebellion, he capitalized on his time at Attica with a *New York Times Magazine* story that he turned into a book. He wrote of Sam, "Melville took a desk across the room from me in the cramped quarters of Cell Study. Nobody talked to him the first few days, which was customary treatment for a new instructor, and he had the added stigma of being anti-U.S. society. . . . Melville was a confirmed Marxist-Leninist. He was also an idealist and, in my opinion, a Romanticist. This all may sound contradictory, but that's exactly the stuff of revolution. . . . I think even he was shocked to some degree by the conditions he found around him at Attica." William R. Coons, "An Attica Graduate Tells His Story," in *Prisons, Protest, and Politics*, ed. by Burton M. Atkins and Henry R. Glick (Englewood Cliffs, NJ: Prentice-Hall, 1972), 117–118. Coons's piece was first published in the *New York Times Magazine* on October 10, 1971, and was subsequently expanded into *Attica Diary* (New York: Stein and Day, 1972).

pants slick, or is the Pig *slick*? The Pig gets the cash saving, the labor, and the wages payed to the slave as soon as the Commissary opens.

So, you see Brother-Man, we have the power to stop this. No Riots or Violence but just refusing to cooperate in maintaining our own misery just because we want a crease in our pants and don't want to wash our own dirty underwear. Yes, let's force the Pig to bring in those unionized laundries and pay that $110,880.00 a year to run the laundry. By saving $3.50, we can cost him $110,880.00 that he can't afford.

Brother-Man, now is the time to act!

STOP PAYING!

JUST HOLD BACK AND MAKE THIS COOKIE CRUMBLE !!!!!!!

PEACE & POWER

YOUR (SLAVE) LAUNDRY MAN

RIGHT ON ! ! ! ! ! RIGHT ON ! ! ! ! ! RIGHT ON ! ! ! ! !

May 18, 1971

Dear Swami [John Cohen],

I got the Spring issue of Liberation recently. It's mostly devoted to the war and antiwar efforts. Not much about liberation in the sense I'm coming to know the term. Also a couple of pages of Julius Lester. The more one reads Julius Lester* the more one regrets he doesn't sing & play guitar more. The man is the embodiment of the artistic/intellectual dialectic: while his fingers on the guitar instinctively respond to the surrounding culture, those same fingers become dull stumps when performing on the typewriter.

I hope you're getting Socialist Revolution. I'm very impressed with it and I want to talk with you about it. Those early impressions I spoke about at our last visit were stupid and based on a brief scanning. Comparing SR to Liberation may be unfair but Herbert Gintis reminds us of (SR Vol. I, No. 3, pp. 14, 15) something so many have seemed to have forgotten: Not only might "the oppressed" not have the *power*

---

* SF: Sam knew Julius Lester from working at the *Guardian*. Lester wrote a weekly column there. He also wrote for *Libertarian*, published books, and had a WBAI show and was a recorded folk singer.

to enforce their will, but in common with most individuals they do not evaluate society on the basis of its conformability to the radical's abstract standard of justice. Rather, they act and evaluate on the basis of perceived self-interest, and of value and belief patterns promoted by the ruling class to secure social harmony and integration. . . . A "radical consciousness" will spread among youth only insofar as it responds to their basic needs, and will effect revolution only insofar as it is close to the sources of economic power.

Gintis warns us against hanging our revolutionary hopes entirely on the young, a bag I was into for so long, but the extent the educated youth has revolutionary potential is the extent they realize their status as the emerging proletariat necessarily technicalized to meet the demands of corporate capitalism.

James Weinstein, while I certainly respect his analysis, strikes me as that giant Roc or Simurgh of Sinbad's Persia. Having seen the world thrice destroyed, he is quietly, dispassionately sifting thru the ashes for the perhaps two or three charred members that may fit together.

Notes: If the Militant is the atavism of Lev Bronstein, it looks very bad for the forces of the permanent revolution.

The sentences for Sharon et al were incredible! They must certainly appeal or even go to trial. Four years for an unlit jar of gasoline! Even fascism can't make that kind of shit stick. The Panther news of course was great. Every man in grey up here was ecstatic with "Right On's" and "Power To The People."*

Well I collaborated for two months and still they won't let me be. Last week they moved me back to D block. I've closed my door and refused to work and I'm waiting for either word from Crain or the pigs to capitulate. I may be locked in for quite some time so hurry and send me names and addresses for correspondence and maybe visits.

Love
Sam Melville
#26124

---

* SF: The "Panther news" was the joyous acquittal of every defendant on every charge in the fifteen-month trial of the Panther 21 (a.k.a. Panther 13) trial.

May 19, 1971

Dear Bill,

On Wednesday, May 19, 1971, I was called for an interview with FBI agents Biard & Davison. They told me what they wanted to talk to me about and read off the warning of rights. They then asked if I would speak to them and I said I would have to speak to my lawyer first.

They had asked me if I would answer questions regarding the Milwaukee Federal building explosion in Sept. '69. They then asked if I would answer questions concerning the whereabouts of certain fugitives.

After I said I would have to speak to my lawyer I asked to see the pictures in front of him (Biard). He showed me pix of the four accused of the Wisconsin Univ. Math Center and pix of Jane and Pat Swinton. He asked if I knew any of them and I said I'd have to speak with my lawyer.

I then left the room.

By the way I'm still in keeplock waiting to be either moved again or I hear from you.

Sam

June 2, 1971

Dear Bill,

Still waiting to here from you. They're fucking with my mail, books, and visiting rights. And I'm practicing anal distension to be prepared. I'll either be boxed or shipped out by June 3.

June 4, 1971

Dear Bill,

Without hearing from you I have no way of knowing if my letters are getting thru. Perhaps it is excessive paranoia but, law or no law, the pigs are known to open mail and conveniently lose inmate mail.*

I have been moved into observation (box) [solitary], where all my possessions were taken and are being returned piecemeal. At the assistant superintendent hearing I was sentenced to 30 days in the box and 15 days lost good time.

I have no intention of returning to work. That will mean no good time and probably no parole in addition to remaining boxed for the remainder of the sentence. What I want from you is to force them to give me *all* my literature and my guitar. It's likely the books and papers will be returned eventually but they have said definitely no to the guitar.

Please answer soon.

S

June 5, 1971

Dear brother,

i'm in the box now for refusing work. still allowed visits & mail but no packages. (i enjoyed the last package very much.) We're allowed 5 books plus mags & newspapers. *please do* renew the times sub. it runs out this month. if you can afford it, get a year's sub ($57) because i'm sure it's going up soon due to the mail rates.

re visits: a gentle young woman and man i know from philly paid a surprise visit 3 weeks ago. a beautiful time. the rule is: *anyone* may apply for one visit and will be granted permission at the discretion of the warden. the philly people were granted permission as soon as they applied, visits or correspondence on a permanent basis will be considered after. caveats: fingerprinting required; no ex-convicts; no press;

---

* SF: The phrase "law or no law" refers to *Sostre v. Rockefeller*.

avoid weekends if possible; come early—it takes about 90 minutes to process. *all, all, all* and *any* visits will be most welcome.*

more hard reality going down for the left—mao backs bandaranaike against rebels; mao backs west pakistan in another bloodbath, protecting "socialism" under the banner of national survival has doubtless cost more lives in the past 50 years than any catastrophe since the flood. china 1927, spain 1936, USSR 1937, china again 1944, indonesia 1965, greece 1965, now young, brave ceylonese and bangla desh by perhaps the hundreds of thousands. but now it's not just enough to acquiesce; mao has to send planes and tanks to yahya kahn. to any impartial observer, the primary contradiction today is not between the workers and the bourgeoisie; its not between the neo-colonialist and the 3rd world; the primary contradiction has at last been reduced to the simplest of terms: between the armed and the unarmed. so after 100 years of rhetorical wrangling, social darwinism emerges triumphant over "socialism," capitalism, or any other shit man uses to justify, rationalize, deify his actions. so be it.

we've had victories, but some of the flock are getting too fat to fly long distances. and their honking sounds gurgled. and the dark erythric fluid dripping from their beaks makes it disconcerting to embrace them.

read yeats' "to a shade." its a brief ode to parnell. it could have been written yesterday to che.

please come up this month if possible.

Sam Melville
#26124 CE-5

---

* Cohen: After Sam was transferred from West Street in April 1970, I was the only visitor he had—excepting the gentle couple he speaks of here. I saw him once every month for two consecutive days. During the year of his guerrilla activities, Sam stopped seeing most of his old friends, even those who were political, and saw mostly people who were involved in his group. These people could not visit him in prison, and Sam, very conscious of the fact that visiting him might endanger or worry his old friends, was unwilling to ask them to do anything they might feel hesitant about. The surprise visit of the gentle couple apparently made him change his attitude, and we began to arrange for other people to see him.

June 20, 1971

Dear Mr. Oswald,*†

I am in punitive segregation at Attica prison.

Chronology of events:

May 7: Moved without request from C block porter to D block State Shop.

May 10: Interview with Mr. Pfeil to ascertain why I was moved. He said the warden thinks I am better supervised in D block. I refused to work until restored to C block.

May 12: Sentenced to 8 days Keeplock.

May 21: Again refuse to work.

May 22: Sentenced to Keeplock pending interview with Deputy Warden.

June 4: Mr. Vincent sentences me to 30 days in punitive segregation with 15 days lost time.

June 15: When returning from exercise yard I am told to fold my arms (for the first time). I refuse.

June 11: Sentenced to "14 days Keeplock or until he conforms to rules."

I want to be restored to my former position as C block porter and my lost time returned to me. If I am to remain in punitive segregation I want exercise privileges.

Sam Melville
#26124

---

* Cohen: Sent to the commissioner of correction.

† JM: This letter along with "An Anatomy of the Laundry" prompted Oswald to meet with Five Company inmates to discuss reforms. According to conflicting reports, Oswald met only with my father, who was in segregation at the time. (Although despite film showing the two of them within mere feet of each other in D Yard, in his memoir Oswald denies ever meeting my father: "As for me, I never met Mr. Melville at all" [p. 23].) Regardless, it's undisputed that Oswald never met with the rest of Five Company. He claimed his wife had taken ill and left Attica abruptly the next morning. This perceived snub, some claim, is what triggered the uprising several days later.

July 1, 1971

Dear brother

Heres that book list again:
Deutscher: 3 vols Trotsky biography—Oxford Press
Marcuse: Essay on Liberation
Selected Writings on Marxism—Internat. Pub.
Rubin: We Are Everywhere—Simon & Shuster*†
Alinsky: Handbook for Radicals—R H

I also would like some work with an in-depth exam of the Spartacus League of 1918 Germany (Rosa Luxemburg & Karl Liebknecht). Many of the books I have make teasing references to it but nothing more. What I want is a brief chronological history of the League and an explanation of their strategy. Ask the people at Monthly Review or International. They would know where to go.

Also a reliable Spanish-English dictionary.

The RH dictionary at last came. Its a good desk edition—better than Merriam—but I've already found some gross errors:

funk-y^1—overcome with fear; terrified; 2. depressed
funk-y^2—evil smelling; foul.

On page XXXii is a guide to show how to find a word if you can't spell it, that is, the various spellings each pronunciation can have. There's nothing under "l" to show its pronunciation in "colonel." The prefix (not uncommon) "coe" as in coelacouth & coenesthesia is pronounced "see," but you'd never find out from Random House. The Chart of Indo-European Languages on p. X could have been much better done indicating the closer ties of English to French & the other Latins. Realizing the pressures of space, the "Historical Sketch of the English Language" could have said a lot more by eliminating the "mysticism" and adding a chronological chart. The explanation of the development of Modern English (p. XIV) would make Sapir turn in his grave.

---

* DV: In *We Are Everywhere*, Jerry Rubin—a close confidant of FBI informant George Demmerle (who was instrumental in the arrest of Sam)—discusses his relationship, and surprise and dismay, at learning Demmerle was an informant after the Melville arrests.
† JV: Jerry Rubin (1938–1994), along with Abbie Hoffman, founded in 1967 the Youth International Party, or Yippie. The Yippies engaged radical political theatrics, like burning money at the New York Stock Exchange, and preached a message of youth revolution. Rubin and Hoffman were prominent defendants in the Chicago Seven trial.

But, thank you, thank you!

I applied for permission to write to Charles. I get an answer soon.

I really enjoy the visits. They pull me from these ruts of Times-Study-Headstands that I tend to ossify in. As I study & learn, the visits get so much more meaningful. I shed more & more this shroud of incantation I use to hide ignorance. Each return to the cell after a visit makes me attack this ignorance with greater determination.

You are going to talk to Sue about writing and try and locate Robert.*

Love
Sam Melville
#26124

July 2, 1971

Bill

They've taken my earphones away—again for not folding arms. Each time I leave the cell for shower, shave, meet the panel, I get another report for not folding arms. First they took away excercise yard, now earphones. Next it will be light bulb and newspaper and books.

I've decided not to leave my cell anymore which means they'll drag me I guess. Can you get these motherfuckers off my back?

Try Oswald or Field, the appeals court head. Anybody!

July 17, 1971

My dear Charles

I recently received permission to correspond w/ you. I hope thats acceptable. JC is t only person I see or hear from to keep my head together just enough to keep me from letting this time beat me. Perhaps we don't know each other well but I trust you & know you are sincere.

---

* Cohen: Old friends Sam wanted to get in touch with.

Before going into anything please write & let me know if you're interested. Should you like to visit (which I would like very much) you would probably be granted permission for one visit upon writing to t warden. He would give consideration to further visits if we wished them. You would have to submit to finger-printing.

In any event, please do me this one great favor: Random House recently sent me their College Dictionary after I hounded John for months. It was promptly stolen & there's little likelihood I'll recover it. In John's abscence could you pester somebody high up in RH to send me another? Although often plagued by poor expression, I am passionate about dictionaries & vow I'll take great care w/ the next.

I received an offer from Ramparts Press this week to review some books including "Weatherman," which I am not permitted to read. There are many legal, political & aesthetic considerations to be hassled over but I've been walking in t clouds since opening t letter. I've felt *so* useless lately.

Please write soon & let me know if we can have some kind of contact. If your answer must be negative, don't hesitate: I do understand.

My love to you & Emily,
Sam Melville
#26124

July 27, 1971

Ramparts Press,

In re your request for my review of "Weatherman":

As if legal, political & aesthetic hassles weren't enough, Senor Jose Dolores Revueltas further complicates matters by adding moral problems. Precisely how am I to relate to the following: "I believe my secretary wrote you last week concerning this proposal, but being a woman, she does not always phrase these things properly . . . "—is this some kind of put-on? Some dumb machismo making sport of presumably past sexist attitudes? Or is it serious? Can it possibly be serious in this day?? I find it difficult to believe that a beautiful & dedicated sister as

Dolores J. can be associated in any way with Senor (or is it Herr) Jose Dolores Revueltas.*

If Ramparts Press & I are to have any future together, I will deal exclusively with Dolores J. Correspondence from your "Direcotr (sic) of Promotion" will not be acknowledged. Furthermore, I insist that my fee be paid to Dolores J. that she may escalate la lucha toward her liberation.

As to the actual review, I expect I'd feel irked enough to make some kind of response if I could only read the book! Unless sufficient pressure is brought to bear on the local Houghnhnms who determine what I read & write, any arrangement we come to will remain strictly academic. To this date this institution has received "Weatherman," "Black Power & the Garvey Movement," and "Marxism in Our Time." They have not been given to me. There are also restrictions regarding inmates writing for publication.

If you're serious about pressing the matter, and I certainly hope you are, please contact my lawyers, William Crain and Martin Stolar, Law Offices, 640 Broadway, N.Y.C., N.Y., 10012.

In any event, please respond to this so that I may know you received it.

Sam Melville

---

* Cohen: On July 12, Sam received a letter from *Ramparts*, written by Dolores Janiewski, asking him to review *Weatherman*, a book the prison authorities had been holding back from him for several months. Sam had his lawyer working on getting the book in. Then, on July 22, he received a letter from Jose Dolores Revueltas. This is the letter he is responding to here. In reply to this letter, Sam received another letter from Dolores Janiewski, written August 11, explaining that "Your anger was beautiful as you came to the defense of me and my sisters. But I feel ashamed now, because you see Jose Dolores Revueltas is me, it's my nom de guerre. The letter was written because I was afraid the other hadn't gotten through because it wasn't businesslike enough, so I was trying to be as piggy as possible, and also letting out my frustrations from the monotony and the oppressiveness of this job, typing someone else's words all day, so I wrote as they might write if they wrote truthfully and typed their own letters. . . . I hope matters are now set right. I'm sorry if my actions caused you any pain, dear brother. . . . Dolores J.

THE ICED PIG*

Number 1

Attica Newsletter

Power brothers! Poder hermanos!

This is t first issue of what will be a continuing project. A project that will help to bring each other to an understanding of our place & role in neo-fascist Amerika & t American Auschwitz known as Attica.

Of primary importance is t coming awareness of ourselves as *political prisoners*. No matter how heinous t "crime" u have been convicted of, no matter how many people u offed, drugs u pushed, whores u ran, places u robbed, u are a political prisoner just as much as Angela. *Every act has a cause & effect.* T *cause* of your "crime" is that u found yourself in a society that offered no prospects for a life of fulfillment & sharing with your brothers & sisters. A society where u were taught to compete & beat t guy next to u because if u didn't, he'd beat u. A society whose every facet & angle is thoroughly controlled by t Pigdogs of t corporation giants of Amerika. T apparent *effect* of your "crime" is that now u find yourself locked behind tons of steel & concrete, completely brutalized, cut off from any warmth & affection. But t *real effect* is that u have become waste material to Amerika's ruling class. By your "crime" u have shown Amerika's bosses that u can't cooperate in t "free enterprise" system. That is to say, u won't accept $100 a week for breaking your balls while some fat-assed capitalist drives around in t Mercedes u paid for. By your "crime" u were only doing in a crude way what t Rockerfellers & Fords have been doing since they stole this country from t Indians 200 years ago.

Yes brothers, in every sense of t word we are political prisoners. And now we owe it to ourselves & t great masses of struggling humanity, to teach ourselves t truth of Amerika's myth. To forge ourselves into dedicated cadres committed to t construction of a society that will serve t needs of t people & make us into whole human beings at last.

---

* Cohen: This is the first issue of *The Iced Pig*, a clandestine newsletter which Sam wrote. It was handwritten, carbon-copied, and distributed by hand, secretly, passed from one group to the next. This issue came out at the end of July, 1971.

    Since *The Iced Pig* was handwritten—perhaps several times for each issue—Sam used simple time- and space-saving abbreviations: t=the, u=you, w/=with. In the personal letters that Sam wrote at this time he also used these abbreviations.

Future issues of The Iced Pig will discuss strategy & tactics of our role in t coming revolution. Every individual's participation is necessary if we are to continue to grow. Make your contribution known by joining t political rap sessions in your yard.

July 27, 1971

[To his lawyers]
Dear People,

I returned to t population July 11 none t worse for wear. Robin is here now & though we'd hoped to meet in a less restrictive environment, it's good to have him. We've gathered a coterie of young freaks & we rap politics alot. T place is beginning to crawl w/20yearoldnamvetheads busted for dope out of Rochester & Buffalo.

I'm sort of interested in doing t Ramparts review of Weatherman & at least i want to read t damned thing, so I ask that you make some special effort in this. Duplicate t 3 letters for your file; send t 2 letters from t Press back to me; mail my response to: Ramparts Press, 2512 Grove St., Berkeley, Calif., 94704. If you have anything to add, please do. They won't let my response out of here.

As per your instructions, i enclose this month's disciplinary proceedings. Also a copy (for your file) of a complaint against one Thomas Boyle, pig.* We are submitting t original to Mancusi tomorrow (7/28). SOP for dealing w/petitions is to lock all t signers up but we hear they're reluctant to do that now. I know this is one stupid small incident but it's our intention to file these complaints as they occur. We have only one other alternative to meet their aggression, and at this time geography is against that—not to mention technology.

As i asked before: respond soon so I know my mail gets to you. And send back t Ramparts Press letters.

Sam

---

* Cohen: "On Tuesday, July 27, 1971, officer Boyle of 'D' block bullied his way through the corridor near 'C' block, shoving and knocking several inmates of 5 and 2 company who were returning from the mess hall. Mr. Boyle had ample room to make his way without molesting others." This was signed by about fifteen inmates.

August 6, 1971

[To his lawyers]

Dear People

Enclosed is a health report & a draft of demands drawn up by some B block men whom i don't know. I think a revised copy was submitted to Albany recently but its not certain. A new "Manifesto" is currently being prepared, drawing largely from t enclosed with more specifics.

We are in need of one lawyer who can devote a significant part of his or her time to helping us w/ technicalities, keeping our stuff moving in t courts & meeting w/ us once a month for progress reports & *important* other things. Herman Schwartz's* office at t Univ. of Buffalo has helped a lot but he is apparently getting too busy to continue. We have 5 or 7 people (myself included) who would be listed as clients of this lawyer so hopefully we could all meet together—something we cannot do otherwise.

We have heard nothing of our complaint about pig Boyle except to note that rules about staying in line & talking in t corridor are being more strictly enforced.

---

* SF: Herman Schwartz had a significant role in D Yard during the uprising: on the second day of the uprising, September 10, Schwartz (who along with Ed Koren ran the ACLU Prison Rights Project in Buffalo) obtained the famous "no reprisals" injunction. Sam was at the leadership table when Schwartz presented it and, in Jerry Rosenberg's words, "One by one we denounced the thing as it went down the table. It was for only a single day, carried no official seal and was limited to 'administrative reprisals.' Words were exchanged, and Rosenberg tore the Injunction in half as the inmates cheered." Richard X. Clark told Tom Wicker that Schwartz "had a reputation . . . of 'talking down' to inmates and taking too long to handle their appeals." After the injunction debacle, Blyden and Rosenberg thought he was incompetent. Asked in federal court who examined the injunction, Rosenberg testified, "Well, there was me . . . Brother Herb, Sam Melville, Frank Lott, Roger Champen, Richie Clark, I believe there was a Latino brother at the table. I think his name was Carlos . . . they didn't feel the injunction was good." When William Kunstler arrived in D Yard [the following day], the inmates asked his legal opinion of the Schwartz injunction. Kunstler told them, "The injunction is . . . not worth the paper it's written on." The rejection of Schwartz's injunction was a blow to Oswald, because he believed it would end the impasse and he said he was "quite optimistic that the injunction would lead to release of the hostages." Kunstler, *My Life*, 218; Rosenberg Testimony, October 1991, US District Court, Buffalo, 1578, 1506–1516, 1578, 1589–1606; Bob Buyer et al., "Progress Report in Attica Talks," *Buffalo Evening News*, September 11, 1971; Oswald, *Attica: My Story*, 97; Wicker, *A Time to Die*, 23, 39–40; Bello, *Doing Life*, 199–201.

Health Report

For t past several weeks, since shortly after i entered t box, i have had mild headaches almost daily. T doctor gave me a pill called HPC which didn't help. After a week I complained again & this time i received a small pink pill (enclosed). T doctor refuses to tell me what it is. These seemed to help for a while. During t past week, t intensity of t pain has increased a lot. When i exercise my head pounds unbearably. T pills no longer help at all.

I went on sick call Aug 3 & told t doctor (Sternberg) i didn't want to keep taking pills that didn't seem to help much & that i thought i should have an examination. Sternberg said very scornfully that other people are now doing my thinking for me, continue taking the pills & go back to my cell.

I protested, trying to control my anger. He cut me off, saying my records indicate I was in good health when i entered prison. When i said that was nearly 2 years ago, he replied he knew when it was. He gave me a pass & told me to go to first aid. There my blood pressure was taken & i reported back to t doctor w/ a note stating my b.p. Sternberg said my b.p. was normal & to continue taking t pills. He told t guard to escort me to my cell.

I have no history of this kind of thing & i'm a little worried. My head aches virtually all t time now & any strenuous movement triggers a very heavy throbbing behind t eyes. And it's not exactly comforting to know t mortality rate at Attica rivals that of t Bengla Desh.*†

---

* SF: Sam's experiences with Attica's "doctors" were the norm. The lack of decent medical care in New York State prisons was an ongoing travesty that cost many inmates their lives and led to two of the demands in D Yard: on Friday September 10, at 11:30 PM, the removal of Warden Mancusi and Dr. Selden Williams was added to the demands. And the prisoners' earlier manifesto, ignored by Oswald for sixty-four days, had called for "a change in medical staff and medical policy and procedure." (See the manifesto itself in appendix B.) Tom Wicker termed the health care at Attica "primitive," but it was far worse than that. The Attica doctors—Selden Williams and Paul Sternberg—were absolutely hated by the inmates, who to a man thought them cruel, sadistic, inhumane, and deeply racist (particularly Williams).

† SF: It is believed that twenty-five prisoners died of exsanguination in D Yard, including Sam, and many could have been saved if they had received medical treatment. "Failure to Anticipate Need of Medical Care Deplored," *Buffalo Evening News*, September 13, 1972.

August 1971

Sister Barbara,*†

What a beautiful letter u wrote! Warm, informative & hopeful. So different from t form letters i get from Bill Crain. Crain & t others at t N.Y. commune have said they're very much interested in getting into concentration camp reform but so far it's all talk. U & some others seem to be more sincere & are definitely into more action.

Our needs here at Attica are myriad. I stress Attica as opposed to t rest of NYS because, given an ambience of totalitarianism (totalitarianism as specifically defined by Hannah Arendt) that exists throughout t state prison system, different regulations & degree of enforcement apply at different institutions. Even within Attica, different rules exist within in t different blocks.

Going thru unbelievably long court procedures, inmates have, from time to time, successfully challenged t necessity, if not the constitutionality, of some of these rules. Herr Rockerfeller, in Jan 71, at gunpoint (NY City jail riots & Auburn rebellion) bounced t Eichmann that ran t prison system,‡ anointed a twenty-year member of t parole

---

* Cohen: A lawyer who was helping another Attica inmate.

† SF: "Sister Barbara" is Barbara Handschu, a lawyer who performed tireless service to the Attica Brothers. When Sam knew her, she was representing Young Lords and other activists in New York City. In early 1972 she was the first lawyer to uproot her life and move to Buffalo to help organize the Attica Defense Committee. Largely unpaid, she coordinated the overwhelming amount of legal work, recruited law students, helped raise funds, visited Brothers at Attica and the other prisons and took them food packages, and tried to help their families. Handschu was cocounsel with William Kunstler for Attica Brother Dalou on one of the major criminal cases against the D Yard leadership. She had to fight not only ruthless state and prison officials but also the sexism of the male movement lawyers who wanted to take her job away. She was loved by the Attica Brothers, who called her "the first Attica Sister." She never received proper recognition for all she did for them. Barbara Handschu also is known as the lead plaintiff in the famous lawsuit *Handschu v. Special Services*, in which she, Abbie Hoffman, Black Panthers, and others sued to limit unlawful surveillance by the New York City "Red Squad." Known as the "Handschu Agreement" or "Handschu Consent Decree," it was considerably watered down after 9/11 but still carries her name as a living legacy. "Bugging the Red Squad," *Liberated Guardian*, December 1972.

‡ SF: The "Eichmann that ran t prison system" was Paul D. McGinnis, Oswald's predecessor, an old-school tyrant forced into retirement in 1970. Before leaving office, referring to

board w/ impeccable Nazi credentials, & renamed prisons "correctional facilities."*

Oh it's true there have been changes: in t year i've been at Attica they've added a civilian to t disciplinary tribunal; tepid water pitchers now adorn t mess hall tables; basketball courts have been built (completely constructed, designed & financed by inmates); lights out is now at 11 rather than 10 PM. It's true we can gather in groups greater than three w/out being gassed or clubbed. It's true penalties involving one's visiting rights have ceased. Wages have been raised from 10¢ to 25¢ a day (!) (countered by an approximately 30% per unit rise in commissary prices) . . . I'm thinking hard for more, but that's it. Not a mill for educational facilities or training programs & equipment; nothing about censorship of mail; nothing about literature relating to our lives being made available to us; nothing about due process in disciplinary proceedings; nothing about institutional racism where t 20% white population occupy 100% of t privileged jobs and influence other appointments & activities; where blacks number 60% & puerto ricans 20% of t population yet are supervised totally by incredibly stupid local farmboy honky pigs.

I wont go into t mickey mouse bullshit like attire, hair-lengths, talking in t corridor, lining up by height, etc., etc.; those kinds of things will stop when t more important essentials of prison life are changed. Nor do i have t space & understanding yet to go into parole

---

the decreased prison budget and the increased militancy of the inmates, McGinnis told the Associated Press, "If it keeps up like this then blood is going to run at many of the institutions." Associated Press, "Prisons See Trouble Brewing," *New York Daily News*, November 19, 1970; "Prison Authorities Feel Control over Militant Inmates Slipping," *Buffalo Evening News*, November 19, 1970.

* SF: The "twenty-year member of the parole board" was Russell Oswald. Oswald was a New York State Board of Parole member for twelve years, not twenty, and its chair for eleven years. Many older inmates in D Yard had appeared before him in that capacity and felt his rulings were unduly harsh, especially since many had been wrongly charged and convicted in the first place. They naturally remembered that when they saw him again in D Yard. In addition, some of them had been at Auburn during the uprising there. Oswald was not yet corrections commissioner, but some men in D Yard didn't know that and held him responsible for the Auburn reprisals. It was for these two reasons, in particular, that Oswald was not trusted. "Auburn Prisoners Tell Story of Repression," *Workers World*, January 15, 1971, 15; "U.S. Prisons 1971," *Activist*, 1971, 6; Oswald, *Attica: My Story*, 106, 173, 194; Bello, *Doing Life*, 199–201.

violation procedure or t terms of so-called "conditional release." Nor will i dwell on t very lucrative capitalist enterprise prison represents to t state & a few Tweedish motherfuckers at t top. Health facilities are reminiscent of 1942 Buchenwald: all inmates in t state w/ cancer are sent to Attica where they mingle w/ t general population & supposedly receive treatment at Rosewell Park Institute. Medical research indicates there are several forms of cancer that are communicable. Accordingly, t death rate at Attica is 2.2 per month for a population of just over 2000.

T "Attica Anti-Depression League" mentioned in my letter to Frank has drawn up & submitted a list of over 20 "demands," often hazy & unspecific, perhaps because passion leaned too hard on t pen. Men who are politically aware & potential leaders are shuffled frequently & isolated from each other. For instance, t only contact we in A block have w/ t brothers in B block is furtive note-passing in religious services (ask Frank). Consequently, we are thinking now in terms of getting one lawyer assigned to five or eight men as representatives from t different blocks just so we can get a chance to meet regularly & clear up our mutual thinking. This lawyer would come up regularly each month for about 3 hours—making progress reports, helping w/ technical shit in writs—but basically to give us inmates a chance to knock our heads together. That may turn out to be impractical & we're open to any suggestions.

I refer u to two groups who can probably be of much help in any broadside attack: t Fortune Society, somewhere in Greenwich Village, & Youth Against War And Fascism, specifically Maryann Weissman, who is probably *the one* person responsible for preventing t murder of at least six men who took part in t Auburn rebellion.*

---

* SF: The Prisoners Solidarity Committee was formed by the Workers World Party and, as Sam no doubt knew, most of its membership was interchangeable with that of YAWF. Maryann Weissman represented PSC/YAWF at Auburn for court appearances of the Auburn Six, the men who were made scapegoats of the August 1970 Auburn rebellion. In one appearance, the six were beaten in open court while shackled and chained to each other. They also were tear-gassed in the holding area, and tear gas seeped into the courtroom. Maryann Weissman was there, led the fight against that brutality, and helped to publicize what happened. "Hassan of 'Auburn 6' Speaks," *Attica Since the Massacre*, 4–5.

Although i'm sure they know this, tell t beautiful sisters at Westfield i love them w/all my heart.* I didn't know sister Claudia in t street but she is my blood as i am her blood nevertheless. I have too many reports of concern about one sister to dismiss them entirely. I know her as a brave comrade who has faced many bitter frustrations but fought well. U must stress that t reports are based on a profound feeling of love for her. If they are true, everyone who can come into contact w/ her must help her break completely w/ t mysticism & confusion of t past, especially t recent past. She must recommit herself to study & growth. My own perspective is too narrow to speak on this but i think an inundation w/ *bonafide* Marxist criticism & analysis will not do harm. Above all, her confidence must be restored in a genuine foundation—not t sham toughness all of us so often relied on. T wit & energy i remember in her would be a terrible price to pay in pursuit of some ephemeral vision.

Sam

THE ICED PIG[†]

Number 2[‡]

Attica Newsletter

In t aftermath of newspaper articles unfavorable to t prison,[§] Mancusi & company are coming out of their old pig bag again. With their muscle & fascist clubs they are trying to head off t growing tendency,

---

* Cohen: Sharon and Joyce, and Claudia, who were sent to state prison for their roles in firebombing a bank.

† SF: At the same time Sam was singlehandedly writing, copying, and circulating the *Iced Pig* at Attica, Martin Sostre was doing the same thing at Wallkill with *Vanguard*—"The Only Black Revolutionary Newspaper Published Inside The Guts Of The Beast." Just three issues, Sam's newsletter was far more meaningful and influential than *Vanguard* ever was. *Vanguard* seemed targeted toward African American inmates, whereas the *Iced Pig* was aimed at every inmate. It is not known whether Sam Melville and Martin Sostre knew of each other's publishing efforts.

‡ Cohen: This issue was distributed during early August.

§ SF: In *Iced Pig* no. 2, the "newspaper articles unfavorable to t prison" were the Richard Roth stories in the *Buffalo Courier-Express*.

both inside & outside t wall, to treat us as something more than dogs. Corridor rules about lining up, no talking, etc., as well as bullshit messhall regulations are all being strictly enforced now. All t old mickey mouse bullshit hasn't gotten a play in t newspapers so t pig is using them to come down on us. T aim of this harassment is clear: they're trying to intimidate us into silence; into crawling meekly back to our cells & not raising a cry of protest. We must not let this happen! We must make our voices heard.

There are several things we can do—all of which are legal:*

(1)   Every man can write a brief letter requesting an interview with his hometown newspaper. If t pigs don't let it out, so much t better. Save t rejected letter & t written reason for not being able to send it. This is evidence for when we have to bring class action.†

(2)   Write your congressmen (sealed letters) stating t doglike treatment you are receiving as a result of change being forced upon t prison.‡

(3)   Check around t yard for feeling about a one-day work stoppage—not a strike—just a brief vacation to dramatize our conditions to t outside.

We must not sit mute! T opportunity to raise our conditions to a level to produce meaningful understanding of our role in society is very near. If we let it slip thru our hands, t prison system will fall back into t 18th century again. Make your voices heard!

---

* SF: The proposals "which are legal" refer to those parts of *Sostre v. Rockefeller* that were upheld on appeal (see Sam's letter to Bill, March 12, 1971).

† SF: The "class action" was the lawsuit Sam hoped to bring, as discussed in his letters to Bill Crain and Barbara Handschu, since Sam was not a jailhouse lawyer.

‡ SF: The "change being forced upon t prison" refers again to the parts of *Sostre v. Rockefeller* upheld on appeal, and also to the *Sostre v. Otis* decision, which led to more political literature being allowed inside.

August 20, 1971

[To his lawyers]
People,

Presently in KL (14 days) for demanding human treatment. T pigs say I was creating a disturbance in t messhall. Political people in at least 3 blocks have been busted this week for petty shit. (See the newsletter.) Bullock sent word that M.S. is coming up this month to see him & I. Plan on staying more than an hour.
Did you get my Aug 6 letter?

S.

August 71

Poder hermano!*†

I can't tell u what a change has come over t brothers in Attica. So much more awareness & growing consciousness of themselves as potential revolutionaries. Reading, questioning, rapping all t time. Still bigotry & racism, black, white & brown, but u can feel it beginning to crumble in t knowledge so many are gaining that we must build

---

* Cohen: This letter is to a Puerto Rican inmate who was released from Attica in the early summer of '71.
† SF: "Poder hermano!" was written to Jose "G.I." Paris, a Young Lord who was paroled on May 20. On September 11, G.I. was allowed back into Attica as an observer, where Sam saw him again before he died. G.I. and William Kunstler were widely credited with saving the lives of seven observers who went back into D Yard on September 12 following Oswald's treachery in giving a dishonest letter to the inmates. Assemblyman Arthur Eve, considered the de facto chair of the Observers Committee, "insist[ed] that if . . . Jose Paris had not firmly asserted then that Oswald had sent his ultimatum in without the committee's knowledge, they might indeed have been killed or taken hostage." Mary Breasted, "An Epic of Failure," *Village Voice*, September 24–30, 1971, 30. Tom Wicker wrote, "Desperately, [Kunstler] and Jose Paris of the Young Lords convinced Brother Richard that they had not known of the note." Wicker said that Kunstler was "the Observer most trusted by the inmates," but that was not really true—the most trusted was Sam's friend G.I., because less than four months before that he had been one of them. Wicker, *A Time to Die*, 174, 194–195, 223–231; "The Attica Tragedy," *Newsweek*, September 27, 1971, 37.

solidarity against our common oppressor—t system of exploitation of each other & alienation from each other.

Since u left, a group has formed under t title of t "Anti- Depression League," as yet a small group trying to create an alliance between all t various factions—Panthers, Young Lords, white radicals, Five Percenters, Orthodox Muslims, etc. Not an easy task as u well know.

Among t problems we face is how to form revolutionary awareness relating to our prison condition vis-a-vis t street & at t same time avoid t obvious classification of prison reformers. Socialists in t past faced a parallel situation in t building of trade unions. When t working class movement gained t strength to demand bargaining power with t caps [capitalists], t unions were bought out w/ a few larger crumbs from t banquet table that t workers had built but could not sit at.

T example is not exactly t answer of course, but t basic problem is: how to avoid t pitfalls of *economism*, that is, settling for simple reforms, however "far-reaching," as opposed to revolutionary structural change. When u come right down to it of course, there's only *one* revolutionary change as far as t prison system in Amerika is concerned. But until t day comes when enough of our brothers & sisters realize what that one revolutionary change is, we must always be certain our demands will exceed what the pigs are able to grant.

Keep in touch my strong latino brother. Many here remember u and love you.

Sam

August 23, 1971

Dear John,

Don't mistake the brevity of this with personal depression. As we all must be, i am trying to place in perspective the events of the 21st—all three.*

You said you would come up in September and i want you to do some research before: Find out as best you can if there is (and why) a

---

* Cohen: On August 21 George Jackson and two guards were killed at San Quentin prison.

rift between Isaac Deutscher & t SWP [Socialist Workers Party]. specifically, why doesn't Pathfinder Press publish Deutscher's works since he lauds Trotsky so much? Also, t apparent rift between Deutscher & International Pubs. Of course, i realize I.P. is, or was, strongly controlled by the CP [Communist Party], but why is such a committed Marxist anathema to them now?

Also, i'm still anxious to learn as much as possible about the events in Berlin between say mid-1916 to mid-1919, the growth of t Spartacists Group and t circumstances surrounding the assassinations of Liebknecht, Luxemburg, et al.

Charlie said he was trying to come up soon. Try to make it together. I think that would be better.

Sam Melville
#26124

THE ICED PIG

Number 3*

Attica Newsletter

U r beautiful brothers! Strength & Solidarity r t greatest weapons to gain dignity. Strength & Solidarity is what u showed on the 27th. As if one man, there was silence & fasting at t noon mess[†] in memory of our revolutionary brother George Jackson. Many brothers wore black arm bands defying t pigs' barbaric dress code. One brother in A block was locked up behind it but t head pig cut him loose.

U scored two other victories this week too: (1) Behind our more than 500 signature petition, t institution is now providing t prizes for t Labor Day events—no more from our pockets. (2) A new list on t bulletin board shows that now we can read a broader range of literature.[‡]

---

* Cohen: This issue came out at the end of August.

† SF: In the final issue of *Iced Pig*, "noon mess" should have been "breakfast" (an error Sam made because he was in keeplock at the time), although many Brothers did continue the silent fast at lunch

‡ SF: "A broader range of literature" refers to the July 28, 1971, landmark federal court case *Sostre v. Otis*, in which Martin Sostre sued the warden of Wallkill for denying his

These r very small victories but they demonstrate t growing feeling of unity & this means strength. & strength is t road to dignity.

Some of t ruling class media tried to show a racist motive behind t killings of t 2 white prisoners at San Q but nobody's going for it. These 2 were lackey attendants & u dont get to attendant status without wiping t man's ass.

On t day of Jackson's funeral, t Weatherpeople bombed 3 offices of t California Corrections Dept. Unfortunately, no one was hurt. Get it together Weatherfolk!

August 30, 1971

Dear Bill,

Got t letters & suit draft. It seems weak. T only substantive point is censorship. We must somehow work into it t basic terror that people live under in prison: t provocative quality of a club suddenly striking a solid brick or steel surface just behind u, accompanied by a roar to lockin, forward march, etc. Many r numb to it, but t young, new men invariably become enraged. U'r immediate impulse is to strike out at t pig but u'r checked by fear or u'r brothers. So u curse & get KL for 7 to 10 days. I was down to t disciplinary court 2 weeks ago & there were more than 70 men waiting for a hearing. T old timers say it's beginning to look like t old days where u got KL for looking crosseyed at t pig. They're enforcing t tiniest shit now. I'm finishing a 14 day KL for a small mess hall infraction which is usually just a reprimand.

---

right to read and own revolutionary literature of his choosing. Judge Mansfield ruled that, henceforth, every inmate must receive written notice of a withheld item and must be given an opportunity to object to a denial, and a board must be established that would "act fairly" in making the decision. This became the Media Review Committee. (One of its members was Walter Dunbar.) Alan Kohn, "Inmate Wins U.S. Ruling on Censoring of Literature," *New York Law Journal*, July 30, 1971, 1, 3. Oswald and the state hated this decision. The new rules were constantly ignored, prompting the Jones Commission to comment, "Supposedly relaxed rules on incoming publications . . . are still ambivalent enough to have banned issues of the *New York Daily News* and the *Schenectady Gazette*." Edward Hershey, "Study Committee Recommends 33 Prison Reforms," *Niagara Falls Gazette*, March 16, 1972.

T newsletter is a group project. T abbreviations r standard for several writers here. And frankly, nobody on t project gives a fuck if t pig finds out. We have reason to believe he knows anyway.

A hard worker in D block just got a 60-day box bit for having t manifesto & progressive lit in his cell.* He is no "flaming rev," he doesn't challenge t pig usually & is pretty much an easy-going ex-college dope pusher. He worked in t school & was responsible for our "sociology class" where t entire rev caucus met every Thurs morning for interblock strategy sessions. It's clear t pig found out & boxed him on a pretext to shut down t class.

In u'r 8-19 letter u say u'r going to Vermont & that u hope to file our suit before leaving so u will be able to continue working on it. Does this mean if u don't file before u move that u won't be able to help us? Is t commune† breaking up? What's happening?

Further suit points:

(1)   Denial of exercise while in KL
(2)   " " medical treatment (I still have headaches)
(3)   " " Dental "

Plus many of t manifesto points.

                                                            Sam

                                                 Aug. 30, 1971

Brother John

I put in a tab to correspond with Sue‡ today. Probably get an answer next week.

We've had a hectic time here recently. A lot of activity around George Jackson followed by a visit from the Herr Commissioner of correction.§ I've just emerged from a 14-day KL so I get all this second

---

* SF: The "hard worker" in the box was Edward T. "Fred" LeShure.

† Cohen: The law commune, a group of radical lawyers who represented Sam, the Panthers, and other revolutionaries.

‡ Cohen: The prison forces inmates to request permission for correspondence with anyone before a letter can go out or get in.

§ SF: If "Herr Commissioner" refers to Russell Oswald, then either Sam was misinformed or his letter's date is wrong. Oswald didn't arrive at Attica until September 2. Presuming hand, but all the lumpen are very excited at the strong display of solidarity exhibited last Friday. At the midday meal [the large meal in prison], not a man ate or spoke—black, white, brown, red. Many wore black armbands. The priest was asked to say a prayer, & after some to-do, did so. No one can remember anything like it here before.

Of course we all realize the lying & distortions of the media but it doesn't matter here. G.J. was beloved by inmates throughout the country. Nothing the press can say diminishes his stature in our eyes. The only souring note in the episode was the alerting phonecalls made before the trashing of the prison offices on the day of the funeral. Schools, yes. Office bldgs, okay. But them???

The Trotsky biog came along with "We Are Everywhere." The only word for Jerry's book is puerile. If that sounds a little like Jack Smith I'm sorry. It's a fact. I can't believe a significant number of people are gonna reach any radicalization from that kind of thing anymore. In terms of sheer info, Abby's latest is much more efficacious. Those 2 aren't permitted in here but somehow, one finds them around.

My bird has flown to another nest but perhaps he will come back again. I hope so. I certainly miss him.

Tell Charlie I'll write him soon. You see we can only get one free letter a week unless we buy stamps, but I've been prohibited from going to commissary for more than a month.

Sam

September 4, 1971

[To his lawyers]

I was allowed to look at (but not keep) a notice from t pigs saying t following books were reviewed in Albany & I would *not* be permitted to have them:

---

the date is correct, Sam probably refers to one of the deputy commissioners who went there earlier to plan for the now famous "inspection" that was planned to occur the previous week and never happened, sparking mistrust within Five Company.

1. Weatherman*
2. Workers World† (3 copies)
3. Martin Sostre in Court‡
4. A True Revolutionary§
5. Prisoners Call Out Freedom¶
6. U.S. Prisons 1971

T notice said I was to choose between sending t books back to t publishers, holding them in my property, or sending them to someone on my correspondence list.

They are also holding, though no longer admit it, "Seize T Time" (8 months), "Prison Diary of A Revolutionary Priest" (at least 3 months) & "Fire: Reports from t Underground Press" (one month).

Duplicate t 2 Ramparts letters, file one set & return one set to me.

Pig Boyle still terrorizes t halls only now his friends help out.

Have not received Liberated Guardian article.

I have perpetual headaches—no longer taking pills.

Dictionary was stolen from my cell.

---

* SF: *Weatherman* was the *Ramparts* anthology compiled by Harold Jacobs. The chapter "Radical Bombers" (first published in *Hard Times*) refers to Sam. Andrew Kopkind, "The Radical Bombers" in *Weatherman*, ed. by Harold Jacobs (San Francisco: Ramparts, 1970), 500–501.

† SF: *Workers World* was the weekly newspaper published in New York City by the Workers World Party. Each issue had to be examined, article by article, by the Media Review Committee in Albany before an inmate could receive it.

‡ SF: *Martin Sostre in Court* was a pamphlet of Sostre's 1968 Erie County Court trial testimony and speeches he made to the spectators, printed in 1969 by his defense committee. The Media Review Committee in Albany banned all three Sostre books from every inmate in the State, even from Sostre himself.

§ SF: *A True Revolutionary* was a 1970 pamphlet about Lonnie McLucas, a minor Black Panther tried in New Haven with Bobby Seale and Ericka Huggins. McLucas was convicted of conspiracy to murder, sentenced to twelve and a half to fifteen years, and released in 1978. His cause was taken up by YAWF/WWP, which produced this pamphlet. The Seale-Huggins-McLucas trial drew fifteen thousand demonstrators to New Haven on May Day 1970, shutting down Yale and the entire city; seven thousand paratroopers, marines, and national guard troops were called in to keep the peace. Participating at this trial as a daily "student observer" who helped "prepare summaries for the ACLU" was Yale law student Hillary Rodham. Carl Bernstein, *A Woman in Charge* (New York: Alfred A. Knopf, 2007), 66–69.

¶ SF: *Prisoners Call Out Freedom* was a 1971 pamphlet published by the Prisoners Solidarity Committee. It contains letters and poetry by the Auburn Six and commentary on their legal battle.

All rules are now *strictly* enforced. Attire, haircuts, lining up, not talking, no wearing hats—everything. You're busted for dispensing lit, holding meetings, or staring at pigs. We are treated as dogs.

Don't wag your righteous finger at Mancusi & pretend you're shocked. Sue t motherfucker or better yet shoot him. But for christs sake do something.

Sam

APPENDIXES

APPENDICES

A

SAM MELVILLE'S PRISON READING LIST

Collated by Jeremy Varon

SAM MELVILLE BECAME A SELF-STYLED "man of action." His turn to violence reflected, in part, his impatience with endless debate about revolutionary strategy. And yet he read extensively, including after his capture. His prison letters mention numerous individual books and authors. They also chronicle his struggles to have access to certain literature, surely deemed seditious by authorities, while incarcerated.

Melville tried to stay abreast of political and social developments, as discussed in leftist publications like *Monthly Review* and *Trans-Action*. He also was interested in the history of revolutionary movements and figures, evident in such works as Isaac Deutscher's multivolume biography of Leon Trotsky, volumes by Lenin, Trotsky, and Engels, and *Empire and Revolution*, written by New Left radical David Horowitz. (Horowitz later became an incendiary figure of the far right.) *Seize the Time* (1970), an early Panther history by Black Panther leader Bobby Seale, offered a contemporary revolutionary perspective. So too did *An Essay on Liberation* (1969), written by the German Jewish Marxist and New Left icon Herbert Marcuse.

Melville had interest as well in more countercultural publications. These include *The Politics of Experience* (1967) by R. D. Laing, who stressed the psychic and existential damage of postwar American society, and the *Whole Earth Catalog*—a compendium of hippie do-it-yourself technology and holistic wisdom.

Melville even sought to publish his writing from prison. *Ramparts* magazine commissioned a review by him of *Weatherman* (1970), an early anthology of writings by or about Weatherman edited by Harold Jacobs, but prison authorities would not let him have the text.

Title	Letter
Seale, *Seize the Time*	1/17/70
Whole Earth Catalog	1/17/70
Monthly Review	1/26/70
R. D. Laing	2/12/70
Rap Brown	7/13/70
Village Voice	7/26/70
Trans-Action	9/6/70
Deutscher, *Life of Leon Trotsky*	10/3/70
Various authors and texts	2/9/71
David Horowitz, *Empire and Revolution*	3/21/71
Socialist Revolution	4/17/71
Jacobs, *Weatherman*	7/17/71

B

THE ATTICA LIBERATION FACTION MANIFESTO OF DEMANDS AND ANTI-DEPRESSION PLATFORM

WE, THE IMPRISONED MEN OF ATTICA PRISON, SEEK AN END TO THE INJUSTICE SUFFERED BY ALL PRISONERS, REGARDLESS OF RACE, CREED OR COLOR.

THE PREPARATION AND CONTENT OF THIS DOCUMENT HAS BEEN CONSTRUCTED UNDER THE UNIFIED EFFORTS OF ALL RACES AND SOCIAL SEGMENTS OF THIS PRISON.

IT IS A MATTER OF DOCUMENTED RECORD AND HUMAN RECOGNITION THAT THE ADMINISTRATION OF THE NEW YORK PRISON SYSTEM HAVE RESTRUCTURED THE INSTITUTIONS WHICH WERE DESIGNED TO SOCIALLY CORRECT MEN INTO THE FASCIST CONCENTRATION CAMPS OF MODERN AMERICA.

DUE TO THE CONDITIONAL FACT THAT ATTICA PRISON IS ONE OF THE MOST CLASSIC INSTITUTIONS OF AUTHORATA-TIVE INHUMANITY UPON MEN, THE FOLLOWING *MANIFESTO OF DEMANDS* ARE BEING SUBMITTED:

"MAN S RIGHT TO KNOWLEDGE AND FREE USE THEREOF"

WE, THE INMATES OF ATTICA PRISON, HAVE GROWN TO RECOGNIZE BEYOND THE SHADOW OF A DOUBT, THAT

BECAUSE OF OUR POSTURE AS PRISONERS AND BRANDED
CHARACTERS AS ALLEGED CRIMINALS, THE ADMINISTRA-
TION AND PRISON EMPLOYEES NO LONGER CONSIDER OR
RESPECT US AS HUMAN BEINGS, BUT RATHER AS DOMES-
TICATED ANIMALS SELECTED TO DO THEIR BIDDING IN
SLAVE LABOR AND FURNISHED AS A PERSONAL WHIP-
PING DOG FOR THEIR SADISTIC, PSYCHOPATHIC HATE.

WE, THE INMATES OF ATTICA PRISON, SAY TO YOU, THE
SINCERE PEOPLE OF SOCIETY, THE PRISON SYSTEM OF WHICH
YOUR COURTS HAVE RENDERED UNTO, IS WITHOUT QUESTION
THE AUTHORATATIVE FANGS OF A COWARD IN POWER.

RESPECTFULLY SUBMITTED TO THE PEOPLE AS A PROTEST
TO THE VILE AND VICIOUS SLAVEMASTERS:

> THE GOVERNOR OF NEW YORK STATE
> THE N.Y.S. DEPARTMENT OF CORRECTIONS
> THE N.Y.S. LEGISLATURE
> THE N.Y.S. COURTS
> THE UNITED STATES COURTS
> THE N.Y.S. PAROLE BOARD

AND THOSE WHO SUPPORT THIS SYSTEM OF INJUSTICE
THE INMATES OF THIS PRISON HAVE VESTED THE POWER
OF NEGOTIATION REGARDING THE SETTLEMENT OF THE STIPU-
LATED DEMANDS WITHIN THE JUDGEMENT AND CONTROL OF
THESE MEN:

> DONALD NOBLE - 26777
> PETER BUTLER - 26018
> FRANK LOTT - 26148
> CARL JONES-EL - 24534
> HERBERT BLYDEN X. - 22480

ALL AND ANY NEGOTIATION WILL BE CONDUCTED BY
PRISON AND STATE AUTHORITIES WITH THESE FIVE MEN.

THESE DEMANDS ARE BEING PRESENTED TO YOU. THERE IS NO STRIKE OF ANY KIND TO PROTEST THESE DEMANDS. WE ARE *TRYING* TO DO THIS IN A DEMOCRATIC FASHION. WE FEEL THERE IS NO NEED TO DRAMATIZE OUR DEMANDS.

WE, THE MEN OF ATTICA PRISON, HAVE BEEN COMMITTED TO THE N.Y.S. DEPARTMENT OF CORRECTIONS BY THE PEOPLE OF SOCIETY FOR THE PURPOSE OF CORRECTING WHAT HAS BEEN DEEMED AS SOCIAL ERRORS IN BEHAVIOR. ERRORS WHICH HAVE CLASSIFIED US AS SOCIALLY UNACCEPTABLE UNTIL PROGRAMMED WITH NEW VALUES AND MORE THOROUGH UNDERSTANDING AS TO OUR VALUE AND RESPONSIBILITIES AS MEMBERS OF THE OUTSIDE COMMUNITY. THE ATTICA PRISON PROGRAM IN ITS STRUCTURE AND CONDITIONS HAVE BEEN ENSLAVED ON THE PAGES OF THIS MANIFESTO OF DEMANDS WITH THE BLOOD, SWEAT, AND TEARS OF THE INMATES OF THIS PRISON.

THE PROGRAMS WHICH WE ARE SUBMITTED TO UNDER THE FACADE OF REHABILITATION, IS RELATIVE TO THE ANCIENT STUPIDITY OF POURING WATER ON A DROWNING MAN, INAS-MUCH AS WE ARE TREATED FOR OUR HOSTILITIES BY OUR PROGRAM ADMINISTRATORS WITH THEIR HOSTILITY AS A MEDICATION.

IN OUR EFFORTS TO COMPREHEND ON A FEELING LEVEL AN EXISTENCE CONTRARY TO VIOLENCE, WE ARE CONFRONTED BY OUR CAPTORS WITH AS TO WHAT IS FAIR AND JUST, WE ARE VICTIMIZED BY THE EXPLOITATION AND THE DENIAL OF THE CELEBRATED DUE PROCESS OF LAW.

IN OUR PEACEFUL EFFORTS TO ASSEMBLE IN DISSENT AS PROVIDED UNDER THIS NATIONS UNITED STATES CONSTITU-TION, WE ARE IN TURN MURDERED, BRUTALIZED AND FRAMED ON VARIOUS CRIMINAL CHARGES BECAUSE WE SEEK THE RIGHTS AND PRIVILEGES OF ALL AMERICAN PEOPLE.

IN OUR EFFORTS TO INTELLECTUALLY EXPAND IN KEEP-ING WITH THE OUTSIDE WORLD, THROUGH ALL CATEGORIES OF NEWS MEDIA, WE ARE SYSTEMATICALLY RESTRICTED AND

PUNITIVELY OFFENDED TO ISOLATION STATUS WHEN WE INSIST
ON OUR HUMAN RIGHTS TO THE WISDOM OF AWARENESS.

Manifesto of Demands

1) WE DEMAND THE CONSTITUTIONAL RIGHTS OF LEGAL REP-
RESENTATION AT THE TIME OF ALL PAROLE BOARD HEARINGS;
AND THE PROTECTION FROM THE PROCEDURES OF THE PAROLE
AUTHORITIES WHEREBY THEY PERMIT NO PROCEDURAL SAFE-
GUARDS SUCH AS AN ATTORNEY FOR CROSS-EXAMINATION OF
WITNESSES, WITNESSES IN BEHALF OF THE PAROLEE, AT THE
PAROLE REVOCATION HEARINGS.

2) WE DEMAND A CHANGE IN MEDICAL STAFF AND MEDI-
CAL POLICY AND PROCEDURE. THE ATTICA PRISON HOSPI-
TAL IS TOTALLY INADEQUATE, UNDERSTAFFED, PREJUDICED
IN THE TREATMENT OF INMATES. THERE ARE NUMEROUS
"MISTAKES" MADE MANY TIMES, IMPROPER AND ERRONEOUS
MEDICATION IS GIVEN BY UNTRAINED PERSONNEL. WE ALSO
DEMAND PERIODICAL CHECK-UPS ON *ALL* PRISONERS AND SUF-
FICIENT LICENSED PRACTITIONERS 24 HOURS A DAY INSTEAD
OF INMATE HELP THAT IS USED NOW.

3) WE DEMAND ADEQUATE VISITING CONDITIONS AND FACILI-
TIES FOR THE INMATES AND FAMILIES OF ATTICA PRISONERS. THE
VISITING FACILITIES AT THIS PRISON ARE SUCH AS TO PRECLUDE
ADEQUATE VISITING FOR THE INMATES AND THEIR FAMILIES.

4) WE DEMAND AN END TO THE SEGREGATON OF PRISON-
ERS FROM THE MAINLINE POPULATION BECAUSE OF THEIR
POLITICAL BELIEFS. SOME OF THE MEN SEGREGATION UNITS
ARE CONFINED THERE SOLEY FOR POLITICAL REASONS AND
THEIR SEGREGATION FROM OTHER INMATES IS INDEFINITE.

5) WE DEMAND AN END TO THE PERSECUTION AND PUNISH-
MENT OF PRISONERS WHO PRACTICE THE CONSTITUTIONAL

RIGHT OF PEACEFUL DISSENT. PRISONERS AT ATTICA AND OTHER N.Y.S. PRISONS CANNOT BE COMPELLED TO WORK, AS THESE PRISONS WERE BUILT FOR THE PURPOSE OF HOUSING PRISONERS AND THERE IS NO MENTION AS TO THE PRISONERS BEING REQUIRED TO WORK ON PRISON JOBS IN ORDER TO REMAIN IN THE MAINLINE POPULATION AND/OR BE COSIDERED FOR RELEASE. MANY PRISONERS BELIEVE THEIR LABOR POWER IS BEING EXPLOITED IN ORDER FOR THE STATE TO INCREASE ITS ECONOMIC POWER AND TO CONTINUE TO EXPAND ITS CORRECTIONAL INDUSTRIES (WHICH ARE MILLION-DOLLAR COMPLEXES), YET DO NOT DEVELOP WORKING SKILLS ACCEPTABLE FOR EMPLOYMENT IN THE OUTSIDE SOCIETY, AND WHICH DO NOT PAY THE PRISONER MORE THAN AN AVERAGE OF FORTY CENTS A DAY. MOST PRISONERS NEVER MAKE MORE THAN FIFTY CENTS A DAY. PRISONERS WHO REFUSE TO WORK FOR THE OUTRAGEOUS SCALE, OR WHO STRIKE, ARE PUNISHED AND SEGREGATED WITHOUT THE ACCESS TO THE PRIVILEGES SHARED BY THOSE WHO WORK; THIS IS CLASS LEGISLATION, CLASS DIVISION, AND CREATES HOSTILITIES WITHIN THE PRISON.

6) WE DEMAND AN END TO POLITICAL PERSECUTION, RACIAL PERSECUTION, AND THE DENIAL OF PRISONERS' RIGHTS TO SUBSCRIBE TO POLITICAL PAPERS, BOOKS OR ANY OTHER EDUCATIONAL AND CURRENT MEDIA CHRONICLES THAT ARE FORWARDED THROUGH THE UNITED STATES MAIL.

7) WE DEMAND THAT INDUSTRIES BE ALLOWED TO ENTER THE INSTITUTIONS AND EMPLOY INMATES TO WORK EIGHT HOURS A DAY AND FIT INTO THE CATEGORY OF WORKERS FOR SCALE WAGES. THE WORKING CONDITIONS IN PRISONS DO NOT DEVELOP WORKING INCENTIVES PARALLEL TO THE MANY JOBS IN THE OUTSIDE SOCIETY, AND A PAROLLED PRISONER FACES MANY CONTRADICTIONS OF THE JOB THAT ADDS TO HIS DIFFICULTY IN ADJUSTING. THOSE INDUSTRIES OUTSIDE

WHO DESIRE PRISONS SHOULD BE ALLOWED TO ENTER FOR THE PURPOSE OF EMPLOYMENT PLACEMENT.

8) WE DEMAND THAT INMATES BE GRANTED THE RIGHT TO JOIN OR FORM A LABOR UNION.

9) WE DEMAND THAT INMATES BE GRANTED THE RIGHT TO SUPPORT THEIR OWN FAMILIES; AT PRESENT THOUSANDS OF WELFARE RECIPIENTS HAVE TO DIVIDE THEIR CHECKS TO SUPPORT THEIR IMPRISONED RELATIVES WHO, WITHOUT THE OUTSIDE SUPPORT, CAN NOT EVEN BUY TOILET ARTICLES OR FOOD. MEN WORKING ON SCALE WAGES COULD SUPPORT THEMSELVES AND FAMILIES WHILE IN PRISON.

10) WE DEMAND THAT CORRECTIONAL OFFICERS BE PROSECUTED AS A MATTER OF LAW FOR ANY ACTS OF CRUEL AND UNUSUAL PUNISHMENT WHERE IT IS NOT A MATTER OF LIFE OR DEATH.

11) WE DEMAND THAT ALL INSTITUTIONS USING INMATE LABOR BE MADE TO CONFORM WITH THE STATE AND FEDERAL MINIMUM WAGE LAWS.

12) WE DEMAND AN END TO THE ESCALATING PRACTICE OF PHYSICAL BRUTALITY BEING PERPETRATED UPON THE INMATES OF N.Y.S. PRISONS.

13) WE DEMAND THE APPOINTMENT OF THREE LAWYERS FROM THE N.Y.S. BAR ASSOCIATION TO FULL TIME POSITIONS FOR THE PROVISION OF LEGAL ASSISTANCE TO INMATES SEEKING POST-CONVICTION RELIEF, AND TO ACT AS A LAISON BETWEEN THE ADMINISTRATION AND INMATES FOR BRINGING INMATE COMPLAINTS TO THE ATTENTION OF THE ADMINISTRATION.

14) WE DEMAND THE UPDATING OF INDUSTRY WORKING CONDITIONS TO THE STANDARDS PROVIDED FOR UNDER N.Y.S. LAW.

15) WE DEMAND THE ESTABLISHMENT OF INMATE WORKERS INSURANCE PLAN TO PROVIDE COMPENSATION FOR WORK RELATED ACCIDENTS.

16) WE DEMAND THE ESTABLISHMENT OF UNIONIZED VOCATIONAL TRAINING PROGRAMS COMPARABLE TO THAT OF THE FEDERAL PRISON SYSTEM WHICH PROVIDES FOR UNION INSTRUCTIONS, UNION PAY SCALES, AND UNION MEMBERSHIP UPON COMPLETION OF THE VOCATIONAL TRAINING COURSE.

17) WE DEMAND ANNUAL ACCOUNTING OF THE INMATES RECREATION FUND AND FORMULATION OF AN INMATE COMMITTEE TO GIVE INMATES A VOICE AS TO HOW SUCH FUNDS ARE USED.

18) WE DEMAND THAT THE PRESENT PAROLE BOARD APPOINTED BY THE GOVERNOR BE ERADICATED AND REPLACED BY A PAROLE BOARD ELECTED BY POPULAR VOTE OF THE PEOPLE. IN A WORLD WHERE MANY CRIMES ARE PUNISHED BY INDETERMINATE SENTENCES AND WHERE AUTHORITY ACTS WITHIN SECRECY AND WITHIN VAST DISCRETION ARE GIVEN HEAVY WEIGHT TO ACCUSATIONS BY PRISONS EMPLOYEES AGAINST INMATES, INMATES FEEL TRAPPED UNLESS THEY ARE WILLING TO ABANDON THEIR TO BE INDEPENDENT MEN.

19) WE DEMAND THAT THE STATE LEGISLATURE CREATE FULL-TIME SALARIED BOARD OF OVERSEER FOR THE STATE PRISONS. THE BOARD WOULD BE RESPONSIBLE FOR EVALUATING ALLEGATIONS MADE BY INMATES, INMATES FAMILIES, THEIR FRIENDS AND LAWYERS AGAINST EMPLOYEES CHARGED WITH ACTING INHUMANELY, ILLEGALLY OR UNREASONABLY. THE BOARD SHOULD INCLUDED PEOPLE NOMINATED BY A PSYCHOLOGICAL OR PSYCHIATRIC ASSOCIATION, BY THE STATE BAR ASSOCIATION OR BY THE CIVIL LIBERTIES UNION, AND BY GROUPS OF CONCERNED, INVOLVED LAYMEN.

20) WE DEMAND AN IMMEDIATE END TO THE AGITATION OF RACE RELATIONS BY THE PRISON ADMINISTRATION OF THIS STATE.

21) WE DEMAND THE DEPARTMENT OF CORRECTIONS FURNISH ALL PRISONERS WITH THE SERVICES OF ETHNIC COUNSELORS FOR THE NEEDED SPECIAL SERVICES OF THE BROWN AND BLACK POPULATION OF THIS PRISON.

22) WE DEMAND AN END TO THE DISCRIMINATION IN THE JUDGEMENT AND QUOTA OF PAROLE FOR BLACK AND BROWN PEOPLE.

23) WE DEMAND THAT ALL PRISONERS BE PRESENT AT THE TIME THEIR CELLS AND PROPERTY ARE BEING SEARCHED BY THE CORRECTIONAL OFFICERS OF STATE PRISONS.

24) WE DEMAND AN END TO THE DISCRIMINATION AGAINST PRISONERS WHEN THEY APPEAR BEFORE THE PAROLE BOARD. MOST PRISONERS ARE DENIED PAROLE SOLEY BECAUSE OF THEIR PREVIOUS RECORDS. LIFE SENTENCES SHOULD NOT CONFINE A MAN LONGER THAN TEN YEARS AS A SEVEN YEAR DURATION IS THE CONSIDERED STATUTE FOR A LIFETIME OUT OF CIRCULA-TION, AND IF A MAN CONNOT BE REHABILITATED AFTER A MAX-IMUM OF TEN YEARS OF CONSTRUCTIVE PROGRAMS, ETC., THEN HE BELONGS IN A MENTAL HYGIENE CENTER, NOT A PRISON.

25) WE DEMAND AN END TO THE UNSANITARY CONDITIONS THAT EXIST IN THE MESS HALL: I.E., DIRTY TRAYS, DIRTY UTEN-SILS, STAINED DRINKING CUPS AND AN END TO THE PRACTICE OF PUTTING FOOD ON THE TABLES HOURS BEFORE EATING TIME WITHOUT ANY PROTECTIVE COVERING PUT OVER IT.

26) WE DEMAND THAT BETTER FOOD BE SERVED TO THE INMATES. THE FOOD IS A GASTRONOMICAL DISASTER. WE ALSO DEMAND THAT DRINKING WATER BE PUT ON EACH TABLE AND THAT EACH INMATE BE ALLOWED TO TAKE AS MUCH FOOD AS

HE WANTS AND AS MUCH BREAD AS HE WANTS, INSTEAD OF THE SEVERELY LIMITED PORTIONS AND LIMITED (4) SLICES OF BREAD. INMATES WISHING A PORK-FREE DIET SHOULD HAVE ONE, SINCE 85% OF OUR DIET IS PORK MEAT OR PORK-SATURATED FOOD.

27) WE DEMAND THAT THERE BE ONE SET OF RULES GOVERNING ALL PRISONS IN THIS STATE INSTEAD OF THE PRESENT SYSTEM WHERE EACH WARDEN MAKES THE RULES FOR HIS INSTITUTION AS HE SEES FIT.

IN CONCLUSION

WE ARE FIRM IN OUR RESOLVE AND WE DEMAND, AS HUMAN BEINGS, THE DIGNITY AND JUSTICE THAT IS DUE TO US BY RIGHT OF OUR BIRTH. WE DO NOT KNOW HOW THE PRESENT SYSTEM OF BRUTALITY AND DEHUMINIZATION AND INJUSTICES HAS BEEN ALLOWED TO BE PERPETRATED IN THIS DAY OF ENLIGHTENMENT, BUT WE ARE THE LIVING PROOF OF ITS EXISTENCE AND WE CANNOT ALLOW IT TO CONTINUE.

THE TAXPAYERS WHO JUST HAPPEN TO BE OUR MOTHERS, FATHERS, SISTERS, BROTHERS, DAUGHTERS AND SONS SHOULD BE MADE AWARE OF HOW THEIR TAX DOLLARS ARE BEING SPENT TO DENY THEIR SONS, BROTHERS FATHERS AND UNCLES OF JUSTICE, EQUALITY AND DIGNITY.

ATTICA LIBERATION FACTION

DONALD NOBLE - 26777

PETER BUTLER - 26018

FRANK LOTT - 26148

CARL JONES-EL - 24534

HERBERT BLYDEN X. - 22480